Communications
in Computer and Information Science 504

T0212890

Tristan Cazenave   Mark H.M. Winands
Yngvi Björnsson (Eds.)

Computer Games

Third Workshop on Computer Games, CGW 2014
Held in Conjunction with the 21st European Conference
on Artificial Intelligence, ECAI 2014
Prague, Czech Republic, August 18, 2014
Revised Selected Papers

 Springer

Volume Editors

Tristan Cazenave
Université Paris-Dauphine, France
E-mail: cazenave@lamsade.dauphine.fr

Mark H.M. Winands
Maastricht University, The Netherlands
E-mail: m.winands@maastrichtuniversity.nl

Yngvi Björnsson
Reykjavik University, Iceland
E-mail: yngvi@ru.is

ISSN 1865-0929   e-ISSN 1865-0937
ISBN 978-3-319-14922-6   e-ISBN 978-3-319-14923-3
DOI 10.1007/978-3-319-14923-3
Springer Cham Heidelberg New York Dordrecht London

Library of Congress Control Number: 2014959041

Typesetting: Camera-ready by author, data conversion by Scientific Publishing Services, Chennai, India

Printed on acid-free paper

Springer is part of Springer Science+Business Media (www.springer.com)

Preface

These proceedings contain the papers of the Computer Games Workshop (CGW 2014) held in Prague, Czech Republic. The workshop took place August 18, 2014, in conjunction with the 21st European Conference on Artificial Intelligence (ECAI 2014). The workshop received 20 submissions. Each paper was sent to two reviewers. In the end, 12 papers were accepted for presentation at the workshop, of which 11 made it into these proceedings. The Computer and Games Workshop series is an international forum for researchers interested in all aspects of artificial intelligence and computer game playing. Earlier workshops took place in Montpellier, France (2012), and Beijing, China (2013).

The published papers cover a wide range of topics related to computer games. They collectively discuss 11 abstract games: 7 Wonders, Amazons, AtariGo, Ataxx, Breakthrough, Chinese Dark Chess, Connect6, NoGo, Pentalath, Othello, and Catch the Lion. Moreover, two papers are on General Game Playing, and four on video game playing. Below we provide a brief outline of the contributions, in the order in which they appear in the proceedings.

"Minimizing Simple and Cumulative Regret in Monte-Carlo Tree Search," a joint collaboration by Tom Pepels, Tristan Cazenave, Mark Winands, and Marc Lanctot. In the paper a new MCTS variant, called Hybrid MCTS (H-MCTS), is introduced that minimizes cumulative and simple regret in different parts of the tree. H-MCTS uses SHOT, a recursive version of Sequential Halving, to minimize simple regret near the root, and UCT to minimize cumulative regret when descending further down the tree. The results show genuine performance increase in Amazons, AtariGo, and Breakthrough.

"On Robustness of CMAB Algorithms: Experimental Approach," authored by Antonín Komenda, Alexander Shleyfman, and Carmel Domshlak experimentally analyzes the robustness of two state-of-the-art algorithms, Naive Monte Carlo (NMC) and Linear Side-Information (LSI), for online planning with combinatorial actions of the turn-based variant of the strategy game μRTS. The results show that LSI is stronger with smaller budgets and shorter look-ahead.

"Job-Level Algorithms for Connect6 Opening Position Analysis," by Ting-Han Wei, I-Chen Wu, Chao-Chin Liang, Bing-Tsung Chiang, Wen-Jie Tseng, Shi-Jim Yen, and Chang-Shing Lee, investigates job-level (JL) algorithms to analyze opening positions for Connect6. The paper first proposes four heuristic metrics when using JL-PNS to estimate move quality. Next, it introduces a JL Upper Confidence Tree (JL-UCT) algorithm and heuristic metrics, one of which is the number of nodes in each candidate move's subtree. In order to compare these metrics objectively, the paper proposes two kinds of measurement methods to analyze the suitability of these metrics when choosing best moves for a set of benchmark positions. The results show that for both metrics this node count heuristic metric for JL-UCT outperforms all the others, including the four for JL-PNS.

"Monte-Carlo Tree Search and Minimax Hybrids with Heuristic Evaluation Functions," written by Hendrik Baier and Mark Winands, discusses three different approaches to employ minimax search with static evaluation functions in MCTS: (1) to choose moves in the play-out phase of MCTS, (2) as a replacement for the play-out phase, and (3) as a node prior to bias move selection. The MCTS-minimax hybrids are tested and compared with their counterparts using evaluation functions without minimax in the domains of Othello, Breakthrough, and Catch the Lion. Results show that introducing minimax search is effective for heuristic node priors in Othello and Catch the Lion. The MCTS-minimax hybrids are also found to work well in combination with each other.

"Monte-Carlo Tree Search for the Game of '7 Wonders'," written by Denis Robilliard, Cyril Fonlupt, and Fabien Teytaud studies MCTS in the game of 7 Wonders. This card game combines several known challenging properties, such as imperfect information, multi-player, and chance. It also includes an inter-player trading system that induces a combinatorial search to decide which decisions are legal. Moreover, it is difficult to build an efficient evaluation function because the card values are heavily dependent upon the stage of the game and upon the other player decisions. The paper discusses how to effectively apply MCTS to 7 Wonders.

"Small and Large MCTS Playouts Applied to Chinese Dark Chess Stochastic Game," by Nicolas Jouandeau and Tristan Cazenave, presents MCTS modifications to deal with the stochastic game of Chinese Dark Chess. Experiments are conducted with group nodes and chance nodes using various configurations: with different play-out policies, with different play-out lengths, with true or estimated wins. Results show that extending the play-out length is useful for creating more informed play-outs, and the usage of an evaluation function can increase or decrease player's effectiveness through modifying the number of draw possibilities.

"On the Complexity of General Game Playing," authored by Édouard Bonnet and Abdallah Saffidine, discusses the computational complexity of reasoning in General Game Playing (GGP) using various combinations of multiple features of the Game Description Language (GDL). Their analysis offers a complexity landscape for GGP with fragments ranging from NP to EXPSPACE in the single-agent case, and from PSPACE to 2-EXPTIME in the multi-agent case.

"Efficient Grounding of Game Descriptions with Tabling," by Jean-Noël Vittaut and Jean Méhat, presents a method to instantiate game descriptions used in GGP with the tabling engine of a Prolog interpreter. Instantiation is a crucial step for speeding up the interpretation of the game descriptions and increasing the playing strength of general game players. The method allows one to ground almost all of the game descriptions present on the GGP servers in a time that is compatible with the common time settings of the GGP competition. It instantiates descriptions more rapidly than previous published methods.

"SHPE: HTN Planning for Video Games," written by Alexandre Menif, Éric Jacopin, and Tristan Cazenave, describes SHPE (Simple Hierarchical Planning

Engine). It is a hierarchical task network planning system designed to generate dynamic behaviors for real-time video games. SHPE is based on a combination of domain compilation and procedural task application/decomposition techniques in order to compute plans in a very short time-frame. The planner is able to return relevant plans in less than three milliseconds for several problem instances of the *SimpleFPS* planning domain.

"Predicting Player Disengagement in Online Games," by Hanting Xie, Daniel Kudenko, Sam Devlin, and Peter Cowling, introduces a pure data-driven method to foresee whether players will quit the game given their previous activity within the game, by constructing decision trees from historical gameplay data of previous players. The method is assessed on two popular commercial online games: I Am Playr and Lyroke. The former is a football game while the latter is a music game. The results indicate that the decision tree built by their method is valuable for predicting the players' disengagement and that its human-readable form allow us to search out further reasons about which in-game events made them quit.

"Coordinating Dialogue Systems and Stories Through Behavior Composition," a joint effort by Stefano Cianciulli, Daniele Riccardelli, and Stavros Vassos, exploits behavior composition in AI as a formal tool for facilitating interactive storytelling in video games. This is motivated by (1) the familiarity of transition systems in video game development, and (2) the fact that behavior composition extends the spectrum of approaches for non-linear storylines by introducing a new paradigm based on planning for a target desired process instead of a goal state. Moreover, the approach provides support for the debugging of deadlocks in stories at design level. The paper describes the behavior composition framework, and shows the details for an interactive dialogue system scenario in order to illustrate how interactive storytelling can be phrased in terms of the framework. A simple architecture for implementing a demo game over the scenario using existing behavior composition tools is also reported.

These proceedings would not have been produced without the help of many persons. In particular, we would like to mention the authors and reviewers for their help. Moreover, the organizers of ECAI 2014 contributed substantially by bringing the researchers together.

November 2014

Tristan Cazenave
Mark Winands
Yngvi Björnsson

Organization

Program Chairs

Tristan Cazenave   Université Paris-Dauphine, France
Mark Winands   Maastricht University, The Netherlands
Yngvi Björnsson   Reykjavik University, Iceland

Program Committee

Yngvi Björnsson   Reykjavik University, Iceland
Bruno Bouzy   Université Paris-Descartes, France
Tristan Cazenave   Université Paris-Dauphine, France
Rémi Coulom   Université Lille 3, France
Stefan Edelkamp   University of Bremen, Germany
Nicolas Jouandeau   Université Paris 8, France
Peter Kissmann   University Bremen, Germany
Sylvain Lagrue   Université d'Artois, France
Marc Lanctot   Maastricht University, The Netherlands
Viliam Lisý   Czech Technical University in Prague,
    Czech Republic
Jean Méhat   Université Paris 8, France
Jochen Renz   The Australian National University, Australia
Abdallah Saffidine   University of New South Wales, Australia
Fabien Teytaud   Université du Littoral Côte d'Opale, France
Olivier Teytaud   Université Paris-Sud, France
Mark Winands   Maastricht University, The Netherlands

Additional Reviewers

Tom Pepels   Maastricht University, The Netherlands
Stephan Schiffel   Reykjavik University, Iceland
Tsan-sheng Hsu   Institute of Information Science,
    Academia Sinica, Taiwan

Table of Contents

Minimizing Simple and Cumulative Regret in Monte-Carlo Tree Search

Tom Pepels[1], Tristan Cazenave[2], Mark H.M. Winands[1], and Marc Lanctot[1]

[1] Games and AI Group, Department of Knowledge Engineering,
Faculty of Humanities and Sciences, Maastricht University
{tom.pepels,m.winands,marc.lanctot}@maastrichtuniversity.nl
[2] LAMSADE - Université Paris-Dauphine
cazenave@lamsade.dauphine.fr

Abstract. Regret minimization is important in both the Multi-Armed Bandit problem and Monte-Carlo Tree Search (MCTS). Recently, simple regret, *i.e.,* the regret of not recommending the best action, has been proposed as an alternative to cumulative regret in MCTS, *i.e.,* regret accumulated over time. Each type of regret is appropriate in different contexts. Although the majority of MCTS research applies the UCT selection policy for minimizing cumulative regret in the tree, this paper introduces a new MCTS variant, Hybrid MCTS (H-MCTS), which minimizes both types of regret in different parts of the tree. H-MCTS uses SHOT, a recursive version of Sequential Halving, to minimize simple regret near the root, and UCT to minimize cumulative regret when descending further down the tree. We discuss the motivation for this new search technique, and show the performance of H-MCTS in six distinct two-player games: Amazons, AtariGo, Ataxx, Breakthrough, NoGo, and Pentalath.

1   Introduction

The Multi-Armed Bandit (MAB) problem is a decision making problem [3] where an agent is faced with several options. On each time step, an agent selects one of the options and observes a reward drawn from some distribution. This process is then repeated for a number of time steps. Generally the problem is described as choosing between the most rewarding arm of a multi-armed slot machine found in casinos. The agent can explore by pulling an arm and observing the resulting reward. The reward can be drawn from either a fixed or changing probability distribution. Each pull and the returned reward constitutes a sample. Algorithms used in MAB research have been developed to minimize *cumulative regret*. Cumulative regret is the expected regret of not having sampled the single best option in hindsight. This type of regret is accumulated during execution of the algorithm, each time a non-optimal arm is sampled the cumulative regret increases. UCB1 [3] is a selection policy for the MAB problem, which minimizes cumulative regret, converging to the empirically best arm. Once the best arm is

T. Cazenave et al. (Eds.): CGW 2014, CCIS 504, pp. 1–15, 2014.

found by exploring the available options, UCB1 exploits it by repeatedly sampling it, minimizing overall cumulative regret. This policy was adapted to be used in Monte-Carlo Tree Search (MCTS) in the form of UCT [11].

Recently, *simple regret* has been proposed as a new criterion for assessing the performance of both MAB [2,6] and MCTS [7,9,18] algorithms. Simple regret is defined as the expected error between an algorithm's recommendation, and the optimal decision. It is a naturally fitting quantity to optimize in the MCTS setting, because all simulations executed by MCTS are for the mere purpose of learning good moves. Moreover, the final move chosen after all simulations are performed, *i.e.,* the *recommendation*, is the one that has real consequence. Nonetheless, since the introduction of Monte-Carlo Tree Search (MCTS) [11] and its subsequent adoption by games researchers UCT [11], or some variant thereof, has become the "default" selection policy (cf. [5]).

In this paper we present a new, MCTS technique, named Hybrid MCTS (H-MCTS) that utilizes both UCT and Sequential Halving [10]. As such, the new technique uses both simple and cumulative regret minimizing policies to their best effect. We test H-MCTS in six distinct two-player games: Amazons, AtariGo, Ataxx, Breakthrough, NoGo, and Pentalath.

The paper is structured as follows, first MCTS and UCT are introduced in Section 2. Section 3 explains the difference between cumulative and simple regret, and how this applies to MCTS. Next, in Section 4 a recently introduced, simple regret minimizing technique for the MAB problem, Sequential Halving [10], is discussed. Sequential Halving is used recursively in SHOT [7], which is described in detail in Section 5. Together, SHOT and UCT form the basis for the new, hybrid MCTS technique discussed in Section 6. This is followed by the experiments, in Section 7 and finally by the conclusion and an outline of future research, in Section 8.

2   Monte-Carlo Tree Search

Monte-Carlo Tree Search (MCTS) is a best-first search method based on random sampling by Monte-Carlo simulations of the state space of a domain [8,11]. In game play, this means that decisions are made based on the results of randomly simulated play-outs. MCTS has been successfully applied to various turn-based games such as Go [16], Lines of Action [20], and Hex [1]. Moreover, MCTS has been used for agents playing real-time games such as the Physical Traveling Salesman [14], real-time strategy games [4], and Ms Pac-Man [13], but also in real-life domains such as optimization, scheduling, and security [5].

In MCTS, a tree is built incrementally over time, which maintains statistics at each node corresponding to the rewards collected at those nodes and number of times they have been visited. The root of this tree corresponds to the current position. The basic version of MCTS consists of four steps, which are performed iteratively until a computational threshold is reached, *i.e.,* a set number of simulations, an upper limit on memory usage, or a time constraint.

Each MCTS simulation consist of two main steps, 1) the *selection* step, where moves are selected and played inside the tree according to the selection policy until a leaf is *expanded*, and 2) the *play-out*, in which moves are played according to a simulation policy, outside the tree. At the end of each play-out a terminal state is reached and the result is *back-propagated* along the selected path in the tree from the expanded leaf to the root.

2.1 UCT

During the selection step, a policy is required to explore the tree to decide on promising options. For this reason, the widely used Upper Confidence Bound applied to Trees (UCT) [11] was derived from the UCB1 [3] policy. In UCT, each node is treated as a bandit problem whose arms are the moves that lead to different child nodes. UCT balances the exploitation of rewarding nodes whilst allowing exploration of lesser visited nodes. Consider a node p with children $I(p)$, then the policy determining which child i to select is defined as:

$$i^* = argmax_{i \in I(p)} \left\{ v_i + C\sqrt{\frac{\ln n_p}{n_i}} \right\}, \tag{1}$$

where v_i is the score of the child i based on the average result of simulations that visited it, n_p and n_i are the visit counts of the current node and its child, respectively. C is the exploration constant to tune. UCT is applied when the visit count of p is above a threshold T, otherwise a child is selected at random.

Note that UCB1 and consequently UCT incorporate both exploitation and exploration. After a number of trials, a node that is identified as the empirical best is selected more often. In tree search, this has three consequences:

1. Whenever a promising move is found, less time is spent on suboptimal ones. Since UCT is generally time-bounded, it is important to spend as much time as possible exploiting the best moves. Due to the *MinMax* principle, which states that an agent aims to maximize its minimum gain, on each ply we expect a player to perform the best reply to its opponent's move.
2. The valuation of any node in the tree is dependent on the values back-propagated. Given that UCT spends less time on suboptimal moves, any values back-propagated are based on increasingly improved simulations, because they are performed deeper in the tree. In fact, given infinite time, UCT converges to almost exclusively selecting nodes with the highest estimates.
3. The current value of the node can be falsified by searching deeper. In UCT, each simulation increases the depth of the search, and as such may reveal moves as becoming worse over time due to an unpredicted turn of events. If an expected good move is not reselected often, such "traps" [15] are not revealed. More generally, when sampling a game-tree rewards are not necessarily drawn from a fixed distribution.

3 Regret

In this section we discuss regret in both the MAB, and MCTS context. The differences between cumulative and simple regret are explained in Subsection 3.1. Next, we discuss regret in the context of MCTS in Subsection 3.2.

3.1 Cumulative and Simple Regret

Suppose a trial is set-up such that a forecaster (a player, or agent) has K actions, which can be repeatedly sampled over $n \in \{1, 2, \cdots, T\}$ trials. Each arm has a mean reward μ_i, and there exists a maximum mean reward μ^*. Suppose further that the forecaster employs a selection policy $I(n)$ that outputs some a to be sampled at time n, and a recommendation policy $J(n)$ that recommends the best arm at time T.

Cumulative regret is defined as the regret of having not sampled the best single action in hindsight,

$$R_n = \sum_{t=1}^{n} \mu^* - \mu_{I(t)}. \tag{2}$$

In other words, the regret is accumulated over time, for each sample the forecaster takes.

Now suppose that we change the experimental set-up, such that the actions chosen on trials $1, 2, \ldots, T - 1$ are taken under some realistic "simulated environment" that represents the true on-line decision problem but without committing to the actions. The only *real* decision is made after having played all T simulations. In contrast, *simple regret* [6] quantifies only the regret for the recommendation policy J at time T,

$$r_n = \mu^* - \mu_{J(n)}, \tag{3}$$

i.e., the regret of not having recommended the best action.

Given these definitions, a performance metric for a selection technique can be described as the expected cumulative $\mathbb{E}R_n$ or simple regret $\mathbb{E}r_n$ over different experiments. In their analysis of the links between simple and cumulative regret in MABs, Bubeck *et al.* [6] found that upper bounds on $\mathbb{E}R_n$ lead to lower bounds on $\mathbb{E}r_n$, and that the smaller the upper bound on $\mathbb{E}R_n$, the higher the lower bound on $\mathbb{E}r_n$, regardless of the recommendation policy, *i.e.*, the smaller the cumulative regret, the larger the simple regret. As such, no policy can give an optimal guarantee on both simple and cumulative regret at the same time. In the case of an MAB the strategy used depends on the context of the problem.

3.2 Regret in MCTS

Based on the analysis in Subsection 2.1, the minimization of cumulative regret is naturally suitable to tree search, and the UCB1 selection policy can be used nearly unaltered in this setting as UCT. However, there exist two contexts for the MAB problem, also to be considered in MCTS. These are:

1. Each trial results in a direct reward for the agent. As such we want to minimize the number of suboptimal arms pulled in order to achieve a rewards as high as possible. This relates, for example, to slot machines in a casino. Every choice made at each point in the algorithm has a direct effect on the agent's reward. In this case, the reward of the agent is related to the inverse of its **cumulative regret**.

2. The agent can perform a number of trials, without consequence, in a simulated environment. The agent is allowed T trials in this fashion, after which it must make a recommendation. Based on its recommendation, the agent is rewarded. In this case, the performance of the agent is measured by the **simple regret** of its recommendation. A low simple regret implies that the recommendation is close to the actual best option.

In most MCTS literature, UCT is used as selection policy (cf. [5]), suggesting that only the first context applies. However, the second context is a more natural fit when MCTS is used to play games, because the behavior of the agent in the domain is based solely on its recommendations. Nevertheless, simple regret minimization cannot replace UCT in this case without consideration. Unlike in an MAB, sampling does have an immediate impact on performance in MCTS because reward distributions are non-stationary. Spending more time on suboptimal moves when descending the tree decreases the amount of time available to explore nodes expected to have high rewards. Moreover, since all values are back-propagated, we risk underestimating ancestors based on sampling descendants that are known to be bad. This trade-off was also shown in [18] where the authors use a measure based on the Value of Information (VOI) to determine whether to exploit an expected good move, or continue exploring others. This trade-off is also described as a "separation of exploratory concerns" in BRUE [9].

4   Regret Minimization

Non-exploiting selection policies have been proposed to decrease simple regret at high rates. Given that UCB1 [3] has an optimal rate of cumulative regret convergence, and the conflicting limits on the bounds on the regret types shown in [6], policies that have a higher rate of exploration than UCB1 are expected to have better bounds on simple regret. Sequential Halving (SH) [10] is a novel, pure exploration technique developed for minimizing simple regret in the MAB problem. In this section, both SH and its recursive definition SHOT [7] are discussed.

4.1   Sequential Halving

In many problems there are only one or two good decisions to be identified, this means that when using a pure exploration technique, a potentially large portion of the allocated budget is spent sampling suboptimal arms. Therefore, an efficient policy is required to ensure that inferior arms are not selected as often as arms with a high reward. Successive Rejects [2] was the first algorithm to show a high rate of decrease in simple regret. It works by dividing the total computational budget into distinct rounds. After each round, the single worst arm is removed from selection, and the algorithm is continued on the reduced subset of arms. Sequential Halving (SH) [10], was later introduced as an alternative to Successive Rejects, offering better performance in large-scale MAB problems.

Algorithm 1. Sequential Halving [10]

    Input: total budget T, K arms
    Output: recommendation J_T
1 $S_0 \leftarrow \{1, \ldots, K\}$, $B \leftarrow \lceil \log_2 K \rceil - 1$
2 **for** $k=0$ **to** B **do**
3   sample each arm $i \in S_k$, $n_k = \left\lfloor \frac{T}{|S_k| \lceil \log_2 |S| \rceil} \right\rfloor$ times
4   update the average reward of each arm based on the rewards
5      $S_{k+1} \leftarrow$ the $\lceil |S_k|/2 \rceil$ arms from S_k with the best average
6 **return** *the single element of* S_B

SH divides search time into distinct rounds, and during each round arms are sampled uniformly. After each such round, the empirically worst half of the remaining arms are removed until a single arm remains. The rounds are equally distributed such that each round is allocated approximately the same number of trials (budget), but with smaller subset of available arms to sample. Sequential Halving is detailed in Algorithm 1.

In the next section a recently introduced MCTS technique called SHOT, is discussed which uses SH recursively. This technique is the basis for H-MCTS discussed in Section 6.

5   Sequential Halving Applied to Trees

Sequential Halving applied to Trees (SHOT) [7] is a search technique that utilizes Sequential Halving at every node of the search tree. A difference with regular SHOT and Sequential Halving is that SHOT comes back to already visited nodes with an increased budget. When the search returns to an already visited node, instead of distributing the new budget as if it was a new node, SHOT takes into account the budget already spent at the node and how it was spent. In order to apply Sequential Halving, SHOT considers the overall budget as the already spent budget plus the new budget to spend. It then calculates for each move the budget per move using Sequential Halving with this overall budget. The other difference with simple Sequential Halving is that each move already has an associated number of play-outs coming from the previous visits to the node. In order to take into account this already spent budget, SHOT only gives to each move the difference between the new budget for the move and the budget already spent for the move during previous visits. If the new budget is less or equal to the already spent budget the move is not given any budget for the current round.

SHOT has four beneficial properties: 1) it uses less memory than standard UCT, whereas standard UCT creates a new node for each play-out SHOT only creates a new entry in the transposition table when a node has more than one play-out. In practice, for 19×19 NoGo for example, it means that SHOT uses fifty times less memory than standard UCT. 2) SHOT uses less time descending the tree than UCT. Instead of descending the tree for each play-out, SHOT descends in a child for a possibly large number of play-outs. In practice this means that for the same number of play-outs SHOT was shown to be approximately twice as fast as UCT in the game NoGo [7]. 3) SHOT allocates a possibly large number of play-outs to the possible moves. This makes it easy to parallelize the search without loss of information and without changing the behavior of the algorithm. 4) SHOT is parameter free, contrary to UCT, which requires tuning its C constant. On the negative side, in order to run SHOT the total number of play-outs has to be known in advance. This is less convenient than UCT, which is an any-time algorithm.

6   A Hybrid MCTS

Recall that in the MAB context, in which simple regret minimization is appropriate, only the final recommendation made by an algorithm has effect on the agent's reward. In game play, this holds for the nodes of the search tree at the first ply. Only after running all the allocated simulations a recommendation is made, which affects the state of the game being played. Nodes deeper in the tree have an implicit effect on this decision. Because the shape of an MCTS tree is directly related to the potential reward of internal nodes, promising nodes are selected more often to grow the tree in their direction. This both enforces the confidence of the reward of promising nodes, but also ensures that their reward can be falsified based on results deeper in the tree.

Treating a game tree as a recursive MAB thus reveals different objectives for the distinct plies of the tree. At the root, simple regret should be as low as possible, since the recommendation of the algorithm is based on the first ply of the tree. On deeper plies, we want to both sample efficiently, avoiding time wasted on bad options, and back-propagate correct values from leafs to their ancestors. Where the former can be achieved by using selection policies such as Successive Rejects or Sequential Halving, the latter, as discussed in Section 2 is inherently performed by UCT. Intuitively, this leads to the belief that we should only minimize simple regret at the root, and use UCT throughout of the tree, as suggested by [18]. However, considering that at any node, based on the MinMax principle, we want to find the *best reply* to the action of the parent. It may also be beneficial to ensure a lower simple regret on that particular move because this could intrinsically lead to an improved evaluation of the parent.

Using a selection policy based on both SHOT and UCT, Hybrid MCTS (H-MCTS) combines simple and cumulative regret minimization in a tunable algorithm. The rationale is based on the results in [6], which show that given a low sampling budget, UCB empirically realizes lower simple regret. The proposed technique switches from Sequential Halving to UCT whenever the computational budget is below the budget limit B. Consequently, the search tree is composed of a *simple regret tree* at the root, and *UCT trees* rooted at the leafs of the simple regret tree. As shown in Figure 1, initially the simple regret tree is shallow

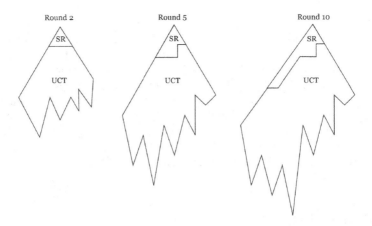

Fig. 1. Example progression of H-MCTS. In the top part of the tree (SR), simple regret is minimized using SHOT. Deeper in the tree, UCT minimizes cumulative regret. The round-numbers represent the Sequential Halving round at the root.

because the computational budget per node is small. Later, when the budget per node increases due to nodes being removed from selection as per Sequential Halving, the simple regret tree grows deeper. Note that since the root's children are sorted in descending order, the left part of the simple regret and UCT tree is always the deepest, since it its root is selected the most.

H-MCTS is outlined in Algorithm 2. Similar to UCT and SHOT, on line 3 terminal conditions are handled, followed by the main feature of the algorithm on line 6 where the initial simulation budget b for each child of the current node is computed. Based on b, a decision is made whether to progress into the UCT tree if $b < B$ or, if $b \geq B$ to continue with SHOT. Note that the $b < B$ check is overridden at the root, since only one cycle is initiated there. Assuming the allocated budget is sufficiently large, at the root simple regret minimization is preferred over cumulative regret minimization. From line 15 the algorithm is similar to the Sequential Halving portion of SHOT. As in SHOT, because multiple play-outs are back-propagated in a single descent from root to leaf, the algorithm returns a tuple t_p, which contains: 1) the number of visits v, and 2) the number of wins per player w_1 and w_2. On line 22, the budget used b_u is incremented by v from the results returned by the recursion. Moreover, the current node's statistics are updated, alongside the cumulative tuple t_p, which are returned to the node's parent. UCT also maintains a tuple of statistics such that it can return the same t_p to the simple regret tree. For the UCT tree, any implementation can be used, as long as it is adapted to return t_p and update the *budgetSpent* value alongside the usual node's visit count because any UCT node in the tree can be "converted" to a simple regret node at any time, when $b > B$ on line 6.

Whenever a UCT node is included in the simple regret tree, all its values are maintained. As such, Sequential Halving has an initial estimate of the values of

---

Algorithm 2. Hybrid Monte-Carlo Tree Search (H-MCTS).

Input: node p, allocated budget *budget*

Output: t_p: number of play-outs, $p1$ and $p2$ wins

1 H-MCTS(node p, *budget*):
2   **if** *isLeaf(p)* **then** $S \leftarrow$ EXPAND(p) $t_p \leftarrow \langle 0, 0, 0 \rangle$
3   **if** *isTerminal(p)* **then**
4   UPDATE t_p, with *budget* wins for the appropriate player, and *budget* visits
5   **return** t_p
6    $b \leftarrow \max\left(1, \left\lfloor \frac{p.budgetSpent+budget}{s \times \lceil log_2|S| \rceil} \right\rfloor \right)$
7   **if** *not isRoot(p)* **and** $b < B$ **then**
8   **for** $i=0$ **to** *budget* **do**
9            $\langle v, w_1, w_2 \rangle_i \leftarrow$ UCT(p)
10   UPDATE p, t_p with $\langle v, w_1, w_2 \rangle_i$
11   **return** t_p
12    $b_u, k \leftarrow 0$
13    $S_0 \leftarrow S$
14    $s \leftarrow |S|$
15   **repeat**
16   **for** $i=1$ **to** s **do**
17            $n_i \leftarrow$ node n at rank i of S_k
18   **if** $b > n_i.visits$ **then**
19                $b_i \leftarrow b - n_i.visits$
20   **if** $i = 0$ **and** $s = 2$ **then**
                      $b_i \leftarrow \max\left(b_i, budget - b_u - (b - n_1.visits)\right)$
                      $b_i \leftarrow \min\left(b_i, budget - b_u\right)$
21                $\langle v, w_1, w_2 \rangle_i \leftarrow$ H-MCTS(n_i, b_i)
22   UPDATE p, b_u, and t_p with $\langle v, w_1, w_2 \rangle_i$
23   break if $b_u \geq budget$
24        $k \leftarrow k + 1$
25        $S_k \leftarrow S_{k-1}$, with the first s elements sorted in descending order
26        $s \leftarrow \lceil s/2 \rceil$
27        $b \leftarrow b + \max\left(1, \left\lfloor \frac{p.budgetSpent+budget}{s \times \lceil log_2|S| \rceil} \right\rfloor \right)$
28   **until** $b_u \geq budget$ **or** $s < 2$
29   UPDATE $p.budgetSpent$ with b_u
30 **return** t_p

the nodes. Based on the budgeting method of SHOT [7], budget is reallocated such that it adheres to Sequential Halving's allocation.

In the scheme presented, a limit on the available budget determines whether to continue in the simple regret tree. However, other methods such as a fixed depth limit for the simple regret tree, or a time-partitioned method, can be viable. Based on the simple regret theory in MABs, pure exploration methods only provide empirically better simple regret than UCB, given a sufficiently large budget. To minimize simple regret given a small budget, UCB with a properly tuned constant should be preferred [6]. Directly applying this result to MCTS means that whenever the available budget is low, UCT with a properly tuned constant should be preferred as selection policy. Therefore, whenever a Sequential Halving round can be initiated with a budget per child higher than B, we continue in the simple regret tree. Otherwise the budget is assigned to UCT, which runs b simulations, and returns the result of their play-outs. Play-outs are only ever initiated in the UCT tree, because UCT immediately takes advantage of the values stored at nodes, whereas Sequential Halving selects all children b times in the first round regardless of their prospects.

As with MCTS, H-MCTS can be separated in four discrete steps:

1. **Budgeting**: A budget is determined for each child. Based on the budget, we enter the UCT tree, or remain in the simple regret tree. If we enter the UCT tree, the four basic MCTS steps apply.
2. **Selection**: In the simple regret tree, nodes are sampled based on Sequential Halving. Nodes in the simple regret tree are assigned a budget, to be spent in their rooted UCT tree, in which play-outs are initiated.
3. **Removal**: Based on the results obtained, children are removed from selection. A new Sequential Halving round starts with half of the best children from the previous round. If the budget is spent, the currently accumulated results are back-propagated.
4. **Back-Propagation**: Since H-MCTS is performed depth-first, the final result is only available after all budget is spent. This results in simultaneous back-propagation of numerous results in the simple regret tree.

In this case Sequential Halving is presented as the simple regret algorithm. However, it is certainly possible to replace it with any other algorithm such as Successive Rejects, or any other form of sequential reduction.

H-MCTS shares its disadvantage of not being able to return a recommendation at any-time with SHOT. It must know its exact computational budget beforehand. However, it does make use of the fact that UCT is any-time. Suppose a node was selected and expanded by H-MCTS, then at each time in the simple regret tree, nodes have an appropriate value based on the results back-propagated by UCT. Thus, when SHOT finishes a round by sorting the nodes by their accumulated values on line 25, UCT's any-time property ensures nodes have a representative value.

To a lesser extent, H-MCTS also shares the speed benefit of SHOT. However, because a part of the search is spent in the UCT tree, H-MCTS still spends more time in the tree than SHOT overall. Given a lower budget limit B, H-MCTS can be tuned to run faster by decreasing time spend in the UCT tree.

In the form presented in Algorithm 2, H-MCTS cannot solve proven wins or losses in the simple regret tree. Although we can employ the MCTS-Solver proposed by Winands *et al.* [19] in the UCT tree, this solver is to be adapted to SHOT to be able to solve nodes in the simple regret tree. Such a mechanism has been developed and details are given in [12].

7   Experiments and Results

In this section we show the results of the experiments performed on six two-player games. H-MCTS and the games were implemented in two different engines. Amazons, Breakthrough, NoGo and Pentalath are implemented in a Java based engine. Ataxx and AtariGo are implemented in a *C++* based engine.

- *Amazons* is played on an 8×8 board. Players each have four Amazons that move as queens in chess. Moves consist of two parts: movement, and blocking a square on the board. The last player to move wins the game.
- *AtariGo*, or first-capture Go, is a variant of Go where the first player to capture any stones wins. Experiments are performed on a 9×9 board.
- *Ataxx* is a game similar to Reversi. Played on a square board, players start with two stones each placed in an opposite corner. Captures are performed by moving a stone alongside an opponent's on the board. In the variant used in this paper, jumps are not allowed. The game ends when all squares are filled, or when a player has no remaining stones. The player with the most stones wins. Experiments are performed on a 7×7 board.
- *Breakthrough* is played on an 8×8 board. Players start with 16 pawns. The goal is to move one of them to the opponent's side.
- *NoGo* is a combinatorial game based on Go. Captures are forbidden and the first player unable to play due to this rule, loses. Experiments are performed on a 9×9 board.
- *Pentalath* is a connection game played on a hexagonal board. The goal is to place 5 pieces in a row. Pieces can be captured by fully surrounding an opponent's group.

A uniform random selection policy is used during the play-outs, unless otherwise stated. The C constant, used by UCT (Equation 1) was tuned in each game and was not re-optimized for H-MCTS, both UCT and H-MCTS use the same C constant in the experiments. The budget limit B which determines the switching point between the simple regret and UCT tree, was optimized for each game independently using a range between 10 and 110, with an interval of 20.

7.1   Results

For each table, the results are shown with respect to the first algorithm mentioned in the captions, along with a 95% confidence interval. For each experiment, the players' seats were swapped such that 50% of the games are played as the first player, and 50% as the second, to ensure no first-player or second-player bias. Because H-MCTS cannot be terminated any-time we present only results for a fixed number of simulations. In each experiment, both players are allocated a budget of both 10,000 and 25,000 play-outs.

Table 1 shows results of the matches played by H-MCTS against a standard UCT player. H-MCTS performs best in Amazons, AtariGo, Ataxx, and Pentalath. For Amazons this is in part due to the high branching factor of approximately $1,200$ moves at the start of the match. Since UCT cannot explore and exploit all options in time, Sequential Halving ensures that only a limited subset of the large action-space is under consideration. For NoGo and Breakthrough we see no significant improvement over UCT. This may be due to the fact that these games are more tactical and have narrow winning-lines, and a more exploiting algorithm applies better by identifying good moves and exploiting them fast.

To determine the effect of UCT in H-MCTS, the results of matches played against SHOT are shown in Table 2. H-MCTS shows significant improvement in 10 of the 12 cases. No use is made of the speed benefits of either technique in these experiments. These results give evidence for the claim that H-MCTS makes use of UCT's any-time property to provide better reward estimates in the simple regret tree. Values back-propagated and averaged by using UCT may be more effective than those back-propagated by SHOT. As a benchmark, SHOT played 1,000 matches against UCT per game in Table 3. The results for NoGo differ from those presented in [7], because our experiment is performed using a fixed budget of play-outs for both players, whereas in [7], results are based on time-based experiments. SHOT performs best against H-MCTS and UCT in the games with the highest branching factors, Amazons and AtariGo. This reinforces the evidence that Sequential Halving is best applied in games with high branching factors. In the games with narrow winning-lines such as Breakthrough and Pentalath, SHOT's performance declines against UCT. However, given SHOT's speed improvement over UCT, it is possible that the technique performs better in a time-based experiment.

Table 1. H-MCTS vs. UCT with random play-outs, 1,000 games

Game	B	10,000 play-outs	25,000 play-outs
Amazons 8×8	50	**65.2** ± 3.0	**62.0** ± 3.0
AtariGo 9×9	30	**60.6** ± 3.1	**60.6** ± 3.1
Ataxx 7×7	30	52.4 ± 3.1	47.2 ± 3.0
Breakthrough 8×8	70	**53.2** ± 3.1	50.4 ± 3.1
NoGo 9×9	30	52.4 ± 3.1	48.8 ± 3.1
Pentalath	30	46.7 ± 3.1	**54.7** ± 3.1

Table 2. H-MCTS vs. SHOT with random play-outs, 1,000 games

Game	B	10,000 play-outs	25,000 play-outs
Amazons 8×8	50	51.2 ± 3.1	**55.4** ± 3.1
AtariGo 9×9	30	50.0 ± 3.1	**57.5** ± 3.1
Ataxx 7×7	30	**54.5** ± 3.1	**56.0** ± 3.1
Breakthrough 8×8	70	**68.4** ± 2.9	**84.0** ± 2.3
NoGo 9×9	30	**56.3** ± 3.1	**55.5** ± 3.1
Pentalath	30	**62.1** ± 3.0	**78.3** ± 2.6

Table 3. SHOT vs. UCT with random play-outs, 1,000 games

Game	10,000 play-outs	25,000 play-outs
Amazons 8×8	**60.2** ± 3.0	**55.2** ± 3.1
AtariGo 9×9	**53.8** ± 3.1	**55.7** ± 3.1
Ataxx 7×7	46.7 ± 3.1	40.8 ± 3.1
Breakthrough 8×8	31.2 ± 3.1	16.4 ± 2.3
NoGo 9×9	44.7 ± 3.1	41.4 ± 3.1
Pentalath	33.7 ± 3.0	22.8 ± 2.6

In Table 4, an informed play-out policy is used to select moves for Breakthrough. A capture move is four times more likely to be selected than a non-capture one, and a defensive capture (near the winning line) is five times more likely to be selected and (anti-)decisive [17] moves are always played when available. UCT with this play-out policy enabled wins approximately 78% of the games played against UCT with random play-outs. H-MCTS benefits more from the informed play-outs than UCT in Breakthrough, winning up to 56.6% of the games against UCT.

The second part of Table 4 shows results for matches played between the H-MCTS Solver presented in [12] and the MCTS-Solver. Breakthrough employs the heuristic play-out policy, for which we see a significant boost in performance proportional to the allocated budget. Overall, the results show some improvement over Table 1 in Pentalath and NoGo with 25,000 play-outs, although the difference is not sufficient to conclude that the Solver performs better in H-MCTS than in UCT in these games with the same C constant.

8   Conclusion and Future Research

In this paper an MCTS technique is presented based on the results of research in regret theory. The conclusions of the research performed in [6] were interpreted into the form of a Hybrid MCTS technique (H-MCTS). Based on minimizing simple regret near the root, where the overall budget is high, and cumulative

Table 4. H-MCTS vs. UCT with heuristic play-outs, with/without solver, 1,000 games

Game	B	10,000 play-outs	25,000 play-outs
		Heuristic play-outs (no solver)	
Breakthrough 8×8	70	50.4 ± 3.1	**56.6** ± 3.1
		H-MCTS Solver	
Amazons 8×8	50	**65.2** ± 3.0	**64.0** ± 3.0
Breakthrough 8×8	70	**56.7** ± 3.1	**61.3** ± 3.0
NoGo 9×9	30	50.5 ± 3.1	50.6 ± 3.1
Pentalath	70	**53.6** ± 3.1	**55.6** ± 3.1

regret deeper in the tree [18]. Depending on the available budget during search H-MCTS' simple regret tree can expand deeper to provide better bounds on simple regret on the best replies of its rooted subtrees. The simple regret tree is traversed using SHOT [7]. H-MCTS requires beforehand knowledge of the available play-out budget and therefore cannot be terminated at any time to provide a recommendation. In tournament-play, when search time is strictly limited, an approximation of the number of simulations per second can be used to determine the available play-out budget.

H-MCTS performed better against SHOT given the same allocation of play-outs in 10 out of 12 experiments. Moreover, results show that in different games, H-MCTS performs either better, or on par with UCT. In Amazons, AtariGo, and Pentalath H-MCTS outperforms UCT by up to 65.2%. In Breakthrough using an informed play-out policy H-MCTS outperformed UCT by up to 61.3% using the solver technique.

Although the hybrid technique is founded on theoretical work in both the MAB context and MCTS, we have not shown that it provides better bounds on simple regret compared to other techniques. This is work for future research. In order to show that H-MCTS exhibits lower simple regret in practice, it should be validated in smaller, proven games for which the game-theoretic value of each action is known. Moreover, investigation is required regarding the effects of the budget limit B in relation to the total allocated number of play-outs, and the interrelation between H-MCTS' B, and UCT's C constant. In the experiments presented in this paper, both were fixed per game, rather than per experiment. Finally, the speed benefits of H-MCTS, combined with parallelization is open to investigation. H-MCTS can be parallelized efficiently by dividing budgets in the simple regret tree over multiple threads [7].

Acknowledgments. This work is partially funded by the Netherlands Organisation for Scientific Research (NWO) in the framework of the project Go4Nature, grant number 612.000.938.

References

1. Arneson, B., Hayward, R., Henderson, P.: Monte-Carlo tree search in Hex. IEEE Trans. Comput. Intell. AI in Games 2(4), 251–258 (2010)
2. Audibert, J., Bubeck, S., Munos, R.: Best arm identification in multi-armed bandits. In: Proc. 23rd Conf. on Learn. Theory, pp. 41–53 (2010)
3. Auer, P., Cesa-Bianchi, N., Fischer, P.: Finite-time analysis of the multiarmed bandit problem. Machine Learning 47(2-3), 235–256 (2002)
4. Balla, R.K., Fern, A.: UCT for tactical assault planning in real-time strategy games. In: Boutilier, C. (ed.) Proc. of the 21st Int. Joint Conf. on Artif. Intel. (IJCAI), pp. 40–45 (2009)
5. Browne, C., Powley, E., Whitehouse, D., Lucas, S.M., Cowling, P.I., Rohlfshagen, P., Tavener, S., Perez, D., Samothrakis, S., Colton, S.: A survey of Monte-Carlo tree search methods. IEEE Trans. on Comput. Intell. AI in Games 4(1), 1–43 (2012)
6. Bubeck, S., Munos, R., Stoltz, G.: Pure exploration in finitely-armed and continuous-armed bandits. Theoretical Comput. Sci. 412(19), 1832–1852 (2010)
7. Cazenave, T.: Sequential halving applied to trees. IEEE Computer Society Press, Los Alamitos (2014)
8. Coulom, R.: Efficient selectivity and backup operators in monte-carlo tree search. In: van den Herik, H.J., Ciancarini, P., Donkers, H.H.L.M(J.) (eds.) CG 2006. LNCS, vol. 4630, pp. 72–83. Springer, Heidelberg (2007)
9. Feldman, Z., Domshlak, C.: Simple regret optimization in online planning for markov decision processes. CoRR abs/1206.3382 (2012)
10. Karnin, Z., Koren, T., Somekh, O.: Almost optimal exploration in multi-armed bandits. In: Proc. of the Int. Conf. on Mach. Learn., pp. 1238–1246 (2013)
11. Kocsis, L., Szepesvári, C.: Bandit based monte-carlo planning. In: Fürnkranz, J., Scheffer, T., Spiliopoulou, M. (eds.) ECML 2006. LNCS (LNAI), vol. 4212, pp. 282–293. Springer, Heidelberg (2006)
12. Pepels, T.: Novel Selection Methods for Monte-Carlo Tree Search. Master's thesis, Department of Knowledge Engineering, Maastricht University, Maastricht, The Netherlands (2014)
13. Pepels, T., Winands, M.H.M., Lanctot, M.: Real-time Monte Carlo Tree Search in Ms Pac-Man. IEEE Trans. Comp. Intell. AI Games 6(3), 245–257 (2014)
14. Powley, E.J., Whitehouse, D., Cowling, P.I.: Monte Carlo tree search with macro-actions and heuristic route planning for the physical travelling salesman problem. In: IEEE Conf. Comput. Intell. Games, pp. 234–241. IEEE (2012)
15. Ramanujan, R., Sabharwal, A., Selman, B.: Understanding Sampling Style Adversarial Search Methods. In: Proceedings of the Conference on Uncertainty in Artificial Intelligence, pp. 474–483 (2010)
16. Rimmel, A., Teytaud, O., Lee, C., Yen, S., Wang, M., Tsai, S.: Current frontiers in computer Go. IEEE Trans. Comput. Intell. AI in Games 2(4), 229–238 (2010)
17. Teytaud, F., Teytaud, O.: On the huge benefit of decisive moves in Monte-Carlo Tree Search algorithms. In: IEEE Conference on Computational Intelligence and Games, pp. 359–364. IEEE (2010)
18. Tolpin, D., Shimony, S.: MCTS based on simple regret. In: Proc. Assoc. Adv. Artif. Intell., pp. 570–576 (2012)
19. Winands, M.H.M., Björnsson, Y., Saito, J.-T.: Monte-Carlo Tree Search Solver. In: van den Herik, H.J., Xu, X., Ma, Z., Winands, M.H.M. (eds.) CG 2008. LNCS, vol. 5131, pp. 25–36. Springer, Heidelberg (2008)
20. Winands, M.H.M., Björnsson, Y., Saito, J.T.: Monte Carlo Tree Search in Lines of Action. IEEE Trans. Comp. Intell. AI Games 2(4), 239–250 (2010)

On Robustness of CMAB Algorithms:
Experimental Approach

Antonín Komenda, Alexander Shleyfman, and Carmel Domshlak

Faculty of Industrial Engineering and Management,
Technion – Israel Institute of Technology, Haifa
{akomenda@tx,alesh@tx,dcarmel@ie}.technion.ac.il

Abstract. In online planning with a team of cooperative agents, a straightforward model for decision making which actions the agents should execute can be represented as the problem of Combinatorial Multi-Armed Bandit. Similarly to the most prominent approaches for online planning with polynomial number of possible actions, state-of-the-art algorithms for online planning with exponential number of actions are based on Monte-Carlo sampling. However, without a proper selection of the appropriate subset of actions these techniques cannot be used. The most recent algorithms tackling this problem utilize an assumption of linearity with respect to the combinations of the actions.

In this paper, we experimentally analyze robustness of two state-of-the-art algorithms NMC and LSI for online planning with combinatorial actions in various setups of Real-Time and Turn-Taking Strategy games.

1 Introduction

In wide range of large-scale sequential decision making problems, analysis of the problem is often reduced to a state-space area that is considered most relevant to the specific decision currently faced by the agent. Thus the agent is required to find the best estimated action for the current state, instead of producing the entire plan as off-line algorithms do. In contrast, on-line planning algorithms focus on the current state of the agent, examine the set of possible courses of action onwards, and use the outcome of that examination to select an action to execute. After the action is executed in the real world, the agent repeats the planning process from the acquired state.

Each sequential problem can be described as a transition system of states and actions. When the number of applicable actions at each state is polynomial in the size of the problem description, the computational complexity of planning grows entirely from the size of the state-space. This "curse of state dimensionality" seems to receive most of the attention in the automated planning research.

Whatever the atomic actions of the agents are, as long as the agent can perform only one (or a small fixed number of) atomic actions simultaneously, the action choices at any state can be efficiently enumerated. However, if we are planning for a team of cooperating agents that each has a number of possible atomic

T. Cazenave et al. (Eds.): CGW 2014, CCIS 504, pp. 16–28, 2014.
© Springer International Publishing Switzerland 2014

actions to execute, then the problem exhibits a "curse of action dimensionality" via the combinatorial structure of the action space.

Real-time strategy games (RTS) are a great example of sequential simultaneous decision problems with combinatorial action spaces, as the players are asked to move sets of units that each by itself forms the force of each player [2,6,7,15,17]. Thus, the set of actions available to a player at each state corresponds to a (sometimes proper, due to some game-specific constraints) subset of the cross-product of explicitly given sets of atomic actions of her units[1].

The problem of combinatorial actions was tackled in work of Ontañón [16], it was suggested considering combinatorial actions in on-line planning through the lens of *combinatorial multi-armed bandit (CMAB)* problems [11,5,16].

In particular, Ontañón suggested a specific Monte-Carlo algorithm for online planning in CMABs, called Naive Monte Carlo (NMC), that is driven by an assumption that the expected value of a combinatorial action can be faithfully approximated by a linear function of its components. Evaluated on the μRTS game, NMC was shown to favorably compete with popular search algorithms such as UCT [14] and alpha-beta considering durations ABCD [7], which avoid dealing with combinatorial actions directly [16].

In our recent paper [18], we presented a family of algorithms (LSI) that substantially outperformed NMC. In this work we continue the study of on-line planning algorithms for CMABs, concentrating on the robust empirical evaluations of both LSI and NMC algorithms, while drawing new conclusions about both quality and responsiveness of those algorithms.

2   Background

The *multi-armed bandit (MAB)* problem is a sequential decision problem defined over a single state. At each stage, the agent has to execute one out of some $k \geq 2$ stochastic actions $\{a_1, \ldots, a_k\}$, with a_i being parameterized with an unknown distribution ν_i, with expectation μ_i. If a_i is executed, the agent gets a reward drawn at random from ν_i.

Most research on MABs has been devoted to the setup of reinforcement learning-while-acting, where the performance of the agent is assessed in terms of its cumulative regret, the sum of differences between the expected reward of the best arm and the obtained rewards. Good algorithms for learning-while-acting in MAB, like UCB1 [1], trade off between exploration and exploitation. These MAB algorithms also gave rise to popular Monte-Carlo tree search algorithms for online planning in multi-state sequential decision problems (e.g., Markov Decision Processes and sequential games), such as ε-MCTS [19], UCT [14], and MaxUCT [13].

However, as it was first studied in depth by Bubeck et al. [4], learning-while-acting and online planning are rather different problems that should favor different techniques. Unlike in learning-while-acting, the agent in online planning

---

[1] From an agent-centric point of view, the player requires acting of her units, therefore we use the game-theoretic terminology of agents instead of units.

may try the actions "free of charge" a given number of times N (not necessarily known in advance) and is then asked to output a recommended arm. The agent in online planning is evaluated by his *simple regret*, i.e., the difference $\mu^* - \mu_i$ between the expected payoff of the best action and the average payoff obtained by his recommendation a_i.

In other words, in online planning for MAB, the agent is judged solely for his final recommendation, and he is provided with a simulator that can be used "free of charge" to evaluate the alternative actions by drawing samples from their reward distributions. Therefore, good algorithms for online planning in MABs, like uniform-EBA [4], Successive Rejects [3], and Sequential Halving [12], are focused solely on exploration, and they already gave rise to efficient Monte-Carlo tree search algorithms for online planning in multi-state sequential decision problems such as BRUE [9] and MaxBRUE [10].

In contrast to regular MAB problems, in which rewards are associated with individual actions and a single action is executed at each stage, in *combinatorial multi-armed bandit (CMAB) problems*, the rewards are associated with certain subsets of actions, and the agents are allowed to simultaneously execute such subsets of actions at each stage [11,5,16,18]. In terms closest to problems that motivated our work in the first place, i.e., sequential decision problems for teams of cooperative agents, a CMAB problem is given by a finite set of $n \geq 1$ classes of actions $\{A_1, \ldots, A_n\}$, with $A_i = \{a_{i;1}, \ldots, a_{i;k_i}\}$, and a constraint $\mathcal{C} \subseteq \mathcal{A} = [A_1 \cup \{\epsilon\}] \times \cdots \times [A_n \cup \{\epsilon\}]$, where ϵ denotes "do nothing", and thus $\mathcal{A}$ is the set of all possible subsets of actions, with at most one representative from each action class. We refer to every set of actions $\mathbf{a} \in \mathcal{A}$ as a combinatorial action, or *c-action*, for short. Each c-action $\mathbf{a}$ is parameterized with an unknown distribution $\nu(\mathbf{a})$, with expectation $\mu(\mathbf{a})$. At each stage, the agents have to execute one out of some $2 \leq K = |\mathcal{C}| \leq \prod_{i=1}^{n} k_i$ c-actions, and if c-action $\mathbf{a}$ is executed, then agents get a reward drawn at random from $\nu(\mathbf{a})$.

Whether our setup is online planning in CMABs or learning-while-planning in CMABs, it is easy to see that CMAB problems with $K = O(poly(n))$ can be efficiently approached with regular MAB algorithms. However, if the problem is only loosely constrained and thus the c-action space grows exponentially with n (as it is typically the case in RTS-like planning problems), then the algorithms for regular MAB problems are no-go because they all rely on assumption that each c-action can be sampled at least once. This led to devising algorithms for CMAB learning-while-planning [11,5] and online planning [16], all making certain assumptions of "side information", usefulness of which depends (either formally or informally) on the properties of μ over the polytope induced by $A_1 \times \cdots \times A_n$. Such a "side information" basically captures the structure of μ targeted by the algorithm, but the algorithm can still be sound for arbitrary expected reward functions. This is, for instance, the case with the Naive Monte Carlo algorithm of Ontañón [16] and Linear Side-Information algorithm [18], which we describe in detail and compare, later on. As a setting we chose the μRTS game that was introduced by Ontañón in [16].

As changing various parameters of the game, we test both algorithms for producing the actions with the highest evaluated reward in the moment. The efficiency of the produced strategies is measured by whether the algorithm won or lost the game.

3   CMAB Algorithms with Linear Side-Information

In contrast to the problems of classic MABs, the area of combinatorial MABs was not so heavily studied so far and the algorithms tackling the problem are sparse. Since we are aiming at RTS games and Monte-Carlo techniques, there are only two candidate algorithms: Ontañón's Naive Monte Carlo (NMC) [16] and our recent Linear Side-Information (LSI) [18].

Both NMC and LSI comprise two distinct sub-processes: (a) generation of the candidate c-actions and (b) evaluation of the generated c-actions. To our knowledge, these are the only approaches to solve CMAB by sampling in general, as for the classic MAB approaches it is unfeasible to work with the whole (exponentially large) set of c-actions $\mathcal{C}$, in other words to tackle the "curse of action space dimensionality". However, the interconnection of these two phases is not fixed. On the one hand, NMC is interleaving both these phases reusing the evaluation of each particular c-action for each particular atomic action. LSI, on the other hand, uses separate phases, i.e., it evaluates atomic actions and based on these evaluations, it generates a set of c-actions $\mathcal{C}^*$.

In the following subsections we describe both algorithms prior to the experimental analysis of their sensitivity to the sampling budget, length of the look-ahead and variants of a RTS game with various action durations.

3.1   NMC

The Naive Monte Carlo algorithm was proposed by Ontañón [16]. The generate and evaluate sub-processes are interleaved in form of ε-greedy strategies and operate under an assumption that μ is linear over the atomic actions of the CMAB, i.e., $\mu(\mathbf{a}) = \sum_{i=1}^{n} \sum_{j=1}^{k_i} 1_{\{a_{i;j} \in \mathbf{a}\}} w_{i;j}$, where $1_{\{.\}}$ is the indicator function, and $w_{i;j} \in \mathbb{R}$. The particular sub-processes are used with probability ε_0 and $(1 - \varepsilon_0)$ respectively:

1. With probability ε_0: The *generation sub-process* forms and samples a candidate c-action $\mathbf{a}$ by selecting atomic actions from each set A_i. The selection is made independently and ε_1-greedily[2]. With probability $(1 - \varepsilon_1)$, the i-th atomic action of $\mathbf{a}$ will be selected from A_i uniformly at random.
2. With probability $(1 - \varepsilon_0)$: The *evaluation sub-process* samples the empirically best action in (the current) set $\mathcal{C}^*$.

---

[2] The selection goes with probability ε_1 for $\mathbf{a}$ which will contain the best atomic action so far from A_i. An action $a_{i;j}$ is the best of A_i if the average reward of the c-action samples involving $a_{i;j}$ is the highest among the atomic actions of A_i

The last best action after spending the whole sampling budget N is used and executed by the agents.

One of the benefits of the algorithm is that it converges to the best c-action from $\mathcal{C}$ in the infinity, even if the assumption of μ's linearity does not hold. The other benefit is that NMC considerably outperforms algorithms such as UCT and ABCD in the μRTS game. However, since the algorithm is interleaving the generation and evaluation sub-processes, a substantial amount of the evaluated samples is used on c-actions based on only small number of samples of the side-information in the generate phase. In addition, the algorithm does not meaningfully guarantee any quality of the recommended action from the generated set of c-actions $\mathcal{C}^*$, as the finally selected (best) c-action can be sampled only once during the whole process. Our more detailed analysis of this effect can be found in [18].

To overcome the weaknesses of NMC, we have recently proposed another Monte-Carlo algorithm [18] to tackle CMABs exploiting linearity of μ with smaller variance of the evaluation of the selected c-action.

3.2 LSI

In contrast to NMC, our recently proposed algorithm [18] Linear Side-Information (LSI) does not interleave the generate and evaluate sub-processes, but uses them in a serial manner, i.e., working in two phases, the *generate phase* and the *evaluate phase*. Each phase has a dedicated sampling budget, partitioned from N into N_g for generation and N_e for evaluation respectively.

In the generate phase, the algorithm evaluates systematically all atomic actions of all agents supplemented by other agents' actions selected with uniform random distribution. The algorithm utilizes all the N_g samples and the particular evaluations are reused for all the atomic actions of all agents (incl. those randomly supplementing the systematically selected one). Based on the evaluations a weight function $\widehat{R}$ is generated from the evaluated atomic actions (adopting the linear side information assumption). Further, a probability distribution $\mathcal{D}_{\widehat{R}}$ over c-action space $\mathcal{C}$ biased "towards" $\widehat{R}$ is formed. Precisely, the atomic action classes are ordered in the increasing order of entropy that is exhibited by the corresponding probability distributions $\mathcal{D}[\{\widehat{R}(a_{i;1}), \ldots, \widehat{R}(a_{i;k_i})\}]$, as measured by an entropy measure H (such as the Shannon entropy, or some other Renyi entropy [8]). These measures quantify the diversity of probability distributions, and minimize on the least diverse distributions, which are uniform distributions. Hence, if c-actions are generated by sampling the atomic action classes sequentially, yet these sequential choices are inter-constrained, sampling the action classes in the increasing order of $H(\mathcal{D}[\{\widehat{R}(a_{i;1}), \ldots, \widehat{R}(a_{i;k_i})\}])$ prioritizes classes in which the different atomic actions actually differ in their purported value, and thus the choice really matters. The generate phase ends with generation of the c-actions based on the probability distribution $\mathcal{D}_{\widehat{R}}$. The resulting set of c-actions enters the following phase as an input.

In the evaluate phase, the generated c-actions are systematically evaluated using the recent *Sequential Halving* algorithm of Karnin et al. [12] for action recommendation (aka online planning) in regular MABs. The algorithm was chosen especially because of its best formal guarantees to date. Sequential Halving is an iterative approach spreading the sampling budget such that the finally selected MAB arm (or c-action in our case) is sampled $\frac{N_e}{\lceil \log_2(N_e) \rceil}$-times, as the algorithm samples uniformly sets of arms in each iteration and keeps only the better half of them to the next iteration. Let us recall that NMC does not guarantee such sampling amount of the best estimated arm and therefore the quality of the final c-action estimation can be in NMC as low as quality of estimation by one sample.

The particular algorithm summarized in this section is one of four algorithms of the LSI family we have proposed in [18]. Precisely, it is LSI$_F^e$, using randomized supplement of the atomic actions in the first phase, thus in the notion of underlying simplex object representing sampling of *Faces* and based on *entropy* measure when forming the probability distribution for the second phase.

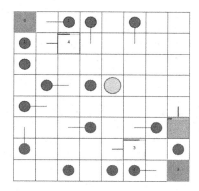

Fig. 1. An example of a mid-game state in μRTS

4   Problem Statement

As a platform for our experiments we chose an instantiation of a Real-time Strategy (RTS) game—μRTS[3]. This two-player zero-sum game simulates the production and maneuvering of various military units with the goal of destroying the opponent forces. In this paper we address both the *real-time* (RT) and *turn-taking* (TT) version of μRTS, where real-time implies actions of different durations and almost simultaneous actions for both players, and turn taking is a standard setting (like Chess or Go), where the actions are issued turn by turn by both players. For the experiments we used an 8×8 grid environment. Each state is fully observable for both players, and each cell on the grid can be occupied either by unit, building, or a resource storage. Each storage has a limited supply of the resource, can be used by both players, and destroyed only when

---

[3] We would like to thank to Santiago Ontañón for making μRTS publicly available.

the resource is exhausted. A player can build working and combat units which can both move and attack enemy units and buildings.

The working units are all identical (*Worker*), they can also transport resources and build buildings. As attackers, however, they are weak. The combat units come in three types—light melee (*LMelee*), heavy melee (*HMelee*), and ranged unit (*Ranged*)—all better attackers than working units, each with its own strengths and weaknesses. In general, movements and attacks are possible only within the 4-connected cells adjacent to the unit location. Additionally, working units and combat units can be built only in *Base* and *Barracks* buildings, respectively. The only difference between real-time and turn-taking version of the game is that the real-time setting all actions may have a different durations and in the TT setting the outcomes of all taken actions will be presented in the next turn, effectively setting all durations to 1. In both cases, actions are not interruptible. Table 1 shows the parameters of units and buildings.

Table 1. Parameters of different buildings and units in μRTS used in [16,18]. *HP* stands for health points, *Cost* is in the resource units, *T(No-op)*, *T(Move)*, *T(Attack)*, and *T(Prod)* represent the durations of an no action (No-op), a single move (in simulated time units), duration of the attack, and duration of producing the unit/building respectively. *Damage* and *Range* represent decrease of *HP* of the target unit and the range of the attack, respectively.

	HP	Cost	T(No-op)	T(Move)	T(Attack)	Damage	Range	T(Prod)
Base	10	10	10	—	—	—	—	250
Barracks	4	5	10	—	—	—	—	200
Worker	1	1	10	10	5	1	1	50
LMelee	4	2	8	8	5	2	1	80
HMelee	4	2	12	12	5	4	1	120
Ranged	1	2	12	12	5	2	3	100

For each player, the initial state of the game contains one *Base*, one *Worker* near the base, and one nearby resource storage. The initial state is the same for both game settings. Even if the resources are gathered optimally, they suffice for 1/3 of the maximal game duration at most, for both the RT and TT games. In Figure 1, one of mid-game states is depicted.

5 Robustness Analysis of NMC and LSI

Although we have experimentally evaluated the LSI algorithm in [18] and showed that it outperforms NMC in the μRTS setup of Ontañón's paper [16], a deeper experimental comparison for different setups of the μRTS game, various sampling budgets and lengths of look-ahead was out of the scope of the paper. In this section, we are filling this gap and adding finer conclusions.

5.1   Turn-Taking Variant of μRTS

The μRTS game was designed by Ontañón as a simplified model of real-time strategy games, therefore the actions of the units/agents differ in duration. Such games require handling not only of what actions are played, but also when they are played, since an appropriate timing of the actions is crucial especially during attacks and retreats.

To evaluate efficiency of LSI and NMC in environment without such timing requirements, we have prepared a variant of μRTS denoted as *1-step*, where the duration of all actions is exactly one simulation step. The parameters of the game are summarized in Table 2.

Table 2. Parameters of μRTS variant forcing the players to do a decision for combinatorial action in each step (*1-step* variant, for $p = 1$) and gradually weakening this requirement with $p > 1$. The explanation of the parameters follows Table 1.

	HP	Cost	T(No-op)	T(Move)	T(Attack)	Damage	Range	T(Prod)
Base	10	10	1	—	—	—	—	p
Barracks	4	5	1	—	—	—	—	p
Worker	1	1	1	p	p	1	1	p
LMelee	4	2	1	p	p	2	1	p
HMelee	4	2	1	p	p	4	1	p
Ranged	1	2	1	p	p	2	3	p

At each simulated time point of the *1-step* game, the decision of what c-action to select has to be done for all the agents, since no agent can be occupied by execution of another action from previous time steps. In contrast to the original μRTS setup, in the *1-step* variant, every decision is combinatorial with the exponential dependence on the current number of agents in the game. A simple experiment showed us that in the original variant of the game, the average number of agents per one decision was 1.55 ± 0.18. While in the *1-step* variant, it is 7.4 ± 0.42. With this observation in mind, we prepared a head-on experiment comparing LSI and NMC in the *1-step* game and we compared the algorithms also with a base-line denoted as noSI describing an approach oblivious to the side-information. noSI is based on the two phase scheme used by LSI, but generates the candidate c-actions randomly. The evaluation phase uses *Sequential Halving* and the evaluation budget of N_e. All experiments used a fixed budget of $N = 2000$ samples and fixed look-ahead of $l = 200$ steps. The results are summarized in Table 3.

The results reveal two notable findings. First, the game is strongly biased towards the first player. In [18], we have reported on a suspicion of such bias in the μRTS simulator, but the effect was negligible in the original variant of the game. The bias is caused by a fixed order of the players and the fact that the second player cannot play actions which are in conflict with the decision already made by the first player, i.e., the game becomes a TT strategy. To compensate for this bias, we measured both player orderings of the match-ups.

Table 3. Comparison of noSI, NMC, LSI in the *1-step* variant of μRTS. The results in brackets are summed up for both orderings of the players of one match-up. The results are in percents of wins/ties/losses of the row algorithm against the column one. Each match-up was measured over 150 games, i.e., each algorithm combination (results in brackets) was measured over 300 games.

w/t/l ↓	noSI	LSI	NMC
noSI		54/22/24 (30/14/56)	71/14/15 (40/17/43)
LSI	87/7/6 (56/14/30)		86/8/6 (61/15/24)
NMC	71/20/9 (43/17/40)	42/21/37 (24/15/61)	

Second, the efficiency results of LSI in the original game holds even stronger for the *1-step* variant. The ratios of the match-up between LSI and NMC is in the *1-step* variant approx. 2.6/0.6/1 (wins/ties/losses) and in the original game it was 1.7/0.5/1. LSI outperforms noSI by ratio 1.9/0.5/1 and it was only by 1.1/0.4/1 in the original game. The comparison of NMC and noSI shows that in the *1-step* game they get on par 1/0.4/1, which is worse result for noSI than in the original variant where it was 1.4/0.3/1 against NMC. Since NMC, similarly to LSI, assumes linearity of the action combination with respect to μ, we conclude that the positive effect of the linear side-information used for candidate selection is getting stronger as the count of c-actions grows, this happens due to increasing number of agents. Additionally, the results strengthen our conclusions on LSI outperforming NMC stated in [18].

With decreasing number of the agents participating in one decision, the number of c-action requiring evaluation decreases exponentially. And therefore the ratio of LSI outperforming NMC should decrease as well. To support this hypotheses, we have prepared an experiment with increasing duration of all actions, precisely for games defined by Table 2 with $p > 1$. The results presented in Figure 2 supports the hypothesis, therefore we conclude that LSI exploits the side-information better than NMC, because with growing durations of the actions the sampling budget per one c-action increases[4].

5.2   Variance of Evaluations

As mentioned before, our hypothesis is that the strength of LSI over NMC is caused by smaller variance in the estimated value of the selected c-action. If it is so, with increasing uncertainty of the c-action evaluations LSI should improve the lead over NMC. Such uncertainty can be caused by two factors in μRTS: (a) by smaller sampling budget and (b) by shorter look-ahead of each sample, i.e., lower number of game steps when the sampling simulates acting of the agents, followed by heuristic evaluation of the last state.

---

[4] The confidence of the results (and therefore strength of the conclusions) is limited by the amounts of the games simulated for the experiments. 300 games for the *1-step* setup and 200 for the rest. The amounts reflects high computational demands on simulation of one game which is in orders of hours

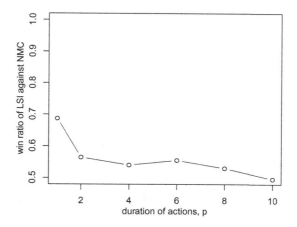

Fig. 2. The win ratio of LSI against NMC with prolonging duration of actions in the game. The ratio is counted as (**wins** + 0.5 · **ties**)/**plays**, i.e., 0.5 means that both algorithms are on par. Each point was measured over 200 games.

All the experiment to this point were using a fixed budget of $N = 2000$ samples and fixed look-ahead of $l = 200$ steps in variants of the game with equal duration of *No-ops* and move actions. For the last batch of experiments, we used a realistic variant of the game with duration of the *No-ops* set to one step (see Table 4) and variable N and l. The results for match-ups of LSI and NMC are summarized in Figure 3.

Table 4. Parameters of a realistic variant of μRTS using unit duration of No-ops. The explanation of the parameters follows Table 1.

	HP	Cost	T(No-op)	T(Move)	T(Attack)	Damage	Range	T(Prod)
Base	10	10	1	—	—	—	—	250
Barracks	4	5	1	—	—	—	—	200
Worker	1	1	1	10	5	1	1	50
LMelee	4	2	1	8	5	2	1	80
HMelee	4	2	1	12	5	4	1	120
Ranged	1	2	1	12	5	2	3	100

For both decreasing budget and shortened look-ahead, we can observe improving tendency of LSI against NMC, which is in line with the hypothesis we proposed.

To rule out the bias caused by comparison of two different algorithm, the final batch of experiments targets sensitivity of the algorithms to decreasing sampling budget and length of the look-ahead when competing against themselves. The results are summarized in Tables 5 and 6.

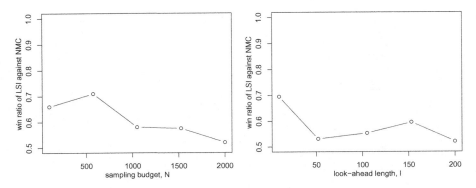

Fig. 3. The win ratio of LSI against NMC with growing sampling budget N (on left) and increasing look-ahead l (on right). The ratio is counted as $(\text{wins}+0.5\cdot\text{ties})/\text{plays}$, 0.5 means that both algorithms are on par. Each point was measured over 200 games.

The difference between plays of algorithms with larger and smaller sampling budgets is most significant for LSI, which indicates that it is the most robust algorithm in respect to the size of the budget and with its highest utilization from the compared algorithms. Similar but weaker effect can be observed in the case of shorter look-ahead. Using the same logic, it means that LSI is more robust with smaller number of losses and higher number of ties against the same algorithm with longer look-ahead.

In summary, all presented experimental results support our hypothesis that LSI outperforms NMC because of the improved utilization of the side-information, as of the guaranteed number of samples dedicated to the evaluation of the c-actions. Additionally, we have shown that LSI has better win-ratio than NMC if the used evaluation is of higher variance in general (caused either by lower budget per c-action or shorter look-ahead).

6   Conclusion

We have shown that LSI is stronger with smaller budgets and shorter look-ahead and therefore we conclude that LSI *is more robust against inaccurate evaluations of the candidate actions, because of the exploitation of the linear side-information*, than NMC in the μRTS game (with confidence of experiments based on 300–200 games per measurement). We have demonstrated this result in various game setups and evaluation parameterizations. These results supplement our recent findings and extend the understanding of the benefits of utilization of side-information in CMAB problems in RTS games.

In the future work, we plan to focus on different games as Arimaa[5], to analyze the findings from RTS games to different turn-taking games designed with combinatorial actions.

---

[5] http://arimaa.com/

Table 5. Comparison of noSI, NMC and LSI with different sampling budgets. The results are in percents of wins/ties/losses of the row setup against the column setup. Each match-up was measured over 200 games.

Table 6. Comparison of noSI, NMC and LSI with different length of the look-ahead. The form of the results follows Table 5

noSI ↓	1525	1050	100
2000	48/13/39	53/11/36	100/0/0
1525		50/11/39	100/0/0
1050			99/0/1

NMC ↓	1525	1050	100
2000	50/9/41	57/8/35	100/0/0
1525		55/11/34	98/0/2
1050			99/0/1

LSI ↓	1525	1050	100
2000	*36/22/42*	55/13/32	100/0/0
1525		*57/11/32*	100/0/0
1050			99/0/1

noSI ↓	153	105	10
200	56/11/33	69/1/30	100/0/0
153		58/4/38	100/0/0
105			100/0/0

NMC ↓	153	105	10
200	53/11/36	68/2/30	100/0/0
153		58/1/41	100/0/0
105			100/0/0

LSI ↓	153	105	10
200	*56/15/29*	70/4/26	100/0/0
153		*60/4/36*	100/0/0
105			100/0/0

Acknowledgments. This work was partly supported by USAF EOARD (grant no. FA8655-12-1-2096), the Technion-Microsoft Electronic-Commerce Research Center, and a Technion fellowship.

References

1. Auer, P., Cesa-Bianchi, N., Fischer, P.: Finite-time analysis of the multiarmed bandit problem. Machine Learning 47(2-3), 235–256 (2002)
2. Balla, R., Fern, A.: UCT for tactical assault planning in real-time strategy games. In: IJCAI, pp. 40–45 (2009)
3. Bubeck, S., Munos, R.: Open loop optimistic planning. In: COLT, pp. 477–489 (2010)
4. Bubeck, S., Munos, R., Stoltz, G.: Pure exploration in finitely-armed and continuous-armed bandits. Theor. Comput. Sci. 412(19), 1832–1852 (2011)
5. Chen, W., Wang, Y., Yuan, Y.: Combinatorial multi-armed bandit: General framework and applications. In: ICML, pp. 151–159 (2013)
6. Chung, M., Buro, M., Schaeffer, J.: Monte Carlo planning in RTS games. In: IEEE-CIG (2005)
7. Churchill, D., Saffidine, A., Buro, M.: Fast heuristic search for RTS game combat scenarios. In: AIIDE (2012)
8. Cover, T.M., Thomas, J.A.: Elements of Information Theory. Wiley, 2 edn. (2006)
9. Feldman, Z., Domshlak, C.: Monte-Carlo planning: Theoretically fast convergence meets practical efficiency. In: UAI (2013)
10. Feldman, Z., Domshlak, C.: On MABs and separation of concerns in Monte-Carlo planning for MDPs. In: ICAPS (2014)

11. Gai, Y., Krishnamachari, B., Jain, R.: Learning multiuser channel allocations in cognitive radio networks: A combinatorial multi-armed bandit formulation. In: IEEE Symposium on New Frontiers in Dynamic Spectrum, pp. 1–9 (2010)
12. Karnin, Z.S., Koren, T., Somekh, O.: Almost optimal exploration in multi-armed bandits. In: ICML, pp. 1238–1246 (2013)
13. Keller, T., Helmert, M.: Trial-based heuristic tree search for finite horizon MDPs. In: ICAPS, pp. 135–143 (2013)
14. Kocsis, L., Szepesvári, C.: Bandit based monte-carlo planning. In: Fürnkranz, J., Scheffer, T., Spiliopoulou, M. (eds.) ECML 2006. LNCS (LNAI), vol. 4212, pp. 282–293. Springer, Heidelberg (2006)
15. Kovarsky, A., Buro, M.: Heuristic search applied to abstract combat games. In: Kégl, B., Lee, H.-H. (eds.) Canadian AI 2005. LNCS (LNAI), vol. 3501, pp. 66–78. Springer, Heidelberg (2005)
16. Ontañón, S.: The combinatorial multi-armed bandit problem and its application to real-time strategy games. In: AIIDE (2013)
17. Saffidine, A., Finnsson, H., Buro, M.: Alpha-beta pruning for games with simultaneous moves. In: Hoffmann, J., Selman, B. (eds.) AAAI 2012 (2012)
18. Shleyfman, A., Komenda, A., Domshlak, C.: On Combinatorial Actions and CMABs with Linear Side Information. In: Schaub, T., Friedrich, G., O'Sullivan, B. (eds.) ECAI 2014. Frontiers in Artificial Intelligence and Applications, vol. 204, pp. 825–830 (2014)
19. Sutton, R.S., Barto, A.G.: Reinforcement Learning: An Introduction. MIT Press (1998)

Job-Level Algorithms for Connect6
Opening Position Analysis

Ting-Han Wei[1], I-Chen Wu[1], Chao-Chin Liang[1], Bing-Tsung Chiang[1],
Wen-Jie Tseng[1], Shi-Jim Yen[2], and Chang-Shing Lee[3]

[1] Department of Computer Science, National Chiao Tung University, Hsinchu, Taiwan
[2] Department of Computer Science and Information Science, National Dong Hwa University,
Hualien, Taiwan
[3] Department of Computer Science and Information Science, National University of Tainan,
Tainan, Taiwan

Abstract. This paper investigates job-level (JL) algorithms to analyze opening
positions for Connect6. The opening position analysis is intended for opening
book construction, which is not covered by this paper. In the past, JL proof-
number search (JL-PNS) was successfully used to solve Connect6 positions.
Using JL-PNS, many opening plays that lead to losses can be eliminated from
consideration during the opening game. However, it is unclear how the information of unsolved positions can be exploited for opening book construction. For
this issue, this paper first proposes four heuristic metrics when using JL-PNS to
estimate move quality. This paper then proposes a JL upper confidence tree (JL-
UCT) algorithm and some heuristic metrics, one of which is the number of
nodes in each candidate move's subtree. In order to compare these metrics
objectively, we proposed two kinds of measurement methods to analyze the suitability of these metrics when choosing best moves for a set of benchmark positions. The results show that for both metrics this node count heuristic metric for
JL-UCT outperforms all the others, including the four for JL-PNS.

Keywords: Job-level computing, opening book generation, Connect6, proof-
number search, Monte-Carlo tree search, upper confidence bound.

1 Introduction

The construction of opening books is critical in designing a strong game-playing program [1,2,3]. While manual construction of opening books have shown success in the
early days, recent efforts have mostly been focused on the automatic generation of
opening books [1,2,3,4,5,6]. The automatic generation of opening books is especially
important to the game of Connect6, a relatively young game that was introduced in
2005 [7], since few expert game records are available for opening book generation.

In the past, many search algorithms such as *alpha-beta search* [8] and *Monte-
Carlo tree search* (MCTS) were applied to explore new opening moves automatically,
as done in Awari [3], Othello [1,3], Amazons [9,10], and Go [4,11]. In [12,13], *job-
level* (JL) *computing* was proposed by Wu et al. to help solve positions by multiple

T. Cazenave et al. (Eds.): CGW 2014, CCIS 504, pp. 29–44, 2014.

simultaneous execution of game-playing programs as jobs. Based on JL computing, they also proposed the *JL proof-number search* (JL-PNS) algorithm to solve various Connect6 positions successfully, many of which were openings, with significant speedups. Saffidine, Jouandeau, and Cazenave [14] also used JL-PNS to solve positions of Breakthrough. Chen et al. [15] proposed a *JL alpha-beta search* (JL-ABS) algorithm to help construct a Chinese chess opening book. Other opening book generation methods similar to JL methods include the *Meta-MCTS* method proposed by Chaslot et al. [5], and the job queue by Schaeffer et al. [16].

Using JL-PNS [12,13], many opening plays that lead to losses can be eliminated from consideration. However, a major drawback to opening book generation using JL-PNS is that it does not yield a good estimate value of positions if the search is terminated before a solution can be obtained. Since many opening positions tend to be difficult to solve, a large amount of computation spent on expanding opening positions may be wasted, if the results from the computation are not used for other purposes. To make most of these computations useful, we attempt to use these results to help construct an opening book.

To utilize these results, four heuristic metrics are proposed to distinguish the best move from all possible candidate moves during JL-PNS analysis. However, none of these heuristic metrics can indicate move quality universally. The main reason is that PNS is designed to prove/solve positions, not to estimate the strengths of positions.

To solve these issues, we also propose a *JL upper confidence tree* (JL-UCT) algorithm. Opening positions are viewed as *multi-armed bandit problems* [17], where each possible move from a given position is treated as a choice. UCT has been successful in balancing between exploiting good moves and exploring new possibilities like the common MCTS [18]. One of the heuristic metrics for JL-UCT simply chooses the move with the maximum number of nodes as most MCTS methods do.

In order to compare these metrics objectively, we propose two kinds of measurement methods to analyze the suitability of these metrics for a set of benchmark positions. The results show that the heuristic metric of node count using JL-UCT outperforms all the others, including the four for JL-PNS in most cases.

The organization of this paper is as follows. Section 2 presents related work. This includes a brief introduction to Connect6 and the game program NCTU6, JL-PNS, and other JL algorithms for opening position analysis. Section 3 outlines the JL-PNS heuristic metrics that are devised to pick out the best candidate move during opening position analysis by JL-PNS, while Section 4 describes the JL-UCT algorithm. Section 5 describes the experiments performed and gives a discussion of the experimental results. Section 6 makes concluding remarks.

2   Previous Work

2.1   Connect6 and NCTU6

Connect6 is a k-in-a-row game proposed by Wu in 2006 [7]. In this game, the first of two players, Black, starts the game by placing a single black stone on an empty square of a typical 19x19 Go board. Each subsequent move is then played by Black or White alternately using two stones of his color on empty squares, starting with White's response to Black's first move. The first player that is able to get six consecutive stones in a line (horizontally, vertically or diagonally) wins. For simplicity of discussion,[1] we call consecutive stones *live* if they are not blocked at either end or *dead* if they are blocked at exactly one end. A common strategy in Connect6 involves playing livefours (L4), creating a so-called *double threat* where the opponent must block both ends of the pattern with two stones or lose immediately. Another example of a double threat involves playing two dead-fours (D4), where each D4 is a *single threat*. Winning by continuously forcing the opponent to block double threats is a common strategy.

NCTU6 is a Connect6 program, developed by the team including some of the authors, which has won multiple Connect6 tournaments and man-machine championships [19,20,21,22,23]. It consists of a solver component, which uses threat space search [24], and an alpha-beta search component [25]. Two features of NCTU6 are particularly important in the scope of this paper.

First, NCTU6 is able to verify victories involving continuous threats, or when such methods fail to find a solution, give an estimate of a position's strength based on the program's evaluation function. The resulting estimate is categorized into 13 distinct game statuses. A winning position for Black is categorized as "B:W"; "B4" indicates the game is extremely favorable for Black, while "B3", "B2", and "B1" indicate Black's advantage in decreasing order. The five game statuses from White's perspective are "W:W", "W4", "W3", "W2", and "W1", also in decreasing order from White winning to the position being slightly favorable for White. For positions where neither player has an advantage, there are three game statuses. "Stable" indicates that the evaluation values for subsequent moves are unlikely to fluctuate significantly. There are two unstable statuses, "unstable1" and "unstable2", where the evaluation fluctuations are greater for the latter. It is worth noting, however, that this fluctuation can also exist for one-sided advantage positions such as B1/W1 through B4/W4 as well.

The second important feature of NCTU6 is that a set of prohibited moves can be given in addition to the position we wish NCTU6 to evaluate. NCTU6 will then calculate and suggest the best move to play that does not exist in the set of prohibited moves, given the input position. If NCTU6 cannot come up with a suggestion that does not exist in the prohibited set without losing, it will consider the position to be a loss with respect to the prohibited set. This feature is critical in applying NCTU6 to the job-level computation model, which we will describe in the next section.

2.2   Job-Level Proof-Number Search (JL-PNS)

This section reviews the JL-PNS algorithm. The overall JL computation model is briefly explained, followed by the generic job-level search. Proof-number search (PNS) and the process of applying it to the generic JL search are then summarized.

---

[1]   Since the playing strategy of Connect6 is not the focus of this paper, we only give a simple intuition for the definitions. Rigorous definitions for live and dead patterns are covered in detail in [7].

JL Computation Model. The job-level computation model starts by defining two parties: the *client*, whose role is to dynamically create tasks, and *workers*, the role of which is to complete these dynamically created tasks. When used in a search algorithm, for example, the client maintains a game tree and may choose a position (which corresponds to a node in the game tree) to encapsulate the move generation and evaluation of this position into a *job*. The system notifies the client when there are idle workers, at which time the client, who plays a passive role, submits jobs that are pending execution. The worker then evaluates this position and returns the result to the client.

Generic JL Search. To apply the JL computation model to a generic search algorithm, we must identify the common phases associated with a search problem. In the scope of computer games, a typical search operation consists of a game tree, for which each node represents a position, while the edges of the tree represent a move from one position to another. There are three common phases to search algorithms such as PNS or MCTS. These three phases are *selection*, *execution*, and *update*.

JL-PNS Algorithm. PNS is an algorithm that outperforms many variants of alpha-beta search when solving game trees [26]. This is made possible by utilizing the *proof-number* (PN) and *disproof-number* (DN) of each explored game tree node. For an arbitrary node n, its PN/DN counts the minimum number of child nodes that must be expanded before n can be solved as a winning/losing position. During the selection phase of PNS, the node that contributes the most to solving the root node of the game tree is chosen. This node is called the *most proving node* (MPN).

To apply PNS to the generic job-level search for Connect6, we use the PNS algorithm for the selection and update phases, while the execution phase is encapsulated as jobs by the client. Workers in this case execute multiple simultaneous instances of NCTU6, each ready to evaluate jobs. As mentioned earlier in the NCTU6 review, the game tree is gradually expanded by supplying each worker with two pieces of information for every job: the position that needs to be examined, and a set of prohibited moves that cannot be returned. When a result is returned to the client, it adds the new node to the game tree and to the set of prohibited moves in the current level so that existing nodes will not be repeatedly added.

In order to apply the domain knowledge, we also initialize the PN/DN of each node based on game statuses given by NCTU6. For example, the PN/DN of a position with B4 are set to 1/18, those for B3 are 2/12, etc. The details of the settings are in [26].

Another detail that is critical to the success of JL-PNS is avoiding selecting the same MPN multiple times before its result is returned. To solve this problem, another phase is added to the generic JL search algorithm called the *pre-update* phase. The pre-update phase is placed after the selection phase but before the execution phase, such that the selected node can be flagged to avoid being chosen multiple times.

2.3   Other JL or JL-Like Methods for Opening Book Generation

In [15], a JL-ABS method was used to help construct a Chinese chess opening book to avoid *weak spots* when dropping out of opening books. Namely, out-of-book positions should still be evaluated as good to the game-playing program.

Chaslot et al. [5] proposed the Meta Monte-Carlo tree search (Meta-MCTS) method in which a two-tiered MCTS is performed to automatically generate an opening book for the game Go. The typical MCTS simulation phase uses a fast routine that follows simple policies, putting little emphasis on playing strength. The Meta-MCTS method replaces this simulation policy with a full game-playing program, which also uses MCTS but in the typical fashion. The upper level is the first tier of the overall algorithm that selects nodes that are worthy of expansion, while MoGo was used for the lower level. This method has been applied to7x7 Go position analysis with success [27].

3   Heuristic Metrics for JL-PNS

In this section, we describe what a heuristic metric is, and then list the four heuristic metrics that were used during the construction of the opening book. To apply JL-PNS to opening book generation, we must first attempt to devise a method of distinguishing good candidate moves from bad ones. A heuristic metric quantifies move quality. This allows us to choose a move to play for any positions that were searched but not solved. Four heuristic metrics that are closely related to the principles of PNS were used to generate the NCTU6 opening book.

3.1   Node Count

PNS is designed to favor exploring moves that allow it to solve a position using the least number of explorations, instead of the strongest moves to play. However, we observe that an MPN as well as its ancestors, which all lie on the *most proving path* (MPP), still tend to be strong moves. Thus, it is likely that the node that is more often included in the MPP tends to be stronger than its less included siblings. Nodes that are more often included in the MPP will have a larger number of nodes in their subtrees, so we may say that nodes with a higher node count are more likely to be stronger moves.

However, there is no guarantee that the node with the largest node count is the best move to play, so the node count metric alone should not be used as a definite sign of a good move. However, it is an important metric to consider when other metrics are used together.

3.2   Proof-Number/Disproof-Number Ratio

The PN and DN are critical to PNS in that they allow the algorithm to locate nodes which contribute most to solving a position. As explained in the PNS review earlier, the PN/DN for a specific node n is the minimum number of child nodes that need to be evaluated in order to prove that n is a winning/losing position. Therefore, we may deduce that a lower PN means that n is likely to be favorable, since it is closer to winning than another node which has a high PN. Similarly, a lower DN is likely to be unfavorable, since n is closer to losing.

To use this as a heuristic metric, we must keep in mind that both PN and DN for a node need to be considered. To do this, we consider the ratio between the PN and DN of a node as a valid heuristic metric. In practice, the PN is divided by the DN, and nodes with the lowest ratio are chosen as the best move when constructing the opening book.

Domain knowledge from NCTU6 is used in the form of PN/DN initialization during JL-PNS. With this in mind, the PN/DN ratio is a mostly adequate metric. However, there are two drawbacks with this metric. First, the actual move quality is highly dependent on the node count metric. In many cases, PN/DN values while the number of child nodes is still relatively small do not indicate move quality definitively. In other words, the PN/DN ratio cannot be used as an indication of move quality with confidence if the node count is not sufficiently large for the node. Second, minimax evaluations are not considered when using the PN/DN ratio metric. Situations may also arise where nodes with similar PN/DN ratios but distinctly different evaluation values are treated similarly when they should not be.

3.3   Minimax Evaluation Value

The minimax value of each internal node, which is computed by NCTU6, can be used to give a rough estimate of the strength of each position. This metric, however, is more of an intermediate one that can be used by another metric rather than a practical one on its own. It is often worse than the other metrics since Connect6 can be a highly unstable game. As described above in Section 2.1, game statuses may vary rapidly, so the minimax evaluation plays a largely variable role in the game's outcome.

3.4   Hybrid Metric

The hybrid method combines the PN/DN ratio with NCTU6's game status estimation to form a heuristic metric. When several moves have the same game status (eg. B1, B2, etc.), the one with the minimum PN/DN ratio is chosen.

While this metric is more accurate than the PN/DN metric, it also depends highly on the node count. The hybrid metric score may still be untrustworthy if the number of nodes in the subtree is insufficient.

4   Job-Level Upper Confidence Tree

In this section, we describe the JL-UCT algorithm. We then list the three heuristic metrics that are used with JL-UCT book generation. Next, the upper confidence bound (UCB) function that is used to balance exploration and exploitation is provided for discussion. Lastly, we discuss the pre-update policy that is used for JL-UCT.

4.1 Algorithm Description

There are two tiers of the JL-UCT search. The lower tier consists of the expansion phase of the generic job-level algorithm. An existing game-playing program, in this case NCTU6, is used to evaluate and suggest the best possible move after excluding the prohibited moves. The upper level is similar to MCTS, where the selection phase chooses the node that has the highest score according to the UCB function, maintaining a UCT as the algorithm continues the search.

4.2 Upper Confidence Bound Function

For the selection phase of the UCT, we chose the commonly used UCB1 function [18].

$$WR + C\sqrt{\frac{log\ (N_p)}{N}}$$

where WR is the win rate for the Black player of the node, C is a pre-defined constant, N_p is the parent visit count, and N is the visit count of the node itself. Similar to JL-PNS, the parameters that are used in the UCB function need to be initialized using domain knowledge from NCTU6. The game statuses returned by NCTU6 are converted into the following win rate initializations.

Table 1. JL-UCT win rate initialization

Status	B:W	B4	B3	B2	B1	Stable	Unstable 2
Win Rate (%)	100	90	80	70	60	50	50

Status	W:W	W4	W3	W2	W1	Unstable 1
Win Rate (%)	0	10	20	30	40	50

4.3 Pre-update Phase

To ensure that the JL algorithm does not choose the same node multiple times during the selection phase, we used the *virtual loss policy* [12]. That is, once a node is selected for expansion, its win rate value is temporarily set to 0% if the move associated with the node is one played by Black, or 100% if it is played by White. By setting the virtual value of the node to a loss, JL-UCT is guaranteed to avoid choosing the same node in subsequent selection phases. Once the job results have been received, the node win rate value is then updated according to the results, removing the virtual loss and allowing the node to be chosen again.

4.4   Heuristic Metrics

Three heuristic metrics are proposed and discussed in this subsection.

Node Count. Similar to the reasoning given in the description for JL-PNS, the number of nodes that belong to a subtree is an intuitive indicator of the move strength that is associated with the root of the subtree. While JL-UCT prefers to devote resources to nodes that have a higher win rate, this is subtly different from JL-PNS where the node that contributes the most to proving the game is given higher priority.

Win Rate. Different from typical MCTS, JL-UCT does not contain a simulation phase where a simple program plays according to a preset policy until game resolution. Therefore the win rates that are used here depend mostly on the initialization values as described in the section above. From this perspective, this metric suffers from the same drawback as the metrics in JL-PNS, where values may not be trustworthy if the node count is insufficient.

Upper Confidence Bound Value. This metric is the one that the JL-UCT algorithm uses during the selection phase to choose the node that is most worthy of expansion. Since the UCB1 function tries to balance exploration with exploitation, this metric will tend to try different options even when they may be weak choices. Therefore this metric exists more as a conceptual point of observation rather than a practical indicator during opening book generation.

5   Experiments and Discussion

5.1   JL-PNS vs. JL-UCT

In our experiments, a set of 22 benchmark game positions was used for analysis and discussion. Each of these positions can be solved as a win for the first player to move. The experiments were designed this way because we were interested in comparing how efficiently an algorithm is able to converge on a single winning move. With a win position for the first player, only one winning move needs to be found for the proof. If we were to choose losing positions for the first player to play instead, all child moves will need to be solved as losses for the first player to play. This is advantageous to JL-PNS since there is no urgency to locate the winning moves, as all moves will eventually be proven as losses, and PNS is inherently superior when it comes to solving game positions. We did not choose unsolved positions for the benchmark because it is difficult to devise an objective metric that can always pick the best choice.[2]

The benchmarks were solved by both JL-PNS and JL-UCT. Each algorithm had access to an 8-core grid consisting of Intel Pentium E2180s. For clarity of discussion, we now define r as the root position of a benchmark, $c_1, c_2, c_3, \ldots, c_k$ as child moves of r, where k is the total number of possible candidate moves from r. As described above, for each benchmark, r is solved as a win for the first player. This implies that some child move, denoted by c_w, can be proven as a win. It is worth mentioning that for some benchmarks there exists more than one c_w. Let n^A denote the total number of nodes required to solve r, using algorithm A.

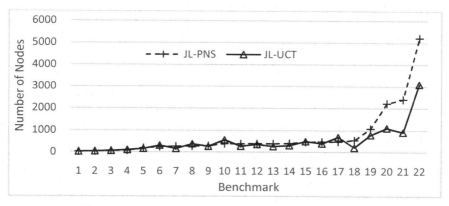

Fig. 1. Number of nodes required to solve each benchmark

The experimental results for n^{PNS} and n^{UCT} are shown in Fig. 1. The benchmarks were numbered according to the increasing order of n^{PNS}. While PNS is intuitively more suitable for solving positions, we can see that JL-UCT does not perform much worse than JL-PNS. In some cases, JL-UCT can even find solutions significantly faster than JL-PNS. This is a somewhat surprising result; while JL-UCT typically needs to expand more nodes to solve AND trees (losing positions) than JL-PNS, it tends to narrow its search towards c_w much earlier and spends less resources verifying the non-winning child moves than JL-PNS in OR trees (winning positions), thereby saving precious computational resources.

5.2   Measuring the Quality of Various Heuristic Metrics

Definitions.

Our second experiment focuses on measuring the quality of various heuristic metrics that are used by JL-PNS and JL-UCT. We introduce two ways of measuring heuristic metric quality, which we will refer to as ε and θ. Namely, heuristic metrics are used to pick the best move to play when a solution cannot be found, while ε and θ are used to measure the quality of heuristic metrics.

---

[2]   It is hard to identify the best moves among several unsolved positions, since the game Connect6 is still new and no experts have given convincing identification of best moves yet.

We define m_i^π as the best move that is chosen by the metric π when the ith job result has been received and its corresponding node has been added in the update phase. That is, m_i^π is the best chosen move by π, after only i jobs have been completed in the JL system. For example, when we are using JL-PNS, m_1^{PNDN} is the best move to play from r according to the PN/DN metric after exactly 1 job has been completed. Using our notation, we can see that $m_N^{PNDN} = c_w$, where $N = n^{PNS}$. **The ε Measuring Method.**

To evaluate the quality of each heuristic metric, we then recorded $\{m_i^{PNS-N}, m_i^{PNDN}, m_i^{Minimax}, m_i^{Hybrid}\}_{i=1,2,\dots,n^{PNS}}$ and $\{m_i^{UCT-N}, m_i^{Winrate}, m_i^{UCB}\}_{i=1,2,\dots,n^{UCT}}$ for all benchmarks. Since all benchmarks are solvable, the winning child move c_w for each benchmark is also known. For any value of i such that $1 \leq i \leq n^A$, we say that the metric π will pick the correct move if $m_i^\pi = c_w$. We can then express the last job for which a metric π is unable to pick the correct move as:

$$\varepsilon^\pi = \arg\max_i (m_i^\pi \neq c_w)$$

In other words, the specified heuristic metric converged on the correct move c_w after ε^π jobs. Therefore, the smaller ε^π is, the better the metric is for the following reason. Assume that a position can be solved eventually with n^A nodes, where n^A is unknown (and quite possibly very large). Then, it is likely that the JL search may stop before r is solved. Between two algorithms, the algorithm with a smaller ε^π is more likely to pick the correct move c_w, even if we do not know what c_w or n^A are, since it converges earlier.

For example, in an extreme case, if for a certain benchmark, ε^{UCT-N} has a value of 0 using the JL-UCT node count heuristic metric, we know that at any given time the subtree of c_w is always the biggest among all other candidate move subtrees. Consequently, if we stop the JL-UCT algorithm at any time, we will be able to pick the correct move to play if we decide to use the node count heuristic metric. Of course, we will not know for certain the move to play is the correct one unless the benchmark is completely solved, but we may conjecture that an algorithm with smaller values of ε^π can find the correct move more often than an algorithm with a larger value.

The results for JL-PNS, JL-UCT, and the best performing metrics for both algorithms are shown in Fig. 2, Fig. 3 and Fig. 4. Since we are interested in examining the ratio between two heuristic metrics, for example ε^{PNS-N} and ε^{PNDN}, and also since ε^π values may vary from less than 10 to well over 1000, we use the base 10 logarithmic scale for all figures in this paper. All values of ε^π are added by 1 so that we may analyze the experiment data with division and the logarithm function.

First of all, we examine the node count and hybrid metrics in Fig. 2. The node count metric was expected to be a moderately adequate metric, while the hybrid metric was expected to perform the best. Surprisingly, the node count metric outperformed the hybrid method in nearly all benchmarks. This contradicts with the practical experiences and observations on the actual games played on the website Little Golem [28], where our NCTU6 JL-PNS player is now currently rated number 1 at an ELO rating of 2421. In the games on Little Golem, for each move, we ran up to 30000 nodes, unless a solution was found. In our observation, the games using the hybrid metric outperformed those for the node count metric. Our conjecture for the pheno-menon is that when playing on Little Golem, very few positions are solvable until late in the game.

Next, from the JL-PNS results in Fig. 2, we can see that the minimax evaluation is indeed a very poor metric. While the PN/DN ratio is much better than the minimax evaluation metric, it does not perform as well as the hybrid metric.

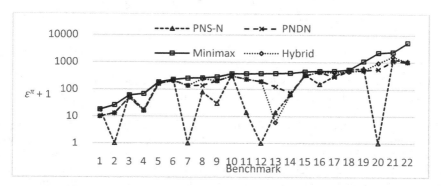

Fig. 2. JL-PNS metric comparison using last incorrect job ε^π. All values of ε^π are added by 1 so that the data may be plotted on a logarithmic scale.

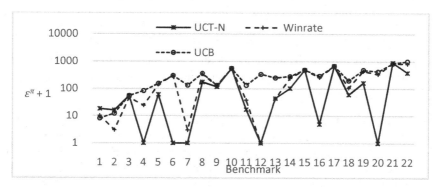

Fig. 3. JL-UCT metric comparison using last incorrect job ε^π. All values of ε^π are added by 1 so that the data may be plotted on a logarithmic scale.

From the JL-UCT results in Fig. 3, we can see that the upper confidence bound value is the worst metric. This is reasonable, since the upper confidence bound value is designed so that it balances between exploration and exploitation, so even poor choices may be indicated as the most suitable move every once in a while. The win rate metric performs reasonably well, but is overall inferior to the node count metric. For many benchmarks, the node count metric is able to stay fixed on the correct move from the very beginning.

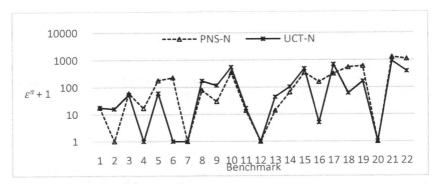

Fig. 4. Best performing metrics PNS-N and UCT-N comparison using last incorrect job ε^π. All values of ε^π are added by 1 so that the data may be plotted on a logarithmic scale.

The best metric from JL-PNS is compared with JL-UCT in Fig. 4. While JL-UCT performs much better for many benchmarks, it sometimes appears to perform worse than JL-PNS, such as in benchmark 2, 8, 9, 10, and 17. Further investigation indicated that while the node count metric seemed to focus on the moves other than the correct move for most of the game in these benchmarks, these seemingly incorrect moves can in fact be solved as well. This fits our intuition that JL-UCT seems to put more emphasis on locating strong moves, which then often lead to solving the position. This is in strong contrast to JL-PNS, which puts solving positions first and foremost for all occasions.

The total sum of ε^{PNS-N} for all benchmarks is 5394, while the total sum of ε^{UCT-N} is 3855. The base-10 logarithm of the ratio between these two metrics, $\frac{\varepsilon^{PNS-N}+1}{\varepsilon^{UCT-N}+1}$, is summed for all benchmarks, yielding a result of 4.103. For two identical metrics, this logarithmic sum should have a value of 0. Therefore we can see that ε^{UCT-N} is the superior metric.

The θ Measuring Method.
We now define a second way of measuring the quality of heuristic metrics. While ε^π is concerned with the last job for which a metric π makes an incorrect choice, we are also interested in the total number of times the metric will lead to an incorrect choice. We define the number of times a metric π chooses incorrect moves for a solved position as follows:

$$\theta^\pi = |\{m_i^\pi | m_i^\pi \neq c_w\}|$$

As a different way of measuring heuristic metric performance, θ^π is interpreted differently from ε^π in the following aspect. Consider an extreme case where $\varepsilon^\pi = n^A - 1$ and $\theta^\pi = 1$. From ε^π, the metric π is poor since we will surely pick c_w after n^A jobs are completed. In contrast, from θ^π, the metric is good since we fail to pick c_w only once, at the time when $n^A - 1$ jobs are completed. However, in general, if ε^π is small like 1, it implies that θ^π is small too and that the heuristic metric is superior; and if θ^π is high like $n^A - 1$, it implies that ε^π is high too and that the heuristic metric is inferior.

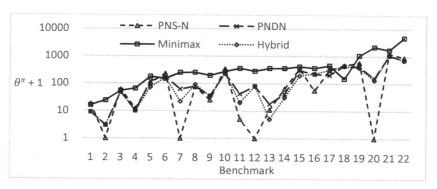

Fig. 5. JL-PNS metric comparison using number of incorrect jobs θ^{π}. All values of θ^{π} are added by 1 so that the data may be plotted on a logarithmic scale.

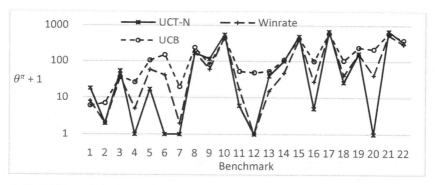

Fig. 6. JL-UCT metric comparison using number of incorrect jobs θ^{π}. All values of θ^{π} are added by 1 so that the data may be plotted on a logarithmic scale.

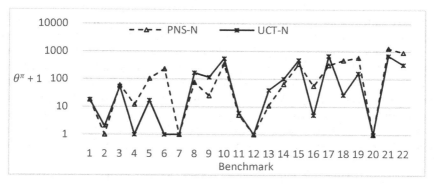

Fig. 7. Best performing metrics PNS-N and UCT-N comparison using number of incorrect jobs θ^{π}. All values of θ^{π} are added by 1 so that the data may be plotted on a logarithmic scale.

Fig. 5, Fig. 6 and Fig. 7 show the comparison between the algorithms and metrics using θ^{π}. The gap between the hybrid metric and the PNS-N metric is not as large as when comparing by ε^{π}. In fact, the θ^{Hybrid} is slightly smaller than θ^{PNS-N} when their values are close, but the PNS-N metric makes up for this disadvantage for benchmarks 2, 7, 12 and 20, where the ratio between θ^{Hybrid} and θ^{PNS-N} is more than 100-fold. Meanwhile, the gap between θ^{UCT-N} and $\theta^{Winrate}$ are also smaller than when comparing by ε^{π}, but it is clear that UCT-N is still the superior metric. For benchmarks 2, 8, 9, 17, UCT-N performs worse than PNS-N, similar to Fig. 4.

Again, we calculate the sum of θ^{PNS-N} and θ^{UCT-N} for all benchmarks, with values of 4938 and 3461, respectively. We then calculate the sum of $\log_{10}\left(\frac{\theta^{PNS-N}+1}{\theta^{UCT-N}+1}\right)$ for all benchmarks for a value of 5.010. We can again see that the JL-UCT algorithm and the UCT-N metric is superior. In addition, since the positions chosen as our benchmarks are all solved, JL-PNS tends to be advantageous in solved positions. For unsolved positions, our conjecture is that JL-UCT would perform even better.

6   Conclusion

In this paper, we applied the previously proposed JL-PNS algorithm to active Connect6 opening book construction. Since PNS is not designed to provide estimates of position strength, we proposed a set of four heuristic metrics that enable us to indicate the best move to play after a game-tree has been generated. These four metrics are the node count, proof/disproof-number ratio, minimax evaluation value, and a hybrid method that uses both proof/disproof-numbers and the minimax evaluation value. These combinations of JL-PNS with the heuristic methods are functional and have shown good utility, but are prone to several drawbacks. The heuristic metrics interact and sometimes the best move to play is not certain. Also, when treated poorly, the opening book may even be detrimental to game program playing strength.

To seek a solution for these problems, this paper proposes the JL-UCT algorithm. JL-UCT treats opening positions as multi-armed bandit problems, and uses the common UCB1 function as its selection criterion in conjunction with the game playing program acting as the expansion mechanism. For performance analysis, we did some experiments and verified that JL-UCT is capable of providing good interim estimates of position strength, and can locate the best move to play more accurately, even from very early stages of the job-level search algorithm. Additionally, JL-UCT simplifies opening book construction in that the node count metric alone can perform well without interaction with other heuristic metrics, eliminating the need for manual adjustment and uncertainty when choosing moves to play. Therefore, it makes it possible to store the entire game tree into the opening book without the need for subtree thresholds.

There is much room for improvement. Future research topics include the actual generation of the opening book using JL-UCT, the tuning of JL-UCT win rate value initializations, additional features in the UCB1 function that deals with variance and instability, verification by actual games such as those on Little Golem, applying JL-UCT to different games (such as 9x9 Go, NoGo, and Hex), and the possibility of applying other multi-armed bandit models.

Acknowledgment. The authors would like to thank National Science Council of the Republic of China (Taiwan) for financial support of this research under the contract numbers NSC 102-2221-E-009-069-MY2, 102-2221-E-009-080-MY2 and 99-2221-E-009-102-MY3.

References

1. Buro, M.: Toward Opening Book Learning. ICCA Journal 22(2), 98–102 (1999)
2. Hyatt, R.M.: Book Learning-a Methodology to Tune an Opening Book Automatically. ICCA Journal 22(1), 3–12 (1999)
3. Lincke, T.R.: Strategies for the Automatic Construction of Opening Books. Computers and Games, 74–86 (2001)
4. Audouard, P., Chaslot, G., Hoock, J.-B., Perez, J., Rimmel, A., Teytaud, O.: Grid Coevolution for Adaptive Simulations: Application to the Building of Opening Books in the Game of Go. In: Giacobini, M., et al. (eds.) EvoWorkshops 2009. LNCS, vol. 5484, pp. 323–332. Springer, Heidelberg (2009)
5. Chaslot, G.M.J.-B., Hoock, J.-B., Perez, J., Rimmel, A., Teytaud, O., Winands, M.H.M.: Meta Monte-Carlo Tree Search for Automatic Opening Book Generation. In: Proceedings of the IJCAI 2009 Workshop on General Intelligence in Game Playing Agents, Pasadena, California, pp. 7–12 (2009)
6. Gaudel, R., Hoock, J.-B., Pérez, J., Sokolovska, N., Teytaud, O.: A Principled Method for Exploiting Opening Books. In: van den Herik, H.J., Iida, H., Plaat, A. (eds.) CG 2010. LNCS, vol. 6515, pp. 136–144. Springer, Heidelberg (2011)
7. Wu, I., Huang, D., Chang, H.: Connect6. ICGA Journal 28(4), 234–242 (2005)
8. Knuth, D.E., Moore, R.W.: An Analysis of Alpha-Beta Pruning. Artificial Intelligence 6(4), 293–326 (1975)
9. Karapetyan, A., Lorentz, R.J.: Generating an opening book for amazons. In: van den Herik, H.J., Björnsson, Y., Netanyahu, N.S. (eds.) CG 2004. LNCS, vol. 3846, pp. 161–174. Springer, Heidelberg (2006)
10. Kloetzer, J.: Monte-carlo opening books for amazons. In: van den Herik, H.J., Iida, H., Plaat, A. (eds.) CG 2010. LNCS, vol. 6515, pp. 124–135. Springer, Heidelberg (2011)
11. Baier, H., Winands, M.H.M.: Active Opening Book Application for Monte-Carlo Tree Search in 19×19 Go. In: 23rd Benelux Conference on Artificial Intelligence (BNAIC 2011), pp. 3–10 (2011)
12. Wu, I.-C., Lin, H.-H., Lin, P.-H., Sun, D.-J., Chan, Y.-C., Chen, B.-T.: Job-level proof-number search for connect6. In: van den Herik, H.J., Iida, H., Plaat, A. (eds.) CG 2010. LNCS, vol. 6515, pp. 11–22. Springer, Heidelberg (2011)
13. Wu, I.-C., Lin, H.-H., Sun, D.-J., Kao, K.-Y., Lin, P.-H., Chan, Y.-C., Chen, P.-T.: Job-Level Proof Number Search. IEEE Transactions on Computational Intelligence and AI in Games 5(1), 44–56 (2013)
14. Saffidine, A., Jouandeau, N., Cazenave, T.: Solving BREAKTHROUGH with race patterns and job-level proof number search. In: van den Herik, H.J., Plaat, A. (eds.) ACG 2011. LNCS, vol. 7168, pp. 196–207. Springer, Heidelberg (2012)
15. Chen, J.-C., Wu, I.-C., Tseng, W.-J., Lin, B.-H., Chang, C.-H.: Job-Level Alpha Beta Search. In: IEEE Transactions on Computational Intelligence and AI in Games (in Press, 2014)
16. Schaeffer, J., Burch, N., Björnsson, Y., Kishimoto, A., Müller, M., Lake, R., Lu, P., Sutphen, S.: Checkers is Solved. Science 317(5844), 1518–1522 (2007)

17. Auer, P., Cesa-Bianchi, N., Fischer, P.: Finite-Time Analysis of the Multiarmed Bandit Problem. Machine Learning 47(2-3), 235–256 (2002)
18. Browne, C.B., Powley, E., Whitehouse, D., Lucas, S.M., Cowling, P.I., Rohlfshagen, P., Tavener, S., Perez, D., Samothrakis, S., Colton, S.: A Survey of Monte Carlo Tree Search Methods. IEEE Transactions on Computational Intelligence and AI in Games 4(1), 1–43 (2012)
19. Lin, P.-H., Wu, I.: NCTU6 Wins Man-Machine Connect6 Championship 2009. ICGA Journal 32(4), 230–232 (2009)
20. Wei, T.-H., Tseng, W.-J., Wu, I., Yen, S.-J.: Mobile6 Wins Connect6 Tournament. ICGA Journal 36(3), 178–179 (2013)
21. Wu, I., Lin, Y.-S., Tsai, H.-T., Lin, P.-H.: The Man-Machine Connect6 Championship 2011. ICGA Journal 34(2), 103–105 (2011)
22. Wu, I.-C., Lin, P.: NCTU6-Lite Wins Connect6 Tournament. ICGA Journal 31(4), 240–243 (2008)
23. Wu, I.-C., Yen, S.-J.: NCTU6 Wins Connect6 Tournament. ICGA Journal 29(3), 157–158 (2006)
24. Wu, I.-C., Lin, P.-H.: Relevance-Zone-Oriented Proof Search for Connect6. IEEE Transactions on Computational Intelligence and AI in Games 2(3), 191–207 (2010)
25. Wu, I.-C., Tsai, H.-T., Lin, H.-H., Lin, Y.-S., Chang, C.-M., Lin, P.-H.: Temporal Difference Learning for Connect6. In: van den Herik, H.J., Plaat, A. (eds.) ACG 2011. LNCS, vol. 7168, pp. 121–133. Springer, Heidelberg (2012)
26. Allis, L.V., van der Meulen, M., van den Herik, H.J.: Proof-Number Search. Artificial Intelligence 66(1), 91–124 (1994)
27. Chou, C.-W., Chou, P.-C., Doghmen, H., Lee, C.-S., Su, T.-C., Teytaud, F., Teytaud, O., Wang, H.-M., Wang, M.-H., Wu, L.-W., Yen, S.-J.: Towards a solution of 7x7 go with meta-MCTS. In: van den Herik, H.J., Plaat, A. (eds.) ACG 2011. LNCS, vol. 7168, pp. 84–95. Springer, Heidelberg (2012)
28. Little Golem, http://www.littlegolem.net

Monte-Carlo Tree Search and Minimax Hybrids with Heuristic Evaluation Functions

Hendrik Baier and Mark H.M. Winands

Games and AI Group, Department of Knowledge Engineering
Faculty of Humanities and Sciences, Maastricht University
Maastricht, The Netherlands
{hendrik.baier,m.winands}@maastrichtuniversity.nl

Abstract. *Monte-Carlo Tree Search* (MCTS) has been found to play suboptimally in some tactical domains due to its highly selective search, focusing only on the most promising moves. In order to combine the strategic strength of MCTS and the tactical strength of minimax, *MCTS-minimax hybrids* have been introduced, embedding shallow minimax searches into the MCTS framework. Their results have been promising even without making use of domain knowledge such as heuristic evaluation functions. This paper continues this line of research for the case where evaluation functions are available. Three different approaches are considered, employing minimax with an evaluation function in the rollout phase of MCTS, as a replacement for the rollout phase, and as a node prior to bias move selection. The latter two approaches are newly proposed. The MCTS-minimax hybrids are tested and compared to their counterparts using evaluation functions without minimax in the domains of Othello, Breakthrough, and Catch the Lion. Results showed that introducing minimax search is effective for heuristic node priors in Othello and Catch the Lion. The MCTS-minimax hybrids are also found to work well in combination with each other. For their basic implementation in this investigative study, the effective branching factor of a domain is identified as a limiting factor of the hybrid's performance.

1 Introduction

Monte-Carlo Tree Search (MCTS) [7, 13] is a sampling-based tree search algorithm using the average result of Monte-Carlo simulations as state evaluations. It selectively samples promising moves instead of taking all legal moves into account like traditional minimax search. This leads to better performance in many large search spaces with high branching factors. MCTS also uses Monte-Carlo simulations of entire games, which often allows it to take long-term effects of moves better into account than minimax. If exploration and exploitation are traded off appropriately, MCTS asymptotically converges to the optimal policy [13], while providing approximations at any time.

While MCTS has shown considerable success in a variety of domains [4], it is still inferior to minimax search with alpha-beta pruning [12] in certain

T. Cazenave et al. (Eds.): CGW 2014, CCIS 504, pp. 45–63, 2014.

games such as Chess and (International) Checkers. Part of the reason could be the selectivity of MCTS, its focusing on only the most promising lines of play. In tactical games such as Chess, a large number of traps exist in the search space [19]. These require precise play to avoid immediate loss, and the selective sampling of MCTS based on average simulation outcomes can easily miss or underestimate an important move.

In previous work [2], the tactical strength of minimax has been combined with the strategic and positional understanding of MCTS in *MCTS-minimax hybrids*, integrating shallow-depth minimax searches into the MCTS framework. These hybrids have shown promising results in tactical domains, despite being independent of a heuristic evaluation function for non-terminal states as typically needed by minimax. In this follow-up paper, we focus on the common case where evaluation functions are available. State evaluations can either result from simple evaluation function calls, or be backpropagated from shallow embedded minimax searches using the same evaluation function. This integration of minimax into MCTS accepts longer computation times in favor of typically more accurate state evaluations.

Three different approaches for integrating domain knowledge into MCTS are considered in this paper. The first approach uses state evaluations to choose rollout moves. The second approach uses state evaluations to terminate rollouts early. The third approach uses state evaluations to bias the selection of moves in the MCTS tree. Only in the first case, minimax has been applied before. The use of minimax for the other two approaches is newly proposed in the form described here.

This paper is structured as follows. Section 2 gives some background on MCTS as the baseline algorithm of this paper. Section 3 provides a brief overview of related work on the relative strengths of minimax and MCTS, on algorithms combining features of MCTS and minimax, and on using MCTS with heuristics. Section 4 outlines three different methods for incorporating heuristic evaluations into the MCTS framework, and presents variants using shallow-depth minimax searches for each of these. Two of these MCTS-minimax hybrids are newly proposed in this work. Section 5 shows experimental results of the MCTS-minimax hybrids in the test domains of Othello, Breakthrough, and Catch the Lion. Section 6 concludes and suggests future research.

2   Background

Monte-Carlo Tree Search (MCTS) is the underlying framework of the algorithms in this paper. MCTS works by repeating the following four-phase loop until computation time runs out [5]. The root of the tree represents the current state of the game. Each iteration of the loop represents one simulated game.

Phase one: *selection*. The tree is traversed starting from the root, choosing the move to sample from each state with the help of a selection policy. This policy should balance the exploitation of states with high value estimates and the exploration of states with uncertain value estimates. In this paper UCB1-TUNED [1] is used as a selection policy.

Phase two: *expansion*. When the selection policy leaves the tree by sampling an unseen move, one or more of its successors are added to the tree. In this paper, we always add the one successor chosen in the current iteration.

Phase three: *rollout*. A rollout (also called *playout*) policy plays the simulated game to its end, starting from the state represented by the newly added node. MCTS converges to the optimal move in the limit even when rollout moves are chosen randomly.

Phase four: *backpropagation*. The value estimates of all states traversed during the simulation are updated with the result of the finished game.

Many variants and extensions of this framework have been proposed in the literature [4]. In this paper, we are using MCTS with the *MCTS-Solver* extension [28] as the baseline algorithm. MCTS-Solver is able to backpropagate not only regular simulation results such as losses and wins, but also game-theoretic values such as proven losses and proven wins whenever the search tree encounters a terminal state. The basic idea is marking a move as a proven loss if the opponent has a winning move from the resulting position, and marking a move as a proven win if the opponent has only losing moves from the resulting position. This avoids wasting time on the re-sampling of game states whose values are already known.

3   Related Work

Several papers by Ramanujan *et al.* [19,21,22] have studied search space properties that influence the performance of MCTS relative to minimax search. In [19], *shallow traps* were identified as a feature of search spaces in which MCTS performs poorly, in particular Chess. A *level-k search trap* was informally defined as the possibility of a player to choose an unfortunate move which leads to a winning strategy for the opponent with a depth of at most k plies. Such traps turned out to be frequent in Chess compared to for example Go. A synthetic tree model allowed the study of MCTS performance at different densities of traps in the search space in [21].

Finnsson and Björnsson [8] found a similar problem to traps, named *optimistic moves*. These are weak moves with relatively easy refutations by the opponent which take MCTS a surprisingly long time to find. In the same paper, the *progression* property was found to be advantageous for MCTS, i.e. the property of a game to progress naturally towards its end with every move made, as compared to games whose ends can be easily delayed or dragged out.

Clune [6] compared the performance of minimax with alpha-beta pruning and MCTS in General Game Playing. He found a stable and accurate evaluation function as well as a relatively low branching factor to give minimax an advantage over MCTS. In this paper, branching factor, evaluation accuracy and trap density help us to understand some of the observed effects.

Previous work on developing algorithms influenced by both MCTS and minimax has taken two principal approaches. On the one hand, one can extract individual features of minimax such as minimax-style backups and integrate them into MCTS. This approach was chosen e.g. in [22], where the algorithm

$UCTMAX_H$ replaces MCTS rollouts with heuristic evaluations and classic averaging MCTS backups with minimaxing backups. In *implicit minimax backups* [14], both minimaxing backups of heuristic evaluations and averaging backups of rollout returns are managed simultaneously. On the other hand, one can nest minimax searches into MCTS searches. This is the approach taken in [2] and this paper.

Various different techniques for integrating domain knowledge into the Monte-Carlo rollouts have been proposed in the literature. The idea of improving rollouts with the help of heuristic knowledge has first been applied to games in [3]. It is now used by state-of-the-art programs in virtually all domains. Shallow minimax in every step of the rollout phase has been proposed as well, e.g. a 1-ply search in [17] for the game of Havannah, or a 2-ply search for Lines of Action [27], Chess [20], and multi-player games [18]. Similar techniques are considered in Subsection 4.1.

The idea of stopping rollouts before the end of the game and backpropagating results on the basis of heuristic knowledge has been explored in Amazons [15], Lines of Action [26], and Breakthrough [16]. A similar method is considered in Subsection 4.2, where we also introduce a hybrid algorithm replacing the evaluation function with a minimax call. Our methods are different from [15] and [26] as we backpropagate the actual heuristic values instead of rounding them to losses or wins. They are also different from [26] as we backpropagate heuristic values after a fixed number of rollout moves, regardless of whether they reach a threshold of certainty.

The idea of biasing the selection policy with heuristic knowledge has been introduced in [9] and [5] for the game of Go. Our implementation is similar to [9] as we initialize tree nodes with knowledge in the form of virtual wins and losses. We also propose a hybrid using minimax returns instead of simple evaluation returns in Subsection 4.3.

This paper represents the continuation of earlier work on MCTS-minimax hybrids [2]. These hybrids MCTS-MR, MCTS-MS, and MCTS-MB have the advantage of being independent of domain knowledge. However, their inability to evaluate non-terminal states makes them ineffective in games with very few or no terminal states throughout the search space, such as the game of Othello. Furthermore, some form of domain knowledge is often available in practice, and it is an interesting question how to use it to maximal effect.

4   Hybrid Algorithms

This section describes the three different approaches for employing heuristic knowledge within MCTS that we explore in this work. For each approach, a variant using simple evaluation function calls and a hybrid variant using shallow minimax searches is considered. Two of the three hybrids are newly proposed in the form described here.

4.1   MCTS with Informed Rollouts (MCTS-IR)

The convergence of MCTS to the optimal policy is guaranteed even with uniformly random move choices in the rollouts. However, more informed rollout policies can greatly improve performance [10]. When a heuristic evaluation function is available, it can be used in every rollout step to compare the states each legal move would lead to, and choose the most promising one. Instead of choosing this *greedy* move, it is effective in some domains to choose a uniformly random move with a low probability ϵ, so as to avoid determinism and preserve diversity in the rollouts. Our implementation additionally ensures non-deterministic behavior even for $\epsilon = 0$ by picking moves with equal values at random both in the selection and in the rollout phase of MCTS. The resulting rollout policy is typically called ϵ-*greedy* [25]. In the context of this work, we call this approach *MCTS-IR-E* (MCTS with informed rollouts using an evaluation function).

The depth-one lookahead of an ϵ-greedy policy can be extended in a natural way to a depth-d minimax search for every rollout move [18,27]. We use a random move ordering in minimax as well in order to preserve non-determinism. In contrast to [27] and [18] where several enhancements such as move ordering, k-best pruning (not searching all legal moves), and killer moves were added to alphabeta, we only use basic alpha-beta search. We are interested in its performance before introducing additional improvements, especially since our test domains have smaller branching factors than e.g. the games Lines of Action (around 30) or Chinese Checkers (around 25-30) used in [27] and [18], respectively. Using a depth-d minimax search for every rollout move aims at stronger move choices in the rollouts, which make rollout returns more accurate and can therefore help to guide the growth of the MCTS tree. We call this approach *MCTS-IR-M* (MCTS with informed rollouts using minimax).

4.2   MCTS with Informed Cutoffs (MCTS-IC)

The idea of rollout cutoffs is an early termination of the rollout in case the rollout winner, or the player who is at an advantage, can be reasonably well predicted with the help of an evaluation function. The statistical noise introduced by further rollout moves can then be avoided by stopping the rollout, evaluating the current state of the simulation, and backpropagating the evaluation result instead of the result of a full rollout to the end of the game [15, 26]. If on average, the evaluation function is computationally cheaper than playing out the rest of the rollout, this method can also result in an increased sampling speed as measured in rollouts per second. A fixed number m of rollout moves can be played before evaluating in order to introduce more non-determinism and get more diverse simulation returns. If $m = 0$, the evaluation function is called directly at the newly expanded node of the tree. As in MCTS-IR, our MCTS-IC implementation avoids deterministic gameplay through randomly choosing among equally valued moves in the selection policy. We scale all evaluation values to $[0, 1]$. We do not round the evaluation function values to wins or losses as proposed in [15], nor do we consider the variant with dynamic m and evaluation function thresholds proposed in [26]. In the following, we call this approach *MCTS-IC-E* (MCTS with informed cutoffs using an evaluation function).

We propose an extension of this method using a depth-d minimax search at cutoff time in order to determine the value to be backpropagated. In contrast to the integrated approach taken in [27], we do not assume MCTS-IR-M as rollout policy and backpropagate a win or a loss whenever the searches of this policy return a value above or below two given thresholds. Instead, we play rollout moves with an arbitrary policy (uniformly random unless specified otherwise), call minimax when a fixed number of rollout moves has been reached, and backpropagate the heuristic value returned by this search. Like MCTS-IR-M, this strategy tries to backpropagate more accurate simulation returns, but by computing them directly instead of playing out the simulation. We call this approach *MCTS-IC-M* (MCTS with informed cutoffs using minimax).

4.3 MCTS with Informed Priors (MCTS-IP)

Node priors [9] represent one method for supporting the selection policy of MCTS with heuristic information. When a new node is added to the tree, or after it has been visited n times, the heuristic evaluation of the corresponding state is stored in this node. This is done in the form of virtual wins and virtual losses, weighted by a prior weight parameter w. For example, if the evaluation value is 0.6 and the weight is 100, 60 wins and 40 losses are stored in the node at hand. We assume evaluation values in $[0, 1]$. Since heuristic evaluations are typically more reliable than the MCTS value estimates resulting from only a few samples, this prior helps to guide tree growth into a promising direction. If the node is visited frequently however, the influence of the prior progressively decreases over time, as the virtual rollout returns represent a smaller and smaller percentage of the total rollout returns stored in the node. Thus, MCTS rollouts progressively override the heuristic evaluation. We call this approach *MCTS-IP-E* (MCTS with informed priors using an evaluation function) in this paper.

We propose to extend this technique with a depth-d minimax search in order to compute the prior value to be stored. It aims at guiding the selection policy through more accurate prior information in the MCTS tree. We call this approach *MCTS-IP-M* (MCTS with informed priors using minimax).

5   Experimental Results

We tested the MCTS-minimax hybrids with heuristic evaluation functions in three different two-player zero-sum games: *Othello*, *Breakthrough*, and *Catch the Lion*. In all experimental conditions, we compared the hybrids as well as their counterparts using heuristics without minimax against regular MCTS-Solver as the baseline. Rollouts were uniformly random unless specified otherwise. Optimal MCTS parameters such as the exploration factor C were determined once for MCTS-Solver in each game and then kept constant for both MCTS-Solver and the MCTS-minimax hybrids during testing. C was 0.7 in Othello and Catch the Lion, and 0.8 in Breakthrough. Draws, which are possible in Othello, were counted as half a win for both players. We used minimax with alpha-beta pruning, but no other search enhancements. Computation time was 1 second per move.

5.1   Games

This section outlines the rules of the three test domains, and the heuristic board evaluation functions used for each of them. The evaluation function from the point of view of the current player is always her total score minus her opponent's total score, normalized to $[0, 1]$ as a final step.

Othello. The game of Othello is played on an 8×8 board. It starts with four discs on the board, two white discs on d5 and e4 and two black discs on d4 and e5. Each disc has a black side and a white side, with the side facing up indicating the player the disc currently belongs to. The two players alternatingly place a disc on the board, in such a way that between the newly placed disc and another disc of the moving player there is an uninterrupted horizontal, vertical or diagonal line of one or more discs of the opponent. All these discs are then turned over, changing their color to the moving player's side, and the turn goes to the other player. If there is no legal move for a player, she has to pass. If both players have to pass or if the board is filled, the game ends. The game is won by the player who owns the most discs at the end.

The evaluation score we use for Othello first determines the number of *stable* discs for the player, i.e. discs that cannot change color anymore. For each stable disc of her color, the player receives 10 points. Afterwards, the number of legal moves for the player is added to her score.

Breakthrough. The variant of Breakthrough used in this work is played on a 6×6 board. The game was originally described as being played on a 7×7 board, but other sizes such as 8×8 are popular as well, and the 6×6 board preserves an interesting search space.

At the beginning of the game, White occupies the first two rows of the board, and Black occupies the last two rows of the board. The two players alternatingly move one of their pieces straight or diagonally forward. Two pieces cannot occupy the same square. However, players can capture the opponent's pieces by moving diagonally onto their square. The game is won by the player who succeeds first at advancing one piece to the home row of her opponent, i.e. reaching the first row as Black or reaching the last row as White.

The evaluation score we use for Breakthrough gives the player 3 points for each piece of her color. Additionally, each piece receives a location value depending on its row on the board. From the player's home row to the opponent's home row, these values are 10, 3, 6, 10, 15, and 21 points, respectively.

Catch the Lion. The game Catch the Lion is a simplified form of Shogi (see [23] for an MCTS approach to Shogi). It is included in this work as an example of chess-like games, which tend to be particularly difficult for MCTS [19]. The game is played on a 3 × 4 board. At the beginning of the game, each player has four pieces: a Lion in the center of her home row, a Giraffe to the right of the Lion, an Elephant to the left of the Lion, and a Chick in front of the Lion. The Chick can move one square forward, the Giraffe can move one square in the vertical and horizontal directions, the Elephant can move one square in the diagonal directions, and the Lion can move one square in any direction. During the game, the players alternatingly move one of their pieces. Pieces of the opponent can be captured. As in Shogi, they are removed from the board, but not from the game. Instead, they switch sides, and the player who captured them can later on drop them on any square of the board instead of moving one of her pieces. If the Chick reaches the home row of the opponent, it is promoted to a Chicken, now being able to move one square in any direction except for diagonally backwards. A captured Chicken, however, is demoted to a Chick again when dropped. The game is won by either capturing the opponent's Lion, or moving your own Lion to the home row of the opponent.

The evaluation score we use for Catch the Lion represents a weighted material sum for each player, where a Chick counts as 3 points, a Giraffe or Elephant as 5 points, and a Chicken as 6 points, regardless of whether they are on the board or captured by the player.

5.2   Game Properties

Two properties of the test domains can help with understanding the results presented in the following subsections. These properties are the *branching factor* and the *tacticality* of the games.

Branching Factor. There are on average 15.5 legal moves available in Breakthrough, but only about 10 in Catch the Lion and 8 in Othello, measured in self-play games of the MCTS-Solver baseline. A higher branching factor makes the application of minimax searches potentially more difficult, especially when basic alpha-beta without enhancements is used as this paper.

Tacticality. The tacticality of a game can be formalized in different ways. [19] proposed the concept of search traps to explain the difficulties of MCTS in some domains such as Chess. This concept was taken up again in [2] to motivate the integration of minimax into MCTS. A tactical game is here understood as a game with a high density of terminal states throughout the search space, which can result in a higher risk of falling into traps especially for selective searches.

As a simple test for this property, MCTS-Solver played 1000 self-play games in all domains. After each move, we measured the number of traps at depth (up to) 3 for the player to move. The result was an average number of 3.7 level-3 traps in Catch the Lion (37% of all legal moves), 2.8 traps in Breakthrough

(18% of all legal moves), and only 0.1 traps in Othello (1.2% of all legal moves). Results were comparable for other trap depths. This indicates that Catch the Lion is the most tactical of the tested games, making the application of minimax searches potentially more useful.

5.3   Experiments with MCTS-IR

MCTS-IR-E was tested for $\epsilon \in \{0, 0.05, 0.1, 0.2, 0.5\}$. Each parameter setting played 1000 games in each domain against the baseline MCTS-Solver with uniformly random rollouts. Figures 1(a) to 1(c) show the results. The best-performing conditions used $\epsilon = 0.05$ in Othello and Catch the Lion, and $\epsilon = 0$ in Breakthrough. They were each tested in 2000 additional games against the baseline. The results were win rates of 79.9% in Othello, 75.4% in Breakthrough, and 96.8% in Catch the Lion. All of these are significantly stronger than the baseline (p<0.001).

MCTS-IR-M was tested for $d \in \{1, \ldots, 4\}$ with the optimal value of ϵ found for each domain in the MCTS-IR-E experiments. Each condition played 1000 games per domain against the baseline player. The results are presented in Figures 1(d) to 1(f). The most promising setting in all domains was $d = 1$. In an additional 2000 games against the baseline per domain, this setting achieved win rates of 73.9% in Othello, 65.7% in Breakthrough, and 96.5% in Catch the Lion. The difference to the baseline is significant in all domains (p<0.001).

In each domain, the best settings for MCTS-IR-E and MCTS-IR-M were then tested against each other in 2000 further games. The results for MCTS-IR-M were win rates of 37.1% in Othello, 35.3% in Breakthrough, and 47.9% in Catch the Lion. MCTS-IR-M is weaker than MCTS-IR-E in Othello and Breakthrough (p<0.001), while no significant difference could be shown in Catch the Lion. This shows that the incorporation of shallow alpha-beta searches into rollouts did not improve MCTS-IR in any of the domains at hand. Depth-1 minimax searches in MCTS-IR-M are functionally equivalent to MCTS-IR-E, but have some overhead in our implementation due to the recursive calls to a separate alpha-beta search algorithm. This results in the inferior performance.

Higher settings of d were not successful because deeper minimax searches in every rollout step require too much computational effort. In an additional set of 1000 games per domain, we compared MCTS-IR-E to MCTS-IR-M at 1000 rollouts per move, ignoring the time overhead of minimax. Here, MCTS-IR-M won 78.6% of games with $d = 2$ in Othello, 63.4% of games with $d = 2$ in Breakthrough, and 89.3% of games with $d = 3$ in Catch the Lion. All of these conditions are significantly stronger than MCTS-IR-E (p<0.001). This confirms MCTS-IR-M is suffering from its time overhead.

Interestingly, deeper minimax searches do not always guarantee better performance in MCTS-IR-M, even when ignoring time. While MCTS-IR-M with $d = 1$ won 50.4% (±3.1%) of 1000 games against MCTS-IR-E in Catch the Lion, $d = 2$ won only 38.0%—both at 1000 rollouts per move. In direct play against each other, MCTS-IR-M with $d = 2$ won 38.8% of 1000 games against MCTS-IR-M with $d = 1$. As standalone players however, a depth-2 minimax beat a depth-1 minimax in 95.8% of 1000 games. Such cases where policies that are stronger as standalone players do not result in stronger play when integrated in MCTS rollouts have been observed before [2, 9, 24].

5.4   Experiments with MCTS-IC

MCTS-IC-E was tested for $m \in \{0, \ldots, 5\}$. 1000 games were played against the baseline MCTS-Solver per parameter setting in each domain. Figures 2(a) to 2(c) present the results. The most promising condition was $m = 0$ in all three domains. It was tested in 2000 additional games against the baseline. The results were win rates of 61.1% in Othello, 41.9% in Breakthrough, and 98.1% in Catch the Lion. This is significantly stronger than the baseline in Othello and Catch the Lion (p<0.001), but weaker in Breakthrough (p<0.001). The evaluation function in Breakthrough may not be accurate enough for MCTS to fully rely on it instead of rollouts. Testing higher values of m showed that as fewer and fewer rollouts are long enough to be cut off, MCTS-IC-E effectively turns into the baseline MCTS-Solver and also shows identical performance. Note that the parameter m can sometimes be sensitive to the opponents it is tuned against. In this paper, we tuned against regular MCTS-Solver only, and both MCTS-Solver and MCTS-IC used uniformly random rollouts.

MCTS-IC-M was tested for all combinations of $m \in \{0, \ldots, 5\}$ and $d \in \{1, 2, 3\}$, with 1000 games each per domain. The results are shown in Figures 2(d) to 2(f). The best performance was achieved with $m = 0$ and $d = 2$ in Othello, $m = 4$ and $d = 1$ in Breakthrough, and $m = 1$ and $d = 2$ in Catch the Lion. Of an additional 2000 games against the baseline per domain, these settings won 62.4% in Othello, 32.4% in Breakthrough, and 99.6% in Catch the Lion. This is again significantly stronger than the baseline in Othello and Catch the Lion (p<0.001), but weaker in Breakthrough (p<0.001).

The best settings for MCTS-IC-E and MCTS-IC-M were also tested against each other in 2000 games per domain. Despite MCTS-IC-E and MCTS-IC-M not showing significantly different performance against the regular MCTS-Solver baseline in Othello and Catch the Lion, MCTS-IC-E won 73.1% of these games in Othello, 58.3% in Breakthrough, and 66.1% in Catch the Lion. All conditions are significantly superior to MCTS-IC-M (p<0.001). Thus, the integration of shallow alpha-beta searches into rollout cutoffs did not improve MCTS-IC in any of the tested domains either.

Just as for MCTS-IR, this is a problem of computational cost for the alpha-beta searches. We compared MCTS-IC-E with optimal parameter settings to MCTS-IC-M at equal rollouts per move instead of equal time in an additional set of experiments. Here, MCTS-IC-M won 65.7% of games in Othello at 10000 rollouts per move, 69.8% of games in Breakthrough at 6000 rollouts per move, and 86.8% of games in Catch the Lion at 2000 rollouts per move (the rollout numbers were chosen so as to achieve comparable times per move). The parameter settings were $m = 0$ and $d = 1$ in Othello, $m = 0$ and $d = 2$ in Breakthrough, and $m = 0$ and $d = 4$ in Catch the Lion. All conditions here are stronger than

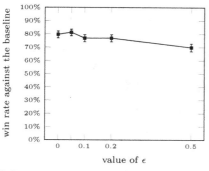

(a) Performance of MCTS-IR-E in Othello.

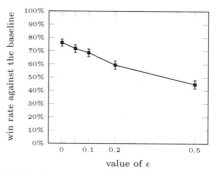

(b) Performance of MCTS-IR-E in Breakthrough.

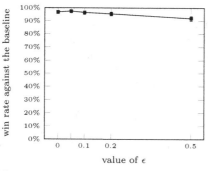

(c) Performance of MCTS-IR-E in Catch the Lion.

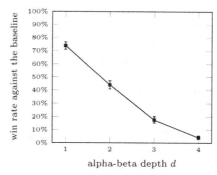

(d) Performance of MCTS-IR-M in Othello. For all conditions, $\epsilon = 0.05$.

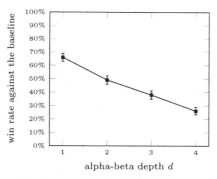

(e) Performance of MCTS-IR-M in Breakthrough. For all conditions, $\epsilon = 0$.

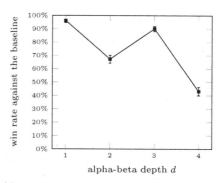

(f) Performance of MCTS-IR-M in Catch the Lion. For all conditions, $\epsilon = 0.05$.

Fig. 1. Performance of MCTS-IR in Othello, Breakthrough and Catch the Lion

MCTS-IC-E (p<0.001). This confirms that MCTS-IC-M is weaker than MCTS-IC-E due to its time overhead.

A seemingly paradoxical observation was made with MCTS-IC as well. In Breakthrough and Catch the Lion, the values returned by minimax searches are not always more effective for MCTS-IC than the values of simple static heuristics, even when time is ignored. In Catch the Lion for example, MCTS-IC-M with $m = 0$ and $d = 1$ won only 2.9% of 1000 test games against MCTS-IC-E with $m = 0$ (at 50000 rollouts per move). With $d = 2$, it won 34.3% (at 25000 rollouts per move). Even with $d = 3$, it won only 34.8% (at 6000 rollouts per move). Once more these results demonstrate that a stronger policy can lead to a weaker search when embedded in MCTS.

5.5   Experiments with MCTS-IP

MCTS-IP-E was tested for all combinations of $n \in \{0, 1, 2\}$ and $w \in \{50, 100, 250, 500, 1000, 2500, 5000\}$. Each condition played 1000 games per domain against the baseline player. The results are shown in Figures 3(a) to 3(c). The best-performing conditions were $n = 1$ and $w = 1000$ in Othello, $n = 1$ and $w = 2500$ in Breakthrough, and $n = 0$ and $w = 100$ in Catch the Lion. In 2000 additional games against the baseline, these conditions achieved win rates of 56.8% in Othello, 86.6% in Breakthrough, and 71.6% in Catch the Lion (all significantly stronger than the baseline with p<0.001).

MCTS-IP-M was tested for all combinations of $n \in \{0, 1, 2, 5, 10, 25\}$, $w \in \{50, 100, 250, 500, 1000, 2500, 5000\}$, and $d \in \{1, \ldots, 5\}$ with 1000 games per condition in each domain. Figures 3(d) to 3(f) present the results, using the optimal setting of d for all domains. The most promising parameter values found in Othello were $n = 2$, $w = 5000$, and $d = 3$. In Breakthrough they were $n = 1$, $w = 1000$, and $d = 1$, and in Catch the Lion they were $n = 1$, $w = 2500$, and $d = 5$. Each of them played 2000 additional games against the baseline, winning 81.7% in Othello, 87.8% in Breakthrough, and 98.0% in Catch the Lion (all significantly stronger than the baseline with p<0.001).

The best settings for MCTS-IP-E and MCTS-IP-M subsequently played 2000 games against each other in all domains. MCTS-IP-M won 76.2% of these games in Othello, 97.6% in Catch the Lion, but only 36.4% in Breakthrough (all of the differences are significant with p<0.001). We can conclude that using shallow alpha-beta searches to compute node priors strongly improves MCTS-IP in Othello and Catch the Lion, but not in Breakthrough. This is once more a problem of time overhead due to the larger branching factor of Breakthrough. At 1000 rollouts per move, MCTS-IP-M with $n = 1$, $w = 1000$, and $d = 1$ won 91.1% of 1000 games against the best MCTS-IP-E setting in this domain.

An interesting observation are the high weights assigned to the node priors in all domains. It seems that at least for uniformly random rollouts, best performance is achieved when rollout returns never override priors for the vast majority of nodes. They only differentiate between states that look equally promising for the evaluation functions used. The exception is MCTS-IP-E in Catch the Lion, where the static evaluations might be too unreliable to give them large weights

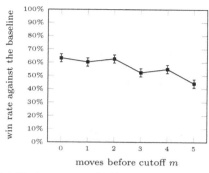

(a) Performance of MCTS-IC-E in Othello.

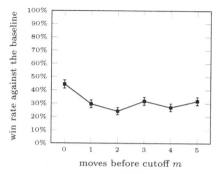

(b) Performance of MCTS-IC-E in Breakthrough.

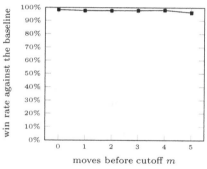

(c) Performance of MCTS-IC-E in Catch the Lion.

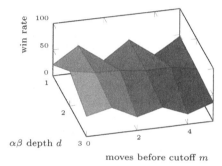

(d) Performance of MCTS-IC-M in Othello.

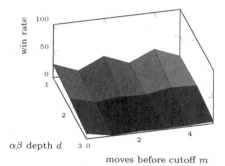

(e) Performance of MCTS-IC-M in Breakthrough.

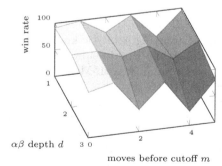

(f) Performance of MCTS-IC-M in Catch the Lion.

Fig. 2. Performance of MCTS-IC in Othello, Breakthrough and Catch the Lion

due to the tactical nature of the game. Exchanges of pieces can often lead to quick and drastic changes of the evaluation values. The quality of the priors in Catch the Lion improves drastically when minimax searches are introduced, justifying deeper searches ($d = 5$) than in the other tested domains despite the high computational cost. However, MCTS-IC still works better in this case, possibly because inaccurate evaluation results are only backpropagated once and are not stored to influence the selection policy for a longer time as in MCTS-IP. In Othello, minimax searches in combination with a seemingly less volatile evaluation function lead to MCTS-IP-M being the strongest hybrid tested in this paper.

The effect of stronger policies resulting in weaker performance when integrated into MCTS can be found in MCTS-IP just as in MCTS-IR and MCTS-IC. In Breakthrough for example, MCTS-IP-M with $n = 1$, $w = 1000$, and $d = 2$ won only 83.4% of 1000 games against the strongest MCTS-IP-E setting, compared to 91.1% with $n = 1$, $w = 1000$, and $d = 1$—both at 1000 rollouts per move. The difference is significant ($p < 0.001$). As standalone players however, depth-2 minimax won 80.2% of 1000 games against depth-1 minimax in the Breakthrough experiments.

5.6   Comparison of Algorithms

Sections 5.3 to 5.5 showed the performance of MCTS-IR, MCTS-IC and MCTS-IP against the baseline MCTS-Solver player. We also tested the best-performing variants of these algorithms against each other. In each condition, 2000 games were played. Figures 4(a) to 4(c) present the results. MCTS-IP-M is strongest in Othello, MCTS-IP-E is strongest in Breakthrough, and MCTS-IC-E is strongest in Catch the Lion.

5.7   Combination of Algorithms

Subsections 5.3 to 5.6 showed the performance of MCTS-IR, MCTS-IC and MCTS-IP in isolation. In order to get an indication whether the different methods of applying heuristic knowledge can successfully be combined, we conducted the following experiments. In Othello, the best-performing algorithm MCTS-IP-M was combined with MCTS-IR-E. In Breakthrough, the best-performing algorithm MCTS-IP-E was combined with MCTS-IR-E. In Catch the Lion, it is not possible to combine the best-performing algorithm MCTS-IC-E with MCTS-IR-E, because with the optimal setting $m = 0$ MCTS-IC-E leaves no rollout moves to be chosen by an informed rollout policy. Therefore, MCTS-IP-M was combined with MCTS-IR-E instead. 2000 games were played in each condition. The results are shown in Figures 4(d) to 4(f). Applying the same knowledge both in the form of node priors and in the form of ϵ-greedy rollouts leads to stronger play in all three domains than using priors alone. In fact, such combinations are the overall strongest players tested in this paper even without being systematically optimized. In Othello, the combination MCTS-IP-M-IR-E won 55.2% of 2000 games against the strongest individual algorithm MCTS-IP-M (stronger with $p = 0.001$). In Breakthrough, the combination MCTS-IP-E-IR-E won 53.9%

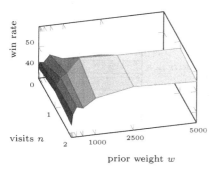

(a) Performance of MCTS-IP-E in Othello.

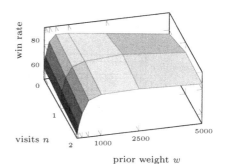

(b) Performance of MCTS-IP-E in Breakthrough.

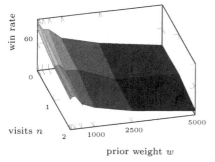

(c) Performance of MCTS-IP-E in Catch the Lion.

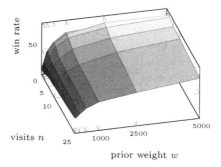

(d) Performance of MCTS-IP-M in Othello. For all conditions, $d = 3$.

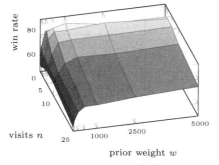

(e) Performance of MCTS-IP-M in Breakthrough. For all conditions, $d = 1$.

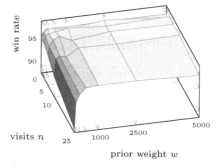

(f) Performance of MCTS-IP-M in Catch the Lion. For all conditions, $d = 5$.

Fig. 3. Performance of MCTS-IP in Othello, Breakthrough and Catch the Lion

against the best-performing algorithm MCTS-IP-E (stronger with p<0.05). In Catch the Lion, the combination MCTS-IP-M-IR-E with $n = 1$, $w = 2500$, and $d = 4$ won 61.1% of 2000 games against the strongest algorithm MCTS-IC-E (stronger with p<0.001, not shown in Figure 4(f)).

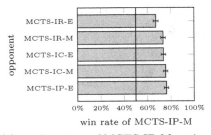

(a) Performance of MCTS-IP-M against the other hybrids in Othello.

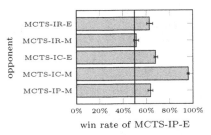

(b) Performance of MCTS-IP-E against the other hybrids in Breakthrough.

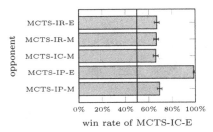

(c) Performance of MCTS-IC-E against the other hybrids in Catch the Lion.

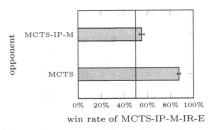

(d) Performance of MCTS-IP-M combined with MCTS-IR-E in Othello.

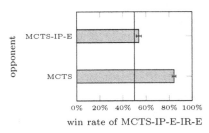

(e) Performance of MCTS-IP-E combined with MCTS-IR-E in Breakthrough.

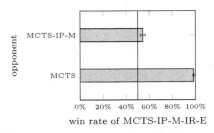

(f) Performance of MCTS-IP-M combined with MCTS-IR-E in Catch the Lion.

Fig. 4. Comparisons and combinations of the MCTS-minimax hybrids

6   Conclusion and Future Research

In this paper, we considered three approaches for integrating heuristic state evaluation functions into MCTS. MCTS-IR uses heuristic knowledge to improve the rollout policy. MCTS-IC uses heuristic knowledge to terminate rollouts early. MCTS-IP uses heuristic knowledge as prior for tree nodes. In all three approaches, we also examined the computation of state evaluations with shallow-depth minimax searches using the same heuristic knowledge. This has only been done for MCTS-IR before.

Experimental results in the domains of Othello, Breakthrough and Catch the Lion showed that the best individual players tested in Othello and Breakthrough make use of priors in order to combine heuristic information with rollout returns. Because of the different branching factors, computing these priors works best by embedding shallow minimax searches in Othello, and by a simple evaluation function call in Breakthrough. In Catch the Lion, random rollouts may too often return inaccurate results due to the tacticality and possibly also due to the non-converging nature of the domain. Replacing these rollouts with the evaluation function turned out to be the most successful of the individually tested approaches. Preliminary experiments with combining the different approaches showed that in both Othello and Catch the Lion, using minimax to compute node priors and applying simple ϵ-greedy rollouts resulted in the overall most successful players tested in this paper.

The fact that some combinations of algorithms play at a higher level than the algorithms in isolation may mean we have not yet found a way to fully and optimally exploit our heuristic knowledge. This is a first direction for future research.

Second, differences between test domains such as their density of terminal states, their density of hard and soft traps [20], or their progression property [8] could be studied in order to understand the behavior of MCTS-minimax hybrids. Artificial game trees could be a valuable tool to separate the effects of individual properties.

Third, all three approaches for using heuristic knowledge have shown cases where embedded minimax searches did not lead to stronger MCTS play than shallower minimax searches or even simple evaluation function calls. This phenomenon has only been observed in MCTS-IR before and deserves further study.

Finally, the main problem of MCTS-minimax hybrids seems to be their sensitivity to the branching factor of the domain. This explains their weak performance in Breakthrough. However, the minimax implementation used in this paper was a simple, unenhanced alpha-beta search. An improved implementation with e.g. static move ordering, k-best pruning, and killer moves has been shown to allow for successful MCTS-IR-M even in Lines of Action, a domain with an average branching factor twice as high as 6×6 Breakthrough [26]. These techniques could drastically increase the branching factor for which all MCTS-minimax hybrids are viable.

Acknowledgment. This work is funded by the Netherlands Organisation for Scientific Research (NWO) in the framework of the project Go4Nature, grant number 612.000.938.

References

1. Auer, P., Cesa-Bianchi, N., Fischer, P.: Finite-Time Analysis of the Multiarmed Bandit Problem. Machine Learning 47(2-3), 235–256 (2002)
2. Baier, H., Winands, M.H.M.: Monte-Carlo Tree Search and Minimax Hybrids. In: 2013 IEEE Conference on Computational Intelligence and Games, CIG 2013, pp. 129–136 (2013)
3. Bouzy, B.: Associating Domain-Dependent Knowledge and Monte Carlo Approaches within a Go Program. Information Sciences 175(4), 247–257 (2005)
4. Browne, C., Powley, E.J., Whitehouse, D., Lucas, S.M., Cowling, P.I., Rohlfshagen, P., Tavener, S., Perez, D., Samothrakis, S., Colton, S.: A Survey of Monte Carlo Tree Search Methods. IEEE Transactions on Computational Intelligence and AI in Games 4(1), 1–43 (2012)
5. Chaslot, G.M.J.B., Winands, M.H.M., van den Herik, H.J., Uiterwijk, J.W.H.M., Bouzy, B.: Progressive Strategies for Monte-Carlo Tree Search. New Mathematics and Natural Computation 4(3), 343–357 (2008)
6. Clune, J.E.: Heuristic Evaluation Functions for General Game Playing. Ph.D. thesis, University of California, Los Angeles, USA (2008)
7. Coulom, R.: Efficient Selectivity and Backup Operators in Monte-Carlo Tree Search. In: van den Herik, H.J., Ciancarini, P., Donkers, H.H.L.M(J.) (eds.) CG 2006. LNCS, vol. 4630, pp. 72–83. Springer, Heidelberg (2007)
8. Finnsson, H., Björnsson, Y.: Game-Tree Properties and MCTS Performance. In: IJCAI 2011 Workshop on General Intelligence in Game Playing Agents (GIGA 2011), pp. 23–30 (2011)
9. Gelly, S., Silver, D.: Combining Online and Offline Knowledge in UCT. In: Ghahramani, Z. (ed.) 24th International Conference on Machine Learning, ICML 2007. ACM International Conference Proceeding Series, vol. 227, pp. 273–280 (2007)
10. Gelly, S., Wang, Y., Munos, R., Teytaud, O.: Modification of UCT with Patterns in Monte-Carlo Go. Tech. rep., HAL - CCSd - CNRS, France (2006)
11. van den Herik, H.J., Xu, X., Ma, Z., Winands, M.H.M. (eds.): CG 2008. LNCS, vol. 5131. Springer, Heidelberg (2008)
12. Knuth, D.E., Moore, R.W.: An Analysis of Alpha-Beta Pruning. Artificial Intelligence 6(4), 293–326 (1975)
13. Kocsis, L., Szepesvári, C.: Bandit Based Monte-Carlo Planning. In: Fürnkranz, J., Scheffer, T., Spiliopoulou, M. (eds.) ECML 2006. LNCS (LNAI), vol. 4212, pp. 282–293. Springer, Heidelberg (2006)
14. Lanctot, M., Winands, M.H.M., Pepels, T., Sturtevant, N.R.: Monte Carlo Tree Search with Heuristic Evaluations using Implicit Minimax Backups. In: 2014 IEEE Conference on Computational Intelligence and Games, CIG 2014, pp. 341–348 (2014)
15. Lorentz, R.J.: Amazons Discover Monte-Carlo. In: van den Herik (ed.) [11], pp. 13–24
16. Lorentz, R., Horey, T.: Programming breakthrough. In: van den Herik, H.J., Iida, H., Plaat, A. (eds.) CG 2013. LNCS, vol. 8427, pp. 49–59. Springer, Heidelberg (2014)
17. Lorentz, R.J.: Experiments with Monte-Carlo Tree Search in the Game of Havannah. ICGA Journal 34(3), 140–149 (2011)
18. Nijssen, J(P.) A.M., Winands, M.H.M.: Playout Search for Monte-Carlo Tree Search in Multi-player Games. In: van den Herik, H.J., Plaat, A. (eds.) ACG 2011. LNCS, vol. 7168, pp. 72–83. Springer, Heidelberg (2012)

19. Ramanujan, R., Sabharwal, A., Selman, B.: On Adversarial Search Spaces and Sampling-Based Planning. In: Brafman, R.I., Geffner, H., Hoffmann, J., Kautz, H.A. (eds.) 20th International Conference on Automated Planning and Scheduling, ICAPS 2010, pp. 242–245. AAAI (2010)
20. Ramanujan, R., Sabharwal, A., Selman, B.: Understanding Sampling Style Adversarial Search Methods. In: Grünwald, P., Spirtes, P. (eds.) 26th Conference on Uncertainty in Artificial Intelligence, UAI 2010, pp. 474–483 (2010)
21. Ramanujan, R., Sabharwal, A., Selman, B.: On the Behavior of UCT in Synthetic Search Spaces. In: ICAPS 2011 Workshop on Monte-Carlo Tree Search: Theory and Applications (2011)
22. Ramanujan, R., Selman, B.: Trade-Offs in Sampling-Based Adversarial Planning. In: Bacchus, F., Domshlak, C., Edelkamp, S., Helmert, M. (eds.) 21st International Conference on Automated Planning and Scheduling, ICAPS 2011. AAAI (2011)
23. Sato, Y., Takahashi, D., Grimbergen, R.: A Shogi Program Based on Monte-Carlo Tree Search. ICGA Journal 33(2), 80–92 (2010)
24. Silver, D., Tesauro, G.: Monte-Carlo Simulation Balancing. In: Danyluk, A.P., Bottou, L., Littman, M.L. (eds.) 26th Annual International Conference on Machine Learning, ICML 2009. ACM International Conference Proceeding Series, vol. 382, pp. 945–952. ACM (2009)
25. Sturtevant, N.R.: An Analysis of UCT in Multi-Player Games. ICGA Journal 31(4), 195–208 (2008)
26. Winands, M.H.M., Björnsson, Y., Saito, J.-T.: Monte Carlo Tree Search in Lines of Action. IEEE Transactions on Computational Intelligence and AI in Games 2(4), 239–250 (2010)
27. Winands, M.H.M., Björnsson, Y.: Alpha-Beta-based Play-outs in Monte-Carlo Tree Search. In: Cho, S.-B., Lucas, S.M., Hingston, P. (eds.) 2011 IEEE Conference on Computational Intelligence and Games, CIG 2011, pp. 110–117. IEEE (2011)
28. Winands, M.H.M., Björnsson, Y., Saito, J.T.: Monte-Carlo Tree Search Solver. In: van den Herik, et al. (eds.) [11], pp. 25–36

Monte-Carlo Tree Search for the Game of "7 Wonders"

Denis Robilliard, Cyril Fonlupt, and Fabien Teytaud

LISIC, ULCO, Univ Lille–Nord de France, France

Abstract. Monte-Carlo Tree Search, and in particular with the Upper Confidence Bounds formula, has provided large improvements for AI in numerous games, particularly in Go, Hex, Havannah, Amazons and Breakthrough. In this work we study this algorithm on a more complex game, the game of "7 Wonders". This card game gathers together several known challenging properties, such as hidden information, multi-player and stochasticity. It also includes an inter-player trading system that induces a combinatorial search to decide which decisions are legal. Moreover, it is difficult to hand-craft an efficient evaluation function since the card values are heavily dependent upon the stage of the game and upon the other player decisions. We show that, in spite of the fact that "7 Wonders" is apparently not so related to classic abstract games, many known results still hold.

1 Introduction

Games are a typical AI research subject, with well-known successful results on games like chess, checkers, or backgammon. However, complex board games (sometimes nicknamed Euro-games) still constitute a challenge, which has been initiated by such works as [16] or [17] on the game "Settlers of Catan", or [22] on the game "Dominion". Most often these games combine several characteristics among multi-player, hidden information and chance, together with little formalized expert knowledge on the subject. Monte-Carlo Tree Search (MCTS), which gained much fame from the game of Go, seems a method of interest in this context.

In order to simplify the obtaining of an AI, many published works use only a limited subset of the game rules: e.g. no trade interactions between players [17], or only a subset of the possible cards in [22]. In this paper we focus on the creation of a MCTS-based AI player for the recent game of "7 Wonders" (see also [10]). One of our goals is to tackle the complete rule set of the game, including the trading mechanism. The way we deal with the trading mechanism is quite a novelty as in the usual case more than one hundred new branches can be created just for the different ways of buying/selling goods. The simulation cannot cope with such a fact and we use a smart stochastic approach to deal with this problem introduced in Section 5.

In the first section we introduce the "7 Wonders" game and its rules, before presenting MCTS. Then we focus on specific issues that arose during implementation, before presenting a set of experiments and their results.

2 "7 Wonders" Game Description

Board games are increasingly numerous, with more than 500 games presented each year at the international Essen game fair. Among these, the game "7 Wonders" (7W)

T. Cazenave et al. (Eds.): CGW 2014, CCIS 504, pp. 64–77, 2014.

issued in 2011 by Antoine Bauza, obtains a fair amount of success, with about 100,000 copies sold per year. It is basically a card game, whose theme is similar to the many existing "civilization" games, where players develop a virtual country using production of resources, trade, military and cultural improvements.

Before heading onto the game mechanisms, let introduce a game classification based on their characteristics. A game can be:

- Fully or partially observable, depending on whether there is hidden information or not.
- Solitaire, two-player or multi-player (standing for N-player with $N > 2$).
- Competitive or cooperative: in competitive games, players have their own goal, while they share the same objective in cooperative games.
- Deterministic or stochastic.

For instance, chess would belong to the family of fully observable, 2-player, competitive, deterministic games. The game of 7W is almost in opposite categories, being in the family of partially observable, multi-player, stochastic, and also competitive games. While this game is competitive under this classification, note that in an N-player game with $N > 2$, several players may share cooperative sub-goals, such as hindering the progress of the current leading player. All these characteristics suggest that 7W is a difficult challenge for AI.

In a 7W game, from 3 to 7 players[1] are first given a random personal board among the 7 available, before playing the so-called 3 ages (phases) of the game. At the beginning of each game age, each player gets a hidden hand of 7 cards. Then there are 6 playing card rounds, where every player simultaneously selects a card from his hand and either:

- puts it on the table in his personal space;
- or puts it under his personal board to unlock some specific power;
- or can discard it for 3 units of the game money.

The last decision (or move) is always possible, while the first two possible moves depend on the player ability to gather enough resources from his board or from the production cards he already played in his personal space. He can also buy, with game money, resources from cards previously played by his left and right neighbors. This trading decision cannot be opposed by the opponent player(s) and the price is determined by the cards already played.

After playing their card, there is a so-called drafting phase, where all players give their hand of remaining cards to their left (age 1 and 3) or to their right (age 2) neighbor. Thus the cards circulate from player to player, reducing the hidden information. When there are less than 6 players, some cards from his original hand will eventually come back to every player. On the 6th turn, when the players receive only two cards in hand, they play one of the two and discard the other.

The goal of the game is to score the maximum victory points (VP), which are awarded to the players at the end of the game, depending on the cards played on the table, under the boards and the respective amounts of game money. The cards are almost all different, but come in families distinguished by color: resources (brown and

---

[1] While the rule allows 2 player games, these are played by simulating a 3rd "dumb" player.

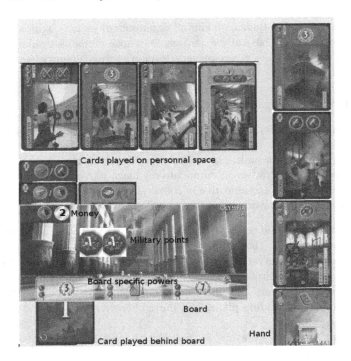

Fig. 1. Illustration of a player board and personal space in the middle of a game. Cards in hand are shown vertically on the right, cards played in the personal space are above the board with only the top of resources cards shown, cards put under the board are shown below the board with hidden face.

grey), military (red), administrative (blue), trade (yellow), sciences (green) and guilds (purple). The green family is itself sub-divided between three symbols used for VP count. See Figure 1 for an illustration of a player situation.

This game presents several interesting traits for AI research, that also probably explain its success among gamers:

- it has a complex scoring scheme combining linear and non-linear features: blue cards provide directly VPs to their owner, red cards offer points only to the owner of the majority of red cards symbols, yellow ones allow to save or earn game money, green ones give their owner the number of identical symbols to the square, with extra points for each pack of three different symbols.
- resource cards have delayed effect: they mainly allow a player to put VPs awarding cards on later turns; this is also the case of green cards that, apart from the scoring of symbols, allow some other cards to be played for free later on.
- there is hidden information when the players receive their hand of cards at the beginning of each age of the game.
- there is a great interactivity between players as they can buy resources from each other to achieve the playing of their own cards. Some cards also give benefits or

VPs depending on which cards have been played by the neighbors. Moreover the drafting phase confronts players with the difficult choice of either playing a card that gives them an advantage, or another card that would give a possibly greater advantage to one of the neighbors that would receive it after the drafting phase.

- the game is strongly asymmetric relatively to the players, since all player boards are different and provide specific powers (such as resources, or military symbols). Most of these benefits are available when playing a card under the personal board at a given cost in resources. Thus some boards are oriented towards specific strategies, such as maximizing the number of military symbols, or increasing the bonuses of collecting green cards symbols, for example.

The number of different cards (68 for 3 players, from those 5 are removed randomly) and the 7 specific boards, together with the delayed effect of many cards and the non-linear scoring, make it difficult to handcraft an evaluation function. Notably, the number of VPs gained in the first game age is a bad predictor of the final score, since scoring points at this stage of the game usually precludes playing resource cards that will be needed later on.

We can give an approximation of the state space size for 3 players, by considering that there are 68 possible different cards, from those each player will usually play 18 cards. We thus obtain $\binom{68}{18} \times \binom{50}{18} \times \binom{32}{18} = 1E38$ possible combinations, neglecting the different boards and the partition between on-table and behind-the-board cards (which would increase that number).

3 Monte-Carlo Tree Search

The Monte-Carlo Tree Search algorithm (MCTS) has been recently proposed for decision-making problems [14,8]. Applications are numerous and varied, and encompass notable games [12,15,4,1,18]. In games MCTS outperforms alpha-beta techniques when evaluation functions are hard to design. The most known implementation of MCTS is Upper Confidence Bound (UCT), that is presented below. Enhancements have also been proposed, such as progressive widening [7,6,19], that is described at the end of this section.

3.1 UCT Description

Let us first define two functions: mc(s) which plays a uniform random decision (move) from the situation s and returns the new position, and result(s) which returns the score of the final situation s. The idea is to build an imbalanced partial subtree by performing many random simulations from the current state, and simulation after simulation biasing these simulations toward those that give good results. The construction is then done incrementally and consists in three different parts: *descent*, *evaluation* and *growth*, illustrated in Fig. 2.

The *descent* is done by using a bandit formula, i.e. by choosing the node j among all possible nodes C^s which gives the best reward according to the formula:

$$s' \leftarrow \arg\max_{j \in C^s} \left[\bar{x}_j + K_{UCT} \sqrt{\frac{ln(n_s)}{n_j}} \right]$$

with $\bar{x}_j$ the average reward for the node j (it is the ratio of the number of victories over the number of simulations, thus belonging to interval $[0,1]$), n_j the number of simulations for the node j, n_s is the number of simulation in s, and $n_s = \sum_j n_j$. K_{UCT} is the exploration parameter and is used to tune the trade-off between exploitation and exploration. At the end of the *descent* part, a node which is outside the subtree has been reached. In order to evaluate this new node, a so-called *playout* is done: random decisions are taken until the end of the game, when the winner is known. The last part is the *Growth* step which consists in simply adding the new node to the subtree, and updating all the nodes which have been crossed by the simulation. The algorithm is presented in Alg.1.

Algorithm 1. MCTS

---

argument node s, MCTS subtree $\hat{T}$
while there is some time left **do**
  $s' \leftarrow s$
  Initialization: $game \leftarrow \emptyset$
  // *DESCENT*
  while s' in $\hat{T}$ and s' not terminal **do**
    $s' \leftarrow \arg\max_{j \in C^{s'}} [\bar{x}_j + K_{UCT}\sqrt{\frac{ln(n_{s'})}{n_j}}]$
    $game \leftarrow game + s'$
  $S \leftarrow s'$
  // *EVALUATION*
  while s' is not terminal **do**
    $s' \leftarrow mc(s')$
  $r = \text{result}(s')$
  // *GROWTH*
  $\hat{T} \leftarrow \hat{T} + S$
  for each s in $game$ **do**
    $n_s \leftarrow n_s + 1$
    $\bar{x}_s \leftarrow \frac{(\bar{x}_s * (n_s - 1) + r)}{n_s}$

In our implementation, a single N-player game turn (corresponding to the N player simultaneous decisions), is represented in the MCTS subtree by N successive levels, thus for a typical 3-player game with 3 ages and 6 cards to play per age, we get $3 \times 6 = 18$ decisions per player and the depth of the subtree is $18 \times 3 = 54$. Of course we keep the "simultaneous decisions" property, that is the state of the game is updated only when reaching a subtree level whose depth is a multiple of N, thus successive players (either real or simulated) make their decision without knowing their opponent choices. The average branching factor of a node can be estimated: a player has 4 cards in hand on average that can possibly be played in 3 different ways: discard, on the table, and behind the board. These two last options can usually be accomplished by different trading options, 2 trading options being common. This leads to an estimated average branching factor of $4 * (1 + 2 \times 2) = 20$ children per node.

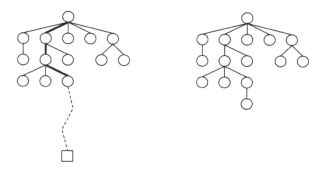

Fig. 2. Illustration of the MCTS algorithm from [3]. Circles represent nodes and the square represents the final node. On the left subtree, the descent part (guided by the bandit formula in the UCT implementation) is illustrated in bold. The evaluation part is illustrated with the dotted line. The subtree after the growth stage is illustrated on the right: the new node has been added.

3.2 Progressive Widening

UCT is an efficient method for balancing exploration and exploitation, however, only few information are provided for decisions loosely explored. Several enhancements have been provided to tackle this problem. The most famous are Progressive Widening [7,6,19] and Rapid Action Value Estimate [12].

The principle of progressive widening is to rank possible decisions according to some heuristics and to discard certain decisions while the number of simulations is not large enough. More precisely, let us rename decisions $y_1 \ldots y_n$, with $i < j$ when decision y_i is better than y_j according to the heuristic. At the mth simulation, all decisions with an index larger than $f(m)$ are discarded. The following formula: $f(m) = \lfloor Qm^P \rfloor$ performs well in the literature [7]. We let the parameter $Q = 1.0$ and tune only P, as reported in the experiment section.

We have chosen a simple ordering heuristic based on human play. This ranking consists in having first alternative resource type cards, then single resource type cards, then military cards, followed by science cards. Other cards are left unordered since for trade cards it is difficult to assess an a priori order, and for civil cards we can expect that they are easier to evaluate by MCTS, since their reward is mostly independent of other cards.

4 MCTS and 7 Wonders

In this section we present how we dealt with partial information and weak moves in playouts.

4.1 Handling Partial Information

In order to handle partial information, we used the determinization paradigm, see [13,2]. This consists in choosing decisions via several simulations of perfect information games that are consistent with what is known of the real, imperfect information, game state. We keep a single MCTS subtree, and the MCTS AI records the whole set of possible cards in its opponents' hands. Any card revealed during play implies a reduction of the opponents' possible cards in hand. When a simulation is done, we perform a determinization by an equiprobable random draw of a real size hand for each opponent, from their set of possible cards. The MCTS subtree is then descended, ignoring children nodes that are not playable with the current determinization, and adding newly available children nodes if required. This way of doing seems similar in principle to what is called information set UCT in [20].

Coping with Weak Decisions. A 7W player has always the choice of putting a card on the discard pile to earn 3 coins of game money. This is the sole option available when the resources needed to play any card are not available, but it can also be a tactical choice, e.g. in order to have enough money to buy resources from neighbors on a later turn. However, most of the time discarding is a worse than average move: notably 3 coins amount to 1 VP, while played cards should bring an average reward of about 3 VPs per card. As any one card can be discarded for money, while not all cards can usually be played, depending on available resources, thus discards are the most common moves and would be the dominant moves explored by a fully random playout procedure. This results in non-informative playouts and a weak MCTS player. The presence of such a class of weak moves is not uncommon in other games too, for instance in Go, all programs discard the "empty triangle" move from their playouts. We act similarly in the playouts, allowing discards only when no other move is possible. On the contrary we keep all moves in the MCTS subtree construction, in order to allow for tactical discards.

5   Managing Trading Decisions

In order to play a card in 7W, a player may choose to buy resources either from the right, left or from both of his two neighbors, at possibly different costs, depending on the resource type. Moreover some of the resource producing cards provide alternate choices: e.g. the "Caravanserai" card provides one unit of either ore, wood, brick or stone. These two game rules induce a combinatorial tree of possible resource trade choices, and it is not uncommon that this tree has several hundred branches, especially during the 3rd game age. Some of the branches are dead end, that is after setting some trade choices, it appears that some required resources cannot be gathered or are now unaffordable to the player. Other branches may offer valid and affordable trade choices, which constitute as many possible game decisions. Note that there is such a tree of possible trade decisions for every card in hand.

While the exploration of the whole tree for every card is recommended for building the MCTS subtree, since one does not want to forget a possible card playing decision, this would greatly impact the speed of play when it is done in playouts. Nonetheless it is not possible to ignore the trade decision tree, since truly random decisions would make nonsense in most cases (such as trying to buy resources from a player that do not own them, or that own them in insufficient number). Thus some sort of exploration of the trade tree has to be done.

We dealt with that issue in playouts by imposing a random order on the branches of the tree of possible trade choices, and fixing a hard limit L on the number of branches explored, depending on the game age: 3rd age cards generally award more VPs and require more resources, so it is sensible to spend more exploration time before deciding if they are playable or not in playouts. If we cannot find a suitable branch in the first L branches explored, then we consider that the card cannot be played (either on the table or under the board), thus it must be discarded.

In Table 1 we show the number of discards in playouts. This number of discards is listed per each game age and for 4 different values of the hard limit L on branch exploration (this is done for 3 players and 15000 simulations per game turn and there is some variance due to the game randomness). Some hands of cards really do not contain any playable card, thus a discard is compulsory by the game rules, but in other cases there are playable cards that are not seen if L is too low: the exploration of trading choices is ended too early. Indeed we see in Table 1 that the number of discards increases when putting too strict limits on trade exploration, meaning that we drop cards that could have been played by allowing a longer search.

In the Table 1 we see that discards are more common in the first age and are not affected by our limit thresholds. This is explained by the fact that not many resources have usually been played by random playouts in the first age, thus discards are often the sole possible decisions. On the contrary, the L threshold impacts the successful discovery of playable moves in age 2 and 3. Discards remain more common in age 3 than in age 2, since age 3 cards require more resources.

Table 1. Number of discards in playouts depending on game age and on the hard limit on the number of trading branches explored

Game age	Limit L on branches explored			
	16 br.	24 br.	32 br.	48 br.
1	35908	40304	38080	36340
2	14540	6727	6009	6191
3	67171	15578	11370	11314

By setting a limit of 8, 24 and 32 branches on respectively age 1, 2 and 3, we gained a more than 5 times speedup against the exploration of the whole trading tree. This allows for about 1000 simulations per second in age 1. The loss of precision in playouts (discards that could have been avoided with a longer search) is more than compensated for by the greater number of simulations allowed in the same time. Note that humans are also confronted to the same problem, and it is not uncommon that a player thinks a card is not playable, while it really is.

6 Experiments and Results

The objective of the experiments is to study the level of efficiency of MCTS to play successfully at 7W. This is done in comparison with a simple handcrafted rule-based AI presented below, and also by studying several values of MCTS parameters and enhancements, such as progressive widening.

Note that our MCTS AI was also successfully matched against experienced human players, even if the number of plays (and players) cannot yet be considered significant and reported here.

6.1 Rule-Based AI Implementation

The rule-based AI (rbAI) is deterministic and is managed, in age 1 and 2, along the principles listed below by priority order (when a card is "always played", it means of course if it is affordable):

- a card providing 2 or more resource types is always played;
- a card providing a single resource type that is lacking to the rbAI is always played;
- a military card is always played if rbAI is not the only leader in military, and the card allows rbAI to become the (or one of the) leading military player(s);
- the civil card with the greatest VP award is always played;
- a science card is always played;
- a random remaining card is played if possible, else a random card is discarded.

In the third game age, the set of rules is superseded by choosing the decision with best immediate VP reward.

6.2 Experimental Setting

All experiments are composed of 1000 runs, and the number of MCTS simulations per game turn is given for the 1st of the 3 ages of the game. This number is multiplied respectively by 1.5 and 2 in the 2nd and 3rd ages, since the shorter playouts allow more simulations in the same time (so a "1000 simulations" means respectively 1000, 1500 and 2000 simulations per turn in ages respectively 1, 2 and 3).

In the MCTS vs rbAI test, we use one instance of MCTS versus 2 instances of the rbAI. Iteratively, 20 sets of personal boards are drawn, and 50 independent random cards distributions are played on every board set.

In the MCTS parameter tuning experiments, we use one instance of the rbAI versus 2 instances of MCTS with different parameters/enhancements, called MCTS-1 and MCTS-2. We draw iteratively 5 board sets where the same board is duplicated for the two MCTS (this duplication of boards is not allowed in the original game rules but is handy to ensure that the MCTS comparison is not biased by the strength of the different boards). For each board setting, 100 independent random card distributions are played, then the two different MCTS instances swap position and the same 100 card distributions are played again. This is to remove any bias that could be generated by the position of each MCTS relatively to the rbAI player.

6.3   MCTS against Simple AI

In this section we compare the success rate of one MCTS player against two instances of the simple rule-based AI. Table 2 shows that MCTS is clearly superior. Adding more simulations improves the MCTS success rate, although with diminishing returns as the number of simulations increases, as expected by the theory.

Table 2. Comparisons of MCTS success rate (SR) versus rule-based AI (rbAI) for several number of simulations per game turn (mean value ± 95% confidence interval)

# sim.	SR MCTS	SR rbAI
125	67.63% ± 2.89	32.37% ± 2.89
250	81.87% ± 2.38	18.13% ± 2.38
500	87.25% ± 2.06	12.75% ± 2.06
1000	92.63% ± 1.62	7.37% ± 1.62

6.4   Comparison of MCTS with Different Parameters

Tuning of the Bandit Formula. First Table 3 shows a comparison of success rate for several values of the exploration constant K_{UCT}, on 1000 games, with 1000 simulations per game turn for each MCTS player. The success rates of the rbAI player are very low when using this number of simulations for MCTS and are not reported here (thus the success rates displayed do not sum up to 100%). The experiment show that good K_{UCT} values can be obtained in the range $[0.3, 1.0]$, although values strictly greater than 0.3 do not yield no much significant improvement. This good 0.3 value is slightly superior to the standard 0.2 found in the literature. This might be explained by the fact that some moves may appear very attractive in a few simulations (e.g. playing a military card) while some other good moves need more simulations to show their robustness (e.g. playing a science card that also allows some good later cards for free).

Scaling of UCT. A second set of experiments, in Table 4 explores the impact of the number of MCTS simulations per game turn. The K_{UCT} value is set to 0.3 for all experiments in this table. For each experiment we compare a given number of simulations against twice as many simulations. The expected gain decreases when the number of simulations rises, which is consistent with the literature (see [11]).

Progressive Widening. We experiment the progressive widening enhancement with 1000 simulations per move and $K_{UCT} = 0.3$. Several values for the P parameter are experimented and results against a standard MCTS are presented in Table 5. Except when P is too small and reduces too much the MCTS exploration, we obtain an improvement for several values of P. While the improvement is small, it appears quite robust in front of P. One point is that we have the same sorting for all moves for all ages. Maybe we should have an independent progressive widening for each age, as the importance of a family of moves could be different in different stages of the game.

Table 3. Comparisons of MCTS success rates (SR) for different values of K_{UCT} and 1000 simulations per game turn (mean value $\pm$ 95% confidence interval, rule-based AI is not reported)

K_{UCT} MCTS-1	K_{UCT} MCTS-2	SR MCTS-1	SR MCTS-2
0.1	0.2	34.20% $\pm$ 2.94	64.2% $\pm$ 2.97
0.2	0.3	42.60% $\pm$ 3.06	55.90% $\pm$ 3.08
0.3	0.4	48.00% $\pm$ 3.10	51.30% $\pm$ 3.10
0.3	0.5	48.70% $\pm$ 3.10	51.20% $\pm$ 3.10
0.3	0.7	49.10% $\pm$ 2.68	50.52% $\pm$ 2.68
0.3	1.0	48.30% $\pm$ 3.10	51.20% $\pm$ 3.10

Table 4. Comparisons of MCTS success rates (SR) for different number of simulations per game turn (mean value $\pm$ 95% confidence interval, rule-based AI is not reported)

# sim. MCTS-1	# sim. MCTS-2	SR MCTS-1	SR MCTS-2
125	250	34.50% $\pm$ 2.95	62.00% $\pm$ 3.01
250	500	39.00% $\pm$ 3.02	59.40% $\pm$ 3.04
500	1000	43.90% $\pm$3.08	55.50% $\pm$3.08
1000	2000	44.80% $\pm$ 3.08	54.60% $\pm$ 3.09
2000	4000	46.20% $\pm$ 3.09	53.50% $\pm$ 3.09
4000	8000	44% $\pm$ 3.08	% 55.90$\pm$ 3.08

Table 5. Comparisons of MCTS success rates (SR) without or with progressive opening of subtrees for different values of the P parameter (mean value $\pm$ 95% confidence interval, rule-based AI is not reported)

P	SR without progressive MCTS-1	SR with progressive MCTS-2
0.15	58.60% $\pm$ 3.05	40.70% $\pm$ 3.04
0.25	46.40% $\pm$ 3.09	53.20% $\pm$ 3.09
0.35	46.40% $\pm$ 3.09	53.30% $\pm$ 3.09
0.45	46.90% $\pm$ 3.09	52.70% $\pm$ 3.09

Using the Real Score of the Game. It has been shown that using an evaluation function instead of a Monte-Carlo policy can improve the global strength of the MCTS algorithm [15,21]. However, building such a function is not always possible and sometimes Monte-Carlo evaluations is the only choice. Sometimes, an intermediate solution consists in taking the real score of the game in order to bias the bandit formula. This is only possible when such a score exists and results are moderate. For instance, in the game of Go, there is only a very small (but significant) improvement [9]. One emphasis reason is that it becomes too greedy to win by more points and takes risks. We try to use the real score to bias the bandit formula as this score exists in the original game. Following [5], the bandit formula becomes then

$$ score_j \leftarrow \bar{x}_j + K_{UCT} * \sqrt{\frac{ln(n_s)}{n_j}} + \frac{K_{score}}{\log(n_j)} * RealScore $$

With this formula, the impact of the real score decreases with the number of simulations.

Results with numerous K_{score} are presented in Table 6. We can note two things: first using only the real score, which is approximated by using a large K_{score} does not work. The problem with this tuning is that the MCTS algorithm tries to win as many points as possible, even if it is a risky strategy. This is not reasonable, since it is better to be sure to win by only one point than to take risks to win by more points. Second, with only a small help of the real score ($K_{score} = 0.1$) it seems possible to obtain a small improvement, although not very significant. Both these results are consistent with the previous literature; in [9] the help of the real score gives a gain of only 0.02 for the game of Go.

Table 6. Comparisons of MCTS success rates (SR) without or with of the use of the real score game for biasing the tree policy (mean value ± 95% confidence interval, rule-based AI is not reported)

K_{score}	SR without the real score MCTS-1	SR with the real score MCTS-2
0.01	50.00% ± 3.10	49.70% ± 3.10
0.05	50.30% ± 3.10	49.20% ± 3.10
0.10	47.40% ± 3.10	52.00% ± 3.10
0.15	51.30% ± 3.10	48.00% ± 3.10
0.20	48.50% ± 3.10	50.60% ± 3.10
0.50	60.00% ± 3.04	39.60% ± 3.03
1.00	69.40% ± 2.86	29.60% ± 2.83
10.00	76.50% ± 2.63	22.20% ± 2.58

7 Conclusion and Future Research

In this paper we investigated Monte-Carlo Tree Search for the complex 7W board game, using all rules. The game of 7W has several challenging properties: multi-player, hidden information, chance and a complex scoring mechanism, that makes it difficult to handcraft an evaluation function. In this context, the MCTS method obtains convincing results, both against a human designed rule-based AI and against experienced human players.

However, the implementation is not straightforward: we use determinization to handle the hidden information element, and we refine the playouts by suppressing a class of weak moves. Moreover, the computing cost of exploiting all possible trading decisions in the playouts is too large to allow enough simulations for real-time play against humans. We solve this problem by approximating the set of allowed trading decisions. Thus the gap between MCTS theory and practice is not negligible.

We notice that the various parameter effects (K_{UCT}, scalability, progressive widening, and adding a score information) are quite similar to what is observed in classic abstract games, despite the fact that this game seems substantially different.

Future works consist in implementing the use of the Rapid Action Value Estimate (RAVE) enhancement [12], which is one the most powerful improvement for several games [12,18]. Another interesting work should be to analyze and improve the enhancements tried in this paper. In particular, having one progressive widening per age seems to be a good idea. The real score could also be incorporated in a similar way, as the relevance of its impact is probably bigger in the last stages of the game. Parallelization of the playouts could have both advantages of increasing the level of play by using more simulations, and allowing enough time to explore all trading moves in playouts. Last but not least, we plan to interface our AI with a gaming website in order to obtain a better assessment of its game level through the confrontation with more human players.

References

1. Arneson, B., Hayward, R.B., Henderson, P.: Monte-Carlo tree search in Hex. IEEE Transactions on Computational Intelligence and AI in Games 2(4), 251–258 (2010)
2. Bjarnason, R., Fern, A., Tadepalli, P.: Lower bounding Klondike Solitaire with Monte-Carlo planning. In: ICAPS (2009)
3. Browne, C.B., Powley, E., Whitehouse, D., Lucas, S.M., Cowling, P.I., Rohlfshagen, P., Tavener, S., Perez, D., Samothrakis, S., Colton, S.: A survey of Monte-Carlo tree search methods. IEEE Transactions on Computational Intelligence and AI in Games 4(1), 1–43 (2012)
4. Cazenave, T.: Monte-carlo kakuro. In: van den Herik, H.J., Spronck, P. (eds.) ACG 2009. LNCS, vol. 6048, pp. 45–54. Springer, Heidelberg (2010)
5. Chaslot, G., Fiter, C., Hoock, J.-B., Rimmel, A., Teytaud, O.: Adding expert knowledge and exploration in monte-carlo tree search. In: van den Herik, H.J., Spronck, P. (eds.) ACG 2009. LNCS, vol. 6048, pp. 1–13. Springer, Heidelberg (2010)
6. Chaslot, G.M.J.-B., Winands, M.H.M., van den Herik, H.J., Uiterwijk, J.W.H.M., Bouzy, B.: Progressive strategies for Monte-Carlo tree search. New Mathematics and Natural Computation 4(3), 343–357 (2008)

7. Coulom, R.: Computing "ELO ratings" of move patterns in the game of Go. ICGA Journal 30(4), 198–208 (2007)
8. Coulom, R.: Efficient selectivity and backup operators in monte-carlo tree search. In: van den Herik, H.J., Ciancarini, P., Donkers, H.H.L.M(J.) (eds.) CG 2006. LNCS, vol. 4630, pp. 72–83. Springer, Heidelberg (2007)
9. Enzenberger, M., Müller, M., Arneson, B., Segal, R.: Fuego–An open-source framework for board games and Go engine based on Monte Carlo tree search. IEEE Transactions on Computational Intelligence and AI in Games 2(4), 259–270 (2010)
10. Gardiner, A.: proposal for an agent that plays 7 Wonders. Tech. rep., Willamette University (2012), http://www.willamette.edu/~bgardine/Thesis_Files/ben_gardiner_proposal_final.pdf
11. Gelly, S., Hoock, J.B., Rimmel, A., Teytaud, O., Kalemkarian, Y., et al.: On the parallelization of Monte-Carlo planning. In: ICINCO (2008)
12. Gelly, S., Silver, D.: Combining online and offline knowledge in UCT. In: Proceedings of the 24th International Conference on Machine Learning, pp. 273–280. ACM (2007)
13. Ginsberg, M.L.: Gib: Imperfect information in a computationally challenging game. J. Artif. Intell. Res. (JAIR) 14, 303–358 (2001)
14. Kocsis, L., Szepesvári, C.: Bandit based Monte-Carlo planning. In: Fürnkranz, J., Scheffer, T., Spiliopoulou, M. (eds.) ECML 2006. LNCS (LNAI), vol. 4212, pp. 282–293. Springer, Heidelberg (2006)
15. Lorentz, R.J.: Amazons discover monte-carlo. In: van den Herik, H.J., Xu, X., Ma, Z., Winands, M.H.M. (eds.) CG 2008. LNCS, vol. 5131, pp. 13–24. Springer, Heidelberg (2008)
16. Pfeiffer, M.: Reinforcement learning of strategies for Settlers of Catan. In: 5th International Conference on Computer Games: Artificial Intelligence, Design and Education, pp. 384–388 (2004)
17. Szita, I., Chaslot, G., Spronck, P.: Monte-Carlo tree search in Settlers of Catan. In: van den Herik, H.J., Spronck, P. (eds.) ACG 2009. LNCS, vol. 6048, pp. 21–32. Springer, Heidelberg (2010)
18. Teytaud, F., Teytaud, O.: Creating an upper-confidence-tree program for havannah. In: van den Herik, H.J., Spronck, P. (eds.) ACG 2009. LNCS, vol. 6048, pp. 65–74. Springer, Heidelberg (2010)
19. Wang, Y., Audibert, J.Y., Munos, R., et al.: Infinitely many-armed bandits. Advances in Neural Information Processing Systems (2008)
20. Whitehouse, D., Powley, E.J., Cowling, P.I.: Determinization and information set Monte-Carlo tree search for the card game Dou Di Zhu. In: 2011 IEEE Conference on Computational Intelligence and Games (CIG), pp. 87–94. IEEE (2011)
21. Winands, M.H.M., Björnsson, Y.: Evaluation function based Monte-Carlo LOA. In: van den Herik, H.J., Spronck, P. (eds.) ACG 2009. LNCS, vol. 6048, pp. 33–44. Springer, Heidelberg (2010)
22. Winder, R.K.: Methods for approximating value functions for the Dominion card game. Evolutionary Intelligence (2013)

Small and Large MCTS Playouts Applied to Chinese Dark Chess Stochastic Game

Nicolas Jouandeau[1] and Tristan Cazenave[2]

[1] LIASD, Université de Paris 8, France
`n@ai.univ-paris8.fr`
[2] LAMSADE, Université Paris-Dauphine, France
`cazenave@lamsade.dauphine.fr`

Abstract. Monte-Carlo Tree Search is a powerful paradigm for deterministic perfect-information games. We present various changes applied to this algorithm to deal with the stochastic game CHINESE DARK CHESS. We experimented with group nodes and chance nodes using various configurations: with different playout policies, with different playout lengths, with true or estimated wins. Results show that extending playout length over the real draw condition is beneficial to group nodes and to chance nodes. It also shows that using an evaluation function can reduce the number of draw games with group nodes and can be increased with chance nodes.

1 Introduction

CHINESE DARK CHESS (CDC) is a popular stochastic two-player game in Asia that is often played on a 4×8 rectangular board where players do not know flipping moves' payoff. The two player (called black and red) start with the same set of pieces: one king, two guards, two bishops, two knights, two rooks, two cannons and five pawns (pieces that are similar to CHINESE CHESS). Before the first move, players do not know their color. The first player move defines the first player color. In classic games, pieces evolve on squares and can move vertically and horizontally from one square to an adjacent free square (*i.e.* up, down, left and right). A piece can capture another piece according to pieces value. Captures are done on vertical and horizontal adjacent squares except for cannons that capture pieces by jumping over another piece. Such jump is performed over a piece (called the jumping piece) and to the target piece. Free spaces can stand between its initial position and the jumping piece and between the jumping piece and the target position. Even if flipping moves imply multiple board possibilities, classic moves can lead to similar positions during the game and capturing rules are different for each piece. Monte-Carlo Tree Search (MCTS) programs have recently improved the most. We show in this paper two different MCTS implementations that can be further improved by using longer playouts, playout policies and an evaluation function.

The paper is organized as follows. Section 2 describes related work. Section 3 presents two MCTS implementations. Section 4 shows experimental results

T. Cazenave et al. (Eds.): CGW 2014, CCIS 504, pp. 78–89, 2014.
© Springer International Publishing Switzerland 2014

achieved with different playout lengths, playout policies and an playout evaluation function. Finally, Section 5 gives the conclusions.

2 Related Work

In this section we discuss related work on CDC. Even though the game has not
been researched extensively, previous research concern methods such as *alpha-beta*, move policies, endgame databases and MCTS.

Chen *et al.* [1] used the *alpha-beta* algorithm with different revealing policies
combined with an *initial-depth flipping* method to reduce the branching factor.
They distinguished opening, middle and endgame to apply different policies.

Chen *et al.* [2] built an endgame databases with retrograde analysis. Created
databases are done for each first move color, up to 8 revealed pieces. They used
2TB of memory to represent 10^{12} positions. Positions status are stored as win,
loss or draw.

Yen *et al.* [3] presented a non-deterministic Monte-Carlo Tree Search model
by combining chance nodes [4] and MCTS. They create shorter simulations by
moderating the three policies named *Capture First*, *Capture Stronger Piece First*
and *Capture and Escape Stronger Piece First*. As draw rate decreases, win rate
increases and simulations are more meaningful for MCTS.

Chang and Hsu [5] solved the 2×4 variant. They created an *Oracle* variant
where every piece is known. Comparing the *Oracle* variant and the classic variant
shows that the first move is crucial on the 2×4 board.

Chen and Hsu [6] presented a policy-oriented search method to build opening
books in case of a very large state space as it is in CDC. Attack, defend, claim
or discover territory are compared according to player's turn. Results show that
player's level is a little stronger with an opening book. As flipping moves can
completely change the game issue, they showed that enhancements provided are
probabilistically acquired.

Safidine *et al.* [7] exploit pieces combinations to reduce endgame databases.
By combining material symmetry identified by relations between pieces and
endgame construction with retrograde analysis, winning positions are recorded
in databases. This general method has been applied to SKAT, DOMINOES and
CDC. Even if the relationship between pieces in CDC creates intricate symme-
tries, they reduced the size of 4-element endgame tables by 9.92 and the size of
8-element endgame tables by 3.68.

Chen *et al.* [8] present equivalence classes computation for endgames with
unrevealed pieces. Boards are identified by threats and pieces' positions that
are compared in a multiple steps algorithm. Compression rates of material have
been studied from 3 to 32 pieces. Endgame databases have been computed of 3
to 8 pieces and its number of elements is reduced by 17.20.

Move groups have been proposed in [10] to address the problem of MCTS in
games with a high branching factor. When there are too many moves, it can be
a good heuristic to regroup the statistics of moves that share some properties.
For example, in the game of Amazons where the branching factor can be of

the order of a thousand moves, a natural way to reduce the branching factor is to separate the queen move from the stone placement [9]. In the imperfect information game Dou Di Zhu, Information Set [11] has been combined with move groups: the player first chooses the base move and then the kicker, as two separate consecutive decision nodes in the tree. Move groups have also been analyzed for an artificial game [12].

3   Stochastic MCTS

In this section, we present the use of chance nodes and of group nodes with MCTS. Group nodes are used to reduce the branching factor created by flipping moves. In a similar manner to move groups that regroup moves, we define group nodes to consider all revealing moves at the same position in a single node. Apart from that, chance nodes are the classic way to manage stochastic information in trees. We present the main loop and the selection function of MCTS with group nodes and with chance nodes. Both algorithms are presented as an anytime interruptible process, that tends to produce a better solution over computing time and that is instantaneously interrupted when time is up or when a winning move is found.

3.1   With Group Nodes

During the game, applying a flipping move can relate to different boards. At the beginning of the game, the first player has 32 possible moves that correspond to 4×10^{36} possibilities. During the game, the number of possible boards linked to flipping moves decreases with the number of unrevealed pieces. For the penultimate flipping move, 2 boards are possible and for the last flipping move, only one board. But as the number of possible boards stays over 120 for more than 5 different pieces, the number of possible boards remains important at most of the time before endgame. To reduce the number of children nodes produced by flipping moves, all possible boards that arise from a flipping move are gathered in a single group node. Therefore, at the beginning of the game, the root node is followed by 32 children that are group nodes. Then the other actions (moves, jumps and captures) are represented in the tree with classic nodes. The main loop of MCTS with group nodes is presented in ALG 1. The selection phase (line 2) returns a node q to expand, its corresponding board and $\mathcal{L}$ the list of moves to apply for expansion. By default, all nodes inserted in the tree have $UNSET$ winning color. If this node is known as winning position, the process is interrupted (line 3). Otherwise each element of $\mathcal{L}$ creates a new child to q and store it in $\mathcal{N}$. For each element of $\mathcal{N}$, the board is modified, a new simulation is applied from the modified board and a new result is backpropagated from the new node up to the root_node. At the end, the bestNext function selects the best next node q_{best} of the root_node that defines the best next move.

The selection function of MCTS with group nodes is presented in ALG 2. The process iterates to find the best node q, its corresponding board and its moves $\mathcal{M}$. There are four different cases:

Algorithm 1. MCTS with group nodes

1. **while** not-interrupted **do**
2. $(q, board, \mathcal{L}) \leftarrow$ select ( )
3.   **if** $q.winning\_color\ != UNSET$ **then break**
4. $\mathcal{N} \leftarrow$ expandAll $(q, \mathcal{L})$
5.   **for** each $e \in \mathcal{N}$ **do**
6. $board' \leftarrow$ applyMove $(e, board)$
7.   simulate $(e, board')$
8.   backpropagate (e)
9.   **end for**
10. **end while**
11. $q \leftarrow$ bestNext $(root\_node)$
12. **return** q

- q is known as winning position. Then the process is interrupted (line 5).
- q is leading a player to a new winning position. Then it returns q with the corresponding *board* and an empty set (line 7).
- q is a new node that has not been extended previously. Then it returns q with the corresponding *board* and new moves that corresponds to the *board* (lines 9 to 11).
- q is a group node previously evaluated with a different flipping outlet that produces new moves that are not yet considered in q children. Then it returns q with the corresponding *board* and new moves that corresponds to only previously unconsidered moves in q group node (line 13 to 15).

The **next** function (ALG 2 line 6) returns all current next nodes of q. The **move** function (line 8) returns all next moves of the current *board*. If $\mathcal{M}$ is empty (line 9), the corresponding node is noted as winning node for the opponent player of the current *board* turn. The test applied line 13, checks if the current situation fits with the current group node. If it fits, then the **best_next** function is applied to select the best nodes inside $\mathcal{M}$ (line 17). If it does not fit, then the selection process is stopped and $\mathcal{M}$ becomes a set of previously unconsidered moves (line 14).

3.2   With Chance Nodes

During the game, moves can lead to the creation of chance nodes. As different pieces are unknown, each flipping move is represented with a chance node. Other board modifications, like moves, jumps and captures, are represented with classic nodes. Chance nodes are composed of classic nodes. At a chance node, each flipping possibility corresponds to a new child. The main loop of MCTS with chance nodes is presented in ALG 3.

According to the MCTS phases, this process applies iteratively selection, simulation and backpropagation. From a selected node q, the simulation leads to a new node q_{new} from which the result of the last simulation is backpropagated toward the *root_node*. At the end, the **bestNext** function selects the best next

---

Algorithm 2. select ( ) with group nodes

---

1. $q \leftarrow root$
2. $board \leftarrow root\_board$
3. $\mathcal{M} \leftarrow \emptyset$
4. **while** not-interrupted **do**
5.   **if** $q.winning\_color \ != UNSET$ **then break**
6. $\mathcal{N} \leftarrow$ next (q)
7.   **if** size $(\mathcal{N}) = 0$ **then break**
8. $\mathcal{M} \leftarrow$ moves $(board)$
9.   **if** size $(\mathcal{M}) = 0$ **then**
10. $q.winning\_color \leftarrow opponent$ $(board.turn)$
11.   **break**
12.   **end if**
13.   **if** $\exists\, e \in \mathcal{M}$ with $e \notin \mathcal{N}$ **then**
14. $\mathcal{M} \leftarrow \mathcal{M} - (\mathcal{M} \cap \mathcal{N})$
15.   **break**
16.   **end if**
17. $(q, board) \leftarrow$ best_next $(q, \mathcal{M})$
18. **end while**
19. **return** $(q, board, \mathcal{M})$

Algorithm 3. MCTS with chance nodes

---

1. **while** not-interrupted **do**
2. $(q, board) \leftarrow$ select ( )
3.   **if** $q_{new}.winning\_color \ != UNSET$ **then break**
4. $q_{new} \leftarrow$ simulate $(q, board)$
5.   backpropagate (q_{new})
6. **end while**
7. $q_{best} \leftarrow$ bestNext $(root\_node)$
8. **return** q_{best}

---

node q_{best} of the *root_node* that defines the best next move. The selection of a chance node can lead to different boards and the selection of a classic node leads to an expected situation. At the beginning, all nodes are inserted in the tree without winning color information. If the selected node is a winning node, the process can be immediately interrupted (line 3 ALG 3 and line 4 ALG 4).

The selection function of MCTS with chance nodes is presented in ALG 4. The process iterates to find the best node q and its corresponding board. From the *root_node* and the *root_board*, the current *board* is updated according to the best move. At each iteration, a set of moves $\mathcal{M}$ is defined according to the selected board position and its turn. If this set is empty (line 6), the corresponding node is noted as winning node for the opponent player of the current *board* turn. If the best move is a new flipping move (line 11), a new chance node and a new node are added in the tree. If initial and final positions differ, a simple classic node is added.

Algorithm 4. select ( ) with chance nodes

1. $q \leftarrow root$
2. $board \leftarrow root\_board$
3. **while** not-interrupted **do**
4.   **if** $q.winning\_color \; ! = UNSET$ **then break**
5. $\mathcal{M} \leftarrow$ moves $(board)$
6.   **if** size $(\mathcal{M}) = 0$ **then**
7. $q.winning\_color \leftarrow opponent \; (board.turn)$
8.   **return** $(q, board)$
9.   **end if**
10.   **if** $(pos_i, pos_f) \leftarrow$ newMove $(q, board, \mathcal{M})$ **then**
11.   **if** $(pos_i = pos_f)$ **then**
12. $q' \leftarrow$ addChanceNode (q)
13. $q_{new} \leftarrow$ addNode (q')
14.   **else**
15. $q_{new} \leftarrow$ addNode (q)
16.   **end if**
17. $board \leftarrow$ play (pos_i, pos_f)
18.   **return** $(q_{new}, board)$
19.   **end if**
20. $(q, board) \leftarrow$ best $(q, board, \mathcal{M})$
21. **end while**

4 Experiments

In this section, we present various experiments to select the fastest policies, to reduce the number of drawn endgames, varying the playout length, and using with or without and evaluation function.

4.1 Fast Policies

In this subsection, we present various policies used to enhance playouts. We present basic and advanced ones and evaluate them to be useful in MCTS with as fast simulations as possible. The fastest policies are considered as most promising and are selected to continue our study.

We have used four basic playout policies, which are natural to use in CDC:

- Random, where players play randomly.
- Capture, where players try to capture opponent pieces.
- Avoid, where players try to avoid opponent's capture.
- Trap, where players try to minimize opponents moves.

According to these basics policies, we settled for the following advanced policies derived from the basic ones:

- Capture and avoid, where players try first to capture one opponent, try second to avoid opponents and otherwise play randomly.

- Avoid and capture, where players try first to avoid opponents, try second to capture one opponent and otherwise play randomly.
- Capture and trap, where players try first to capture one opponent and otherwise to trap opponents.
- Capture avoid and trap, where players try first to capture an opponent, try second to avoid opponents and otherwise to trap opponents.

All these policies have been tested for 2000 playouts at the beginning, the middle and the end of the game. Results are shown in Fig. 1-3 and in Tab. 1.

Fig. 1 show the board at the beginning of the game, when player colors are unknown. Best moves are colored in gray on the board and are bold in Tab. 1.

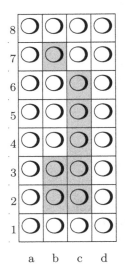

Fig. 1. Beginning

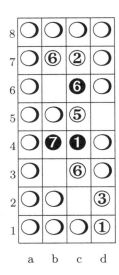

Fig. 2. Middle game

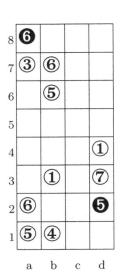

Fig. 3. Endgame

Fig. 2 shows the resulting board situation after the following 10 turns. Unknown pieces are represented with white circles. The 10 moves played are (columns are annotated with letters and rows are annotated with numbers. Flipping moves indicate a revealed piece under parenthesis. Moving and capturing moves indicate two coordinates.):

c4(k) d1(P) ; d2(N) d5(p) ; c2(G) c3(c) ; c5(C) c5-c3 ;
c4(p) c6(M) ; b3(r) c6-c5 ; b3-c3 c2-c3 ; c7(C) c5-d5 ;
b6(g) d5-c5 ; b6-c6 b7(G) ;

It is now first player's turn to play. 19 reveal moves remain. First player is black and its non-flipping possible moves are:

b4-b3 ; c6-b6 ; c6-c7 ; c6-c5 ;

Second player is white (*i.e.* red) and its non-flipping possible moves are:

Table 1. Playing 2000 playouts at beginning, middle game and endgame

Policy	Time	Rem. pieces	Playout length	Without eval. fun. Best	W	L	D	With eval. fun. Best	W	L	D
At beginning											
Random	0.660	12.16 $_{(2.31)}$	106.37 $_{(9.25)}$	d7	-	-	100	b7	69	30	01
Capture	0.375	5.67 $_{(2.20)}$	100.01 $_{(17.69)}$	c2	25	22	53	b3	52	48	-
Avoid	5.973	16.78 $_{(2.88)}$	207.41 $_{(74.49)}$	b2	-	-	100	c8	57	43	-
Capture and avoid	0.598	7.24 $_{(2.25)}$	107.27 $_{(18.05)}$	b1	34	13	53	c8	55	45	-
Avoid and capture	1.049	7.69 $_{(2.20)}$	123.02 $_{(20.15)}$	c4	18	06	76	c6	38	60	02
Trap	140.457	8.95 $_{(2.15)}$	579.69 $_{(115.79)}$	d7	-	-	100	d6	86	14	-
Capture and trap	99.753	15.07 $_{(3.07)}$	610.96 $_{(111.26)}$	c3	02	-	98	c5	52	48	-
Capture avoid and trap	39.799	7.12 $_{(2.52)}$	435.53 $_{(177.59)}$	d3	31	25	44	d1	64	36	-
At middle game											
Random	0.606	12.18 $_{(2.24)}$	91.89 $_{(9.20)}$	d8	-	-	100	c6-c7	43	57	-
Capture	0.348	6.91 $_{(2.17)}$	75.60 $_{(19.26)}$	c6-c7	48	02	50	c6-c7	90	10	-
Avoid	5.072	16.60 $_{(2.72)}$	194.68 $_{(87.18)}$	d4	-	-	100	d4	55	44	01
Capture and avoid	0.585	7.53 $_{(1.96)}$	89.06 $_{(17.93)}$	c6-c7	34	02	64	c6-c7	84	16	-
Avoid and capture	0.885	7.55 $_{(2.02)}$	103.68 $_{(15.79)}$	c6-c7	04	14	82	c6-c7	30	69	01
Trap	157.911	9.68 $_{(1.86)}$	704.73 $_{(62.78)}$	d7	-	-	100	d8	97	03	-
Capture and trap	123.055	14.49 $_{(2.89)}$	711.58 $_{(45.01)}$	b8	01	-	99	d4	76	24	-
Capture avoid and trap	34.201	9.92 $_{(1.59)}$	370.29 $_{(177.85)}$	c6-c7	54	00	46	c6-c7	100	-	-
At endgame											
Random	0.504	8.23 $_{(1.14)}$	42.72 $_{(1.46)}$	a8-a7	-	-	100	a8-a7	-	100	-
Capture	0.469	6.26 $_{(0.94)}$	41.93 $_{(6.02)}$	a8-a7	00	22	78	a8-a7	-	100	-
Avoid	0.781	10.12 $_{(0.54)}$	40.66 $_{(1.55)}$	d2-c2	-	02	98	d2-c2	-	100	-
Capture and avoid	0.733	8.00 $_{(0.00)}$	43.00 $_{(0.00)}$	a8-a7	-	-	100	a8-a7	-	100	-
Avoid and capture	0.817	9.80 $_{(0.53)}$	40.34 $_{(4.36)}$	d2-c2	-	04	96	d2-c2	-	100	-
Trap	11.138	7.00 $_{(0.00)}$	44.00 $_{(0.00)}$	d2-c2	-	-	100	d2-c2	-	100	-
Capture and trap	7.389	11.00 $_{(0.00)}$	40.00 $_{(0.00)}$	d2-c2	-	-	100	d2-c2	-	100	-
Capture avoid and trap	6.030	8.0 $_{(0.00)}$	43.00 $_{(0.00)}$	a8-a7	-	-	100	a8-a7	-	100	-

b7-b6 ; c5-c4 ; c5-d5 ; c3-b3 ; c3-c2 ; c3-c4 ; d2-c2 ;
First player has captured only one C piece and second player has captured 3 pieces that are p c r. Good move for black is c6-c5, or reveal c8 and d7.

Fig. 3 shows an endgame board, where everything is known. Black has clearly lost the game.

As CDC games can end in a draw, we constructed an evaluation function that can evaluate a drawn position. This evaluation function is based on material balance. It allows to assign a numerical value to drawn endgame boards. As we do not know if playing first is an advantage, we allow this evaluation function to reply draw if the material is equal. In some specific cases, the draw depends on piece position and then this function gives a false win detection. In order, pieces {K G M R N C P} are associated to the weights {0.15, 0.1, 0.07, 0.05, 0.03, 0.05, 0.05}.

Tab. 1 compares the time required by basic and advanced policies to achieve 2000 playouts. This table also gives the average of remaining pieces and its standard deviation, the average playout length and its standard deviation, the best moves with and without evaluation function.

It shows that some policies are too slow (*i.e.* Avoid, Avoid and capture, Trap, Capture and trap, Capture avoid and trap) to play a significant number of playouts to be simply used in MCTS. Remaining pieces and playout length showed us that longer playout could be interesting.

4.2   Reducing the Number of Drawn Games

In this subsection, we select the best policies by checking their ability to create as few as drawn games as possible. Results are presented according to various draw conditions.

As some policies are considered as too slow, we only kept *Random* (*i.e.* RND), *Capture* (*i.e.* CAP_RND), *Capture and avoid* (*i.e.* CAP_AVD_RND) and *Avoid and Capture* (*i.e.* AVD_CAP_RND) (where these last three also call random if nothing else can be done).

Table 2. Applying 2000 playouts from begin board

Policy	time[sec]	draw	Rem. pieces	Playout length	Draw condition
RND	0.630	1.00	12.62	106.07	40
	1.067	0.99	6.03	232.11	160
	1.801	**0.67**	3.24	622.37	640
CAP_RND	0.376	0.70	5.66	103.71	40
	0.522	0.46	4.59	171.77	160
	0.802	**0.31**	4.29	335.92	640
CAP_AVD_RND	0.598	0.73	7.15	110.45	40
	0.953	0.53	6.07	185.41	160
	2.139	**0.43**	5.87	403.44	640
AVD_CAP_RND	1.012	0.87	7.77	124.29	40
	1.707	0.69	6.19	223.51	160
	4.353	**0.59**	5.85	550.41	640

Tab. 2 shows the time used to generate 2000 playouts from the begin board. Next columns show the draw ratio, the average number of pieces at the end, the playout length according to different draw conditions. In a normal game, the draw condition is equal to 40 moves without capture or reveal. It shows that the number of draws can be reduced significantly by increasing the draw condition. In the same time, the number of remaining pieces is reduced. It shows that CAP_RND is really efficient for every value of the draw condition. We decided to eliminate the AVD_CAP_RND policy that increases the time with only a slightly better draw reduction than the simple RND policy.

4.3   Group Nodes vs. Chance Nodes

In this subsection, we challenge MCTS players by facing group nodes against chance nodes, with different playout length, with the most promising policies. For each combination, we also checked the influence of the evaluation function. All the players are tested against a reference player, that simply plays randomly when pieces are unrevealed and otherwise applies minimax to find the best move. Results are shown in Tab. 3 for 500 games with half as the first player and half as the second player. Each player has 1 sec to generate a new move. The corresponding number of drawn games is shown in Fig. 4 for MCTS with group nodes and in Fig. 5 for MCTS with chance nodes.

The RND policy is now abbreviated with R, the CAP_RND policy is abbreviated CR and the CAP_AVD_RND) policy is abbreviated CAR. C1 stands for group nodes

Table 3. Playing 500 games against the reference player

	playout length	40		160		640		2560	
		win	lost	win	lost	win	lost	win	lost
chance nodes	C2-R	0	255	4	298	213	109	164	72
	C2-R-h	9	137	104	64	116	43	135	42
	C2-CR	**244**	**16**	242	21	245	15	149	21
	C2-CR-h	131	15	143	14	138	23	129	23
	C2-CAR	199	33	**245**	**27**	239	46	159	47
	C2-CAR-h	129	16	125	25	122	9	104	30
	playout length	40		160		640		2560	
		win	lost	win	lost	win	lost	win	lost
group nodes	C1-R	10	249	51	185	78	187	64	233
	C1-R-h	60	269	103	231	80	219	85	263
	C1-CR	35	46	101	52	146	61	137	66
	C1-CR-h	120	87	167	98	**182**	**88**	147	127
	C1-CAR	41	35	103	52	128	93	72	170
	C1-CAR-h	109	100	167	86	**175**	**97**	130	143

and C2 stands for chance nodes. h mentions evaluation function usage and no h means that only true victories are considered inside the playouts.

Results shows that chance nodes are less effective with evaluation function where group nodes are more effective with evaluation function. It further shows that chance nodes are more dependent on playout length than group nodes. The best group-nodes players achieved 182 and 175 victories when chance nodes achieved 244 and 245 victories.

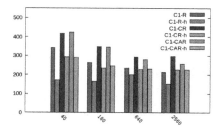

Fig. 4. Group-node draw of Tab 3

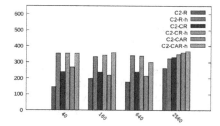

Fig. 5. Chance-node draw of Tab 3

For each policy, Fig. 4 shows that evaluation function reduces the number of draw games with group nodes. Nonetheless the number of draw games is equal or higher with chance nodes (see Fig. 5).

Table 4. Tournament between MCTS players

	C1-CAR-h-640	C2-CR-40	C2-CR-640	C2-CAR-160
C1-CR-h-640	**268** / 169	**282** / 97	176 / **252**	**287** / 131
C1-CAR-h-640		**228** / 137	156 / **285**	236 / 175
C2-CR-40			149 / **220**	176 / 204

Tab. 4 presents a tournament of best chance-nodes and group-nodes players. It shows that:

- Between group nodes, `CR-h-640` (*i.e.* *Capture* with evaluation function and playout length of 640) is the best policy.
- Chance-nodes players even simply with *Capture* policy are better than group nodes.
- Between all players, the best is chance nodes with *Capture*, without evaluation function and with a playout length of 640.

It shows that sophisticated policies are better with group nodes where the basic *Capture* policy is the best with chance nodes. Extending playout length over the real draw condition is beneficial to group nodes and to chance nodes.

5   Conclusion

We have presented different Monte-Carlo Tree Search enhancements that deal with the stochastic game CHINESE DARK CHESS. We have shown relations with playout length, basic or advanced policies and evaluation function usage. While extending the playout length is useful to create more informed playouts, an evaluation function usage can either increase or decrease player's effectiveness through modifying the number of draw possibilities.

References

1. Chen, B.-N., Shen, B.-J., Hsu, T.-S.: Chinese Dark Chess. ICGA Journal 33(2), 93–106 (2010)
2. Chen, J.-C., Lin, T.-Y., Hsu, S.-C., Hsu, T.-S.: Design and Implementation of Computer Chinese Dark Chess Endgame Database. In: TCGA Computer Game Workshop, TCGA 2012 (2012)
3. Yen, S.-J., Chou, C.-W., Chen, J.-C., Wu, I.-C., Kao, K.-Y.: The Art of the Chinese Dark Chess Program DIABLE. In: Proc. of the Int. Computer Symposium (ICS-2012), pp. 231–242 (2013)
4. Lanctot, M., Saffidine, A., Veness, J., Archibald, C., Winands, M.H.M.: Monte Carlo *-Minimax Search. In: 23rd Int. Joint Conf. on Artificial Intelligence (IJCAI-2013), pp. 580–586 (2013)
5. Chang, H.-J., Hsu, T.-S.: A Quantitative Study of 2×4 chinese dark chess. In: van den Herik, H.J., Iida, H., Plaat, A. (eds.) CG 2013. LNCS, vol. 8427, pp. 151–162. Springer, Heidelberg (2014)
6. Chen, B.-N., Hsu, T.-S.: Automatic Generation of Opening Books for Dark Chess. In: van den Herik, H.J., Iida, H., Plaat, A. (eds.) CG 2013. LNCS, vol. 8427, pp. 221–232. Springer, Heidelberg (2014)
7. Saffidine, A., Jouandeau, N., Buron, C., Cazenave, T.: Material symmetry to partition endgame tables. In: van den Herik, H.J., Iida, H., Plaat, A. (eds.) CG 2013. LNCS, vol. 8427, pp. 187–198. Springer, Heidelberg (2014)
8. Chen, J.-C., Lin, T.-Y., Chen, B.-N., Hsu, T.-S.: Equivalence Classes in Chinese Dark Chess Endgames. IEEE Trans. on Computational Intelligence and AI in Games (in press, 2014)

9. Childs, B.E., Brodeur, J.H., Kocsis, L.: Transpositions and move groups in Monte Carlo tree search. In: IEEE Symp. on Computational Intelligence and Games (CIG-2008), pp. 389–395 (2008)
10. Saito, J.-T., Winands, M.H.M., Uiterwijk, J.W.H.M., van den Herik, H.J.: Grouping Nodes for Monte-Carlo Go. In: Computer Games Workshop 2007 (CGW 2007), pp. 125–132 (2007)
11. Cowling, P.I., Powley, E.J., Whitehouse, D.: Information Set Monte Carlo Tree Search. IEEE Trans. on Computational Intelligence and AI in Games 4(2), 120–143 (2012)
12. Van Eyck, G., Müller, M.: Revisiting Move Groups in Monte-Carlo Tree Search. In: van den Herik, H.J., Plaat, A. (eds.) ACG 2011. LNCS, vol. 7168, pp. 13–23. Springer, Heidelberg (2012)

On the Complexity of General Game Playing

Édouard Bonnet[1] and Abdallah Saffidine[2]

[1] LAMSADE
Universit Paris-Dauphine
edouard.bonnet@dauphine.fr
[2] School of Computer Science and Engineering
The University of New South Wales
abdallahs@cse.unsw.edu.au

Abstract. The Game Description Language (GDL) used in General Game Playing (GGP) competitions provides a compact way to express multi-agents systems. Multiple features of GDL contribute to making it a convenient tool to describe multi-agent systems. We study the computational complexity of reasoning in GGP using various combinations of these features. Our analysis offers a complexity landscape for GGP with fragments ranging from NP to EXPSPACE in the single-agent case, and from PSPACE to 2EXPTIME in the multi-agent case.

1 Introduction

General Game Playing (GGP) research aims at developing systems capable of reasoning on a variety of multi-agent situations encoded in the Game Description Language (GDL) [4]. GDL can be seen as a domain specific logic programming language that provides a compact representation for transition systems. As such, GDL can be related both the Planning Domain Description Language (PDDL) and to Datalog.

The similarity between GDL and PDDL stems from the fact that both languages were created to describe dynamic situations. PDDL revolves around the agent's actions and allows modeling the preconditions and effects of actions chosen by a planning system. On the other hand, GDL focusses on predicates that characterize a current state and possible actions and their effects can be inferred via logical reasoning on the state.

While GDL is based on Datalog and incorporates many aspects of it such as negation-as-failure, it features multiple elements absent in Datalog such as nested function constants and more importantly multi-agent system semantics as opposed to a (set of) model(s).

Many language features of GDL make it a convenient tool to describe games and other multi-agent systems. However, this very expressiveness makes reasoning about described systems challenging.

In this paper, we tackle the computational complexity of reasoning about systems described in GDL. We study the impact, or lack thereof, of the most

T. Cazenave et al. (Eds.): CGW 2014, CCIS 504, pp. 90–104, 2014.

notable language features on the problems of finding a winning strategy for a given agent, and on the reachability problem.

Some standard results on the complexity of logic programming can be lifted to GDL [3]. While these results apply to the static part of GDL: state queries such as computing the legal moves for each agent, they do not tell much about the dynamical aspects of the game. Indeed, few complexity results for GGP have been established before. In particular, the multi-agent propositional fragment was known to be EXPTIME-complete [10]. In this paper, we provide the first comprehensive analysis of the complexity of GDL and its dependency on the language features used. Our results are summarized in Table 1.

Table 1. Complexity of the reachability problem with rational agents. This can also be seen as the complexity of determining whether a given player has a winning strategy. The multi-agent results hold with as few as one rational agent in a stochastic environment, i.e., with Nature as a player, as well as with two rational agents with conflicting goals. Markov chain features a single agent which is Nature.

Fragment	Single-agent	Markov chain	Multi-agent
Prop. and Monot.	NP-c	PP-c	PSPACE-c
Propositional	PSPACE-c	PSPACE-c	EXPTIME-c
Monotonic	NEXPTIME-c	PEXPTIME-c	EXPSPACE-c
Bounded	EXPSPACE-c	EXPSPACE-c	2EXPTIME-c
Full	UNDEC	UNDEC	UNDEC

Several researchers have investigated the complexity of planning in other description languages such as STRIPS [1] or PDDL [9].

After defining the syntax, semantics, and fragments of GDL, we introduce the complexity theoretic framework in which we carry our analysis. We then proceed to the core of the paper, establishing upper complexity bounds for the fragments of GDL and a reduction from the word problem for Turing Machines (TMs) with space or time restrictions to GDL providing matching lower bounds.

2 The Game Description Language

The Game Description Language (GDL) has been developed to formalize the rules of any finite game with complete information in such a way that the description can be automatically processed by a general game player.

GDL game descriptions are sets of *normal logic program clauses* [3] written in prefix notation using s-expressions, where variables are indicated by a leading ?. A language especially designed for game descriptions, GDL uses a few pre-defined predicate symbols shown in Table 2.

In GDL it is assumed that gameplay happens synchronously, that is, all players move simultaneously and the world changes only in response to moves.

Table 2. Predefined GDL predicates and their interpretation

Predicate instance	Meaning
(role r)	r is a player
(init f)	f holds in the initial position
(true f)	f holds in the current position
(legal r m)	player r has legal move m
(does r m)	player r does move m
(next f)	f holds in the next position
terminal	the current position is terminal
(goal r n)	player r gets goal value n

GDL imposes some syntactic restrictions on a set of clauses with the intention to ensure uniqueness and finiteness of the set of derivable predicate instances [6]. Specifically, the program must be stratified and satisfy the *recursion restriction*. Stratified logic programs are known to admit a unique stable model [3].

Definition 1. *A GDL program satisfies the* recursion restriction *if the following holds for every rule R. If the body of R contains a predicate q depending on the head of R, p, then at least one of the following must hold for every argument v_j of q in R. Either v_j is ground, or v_j appears as an argument of p in R, or v_j appears as an argument of another predicate r of R such that r does not depend on p.*

The semantics of a set of game rules has been informally described by a state transition system [4] and later formalized as follows [12]. Let $G \models A$ denote that atom A is true in the unique answer set of a stratified set of rules G. The *players* in game G are $R = \{r : G \models (\text{role } r)\}$. The *initial state* is $\{f : G \models (\text{init } f)\}$. A move m of player $r \in R$ is *legal in state* S if $G \cup S^{\text{true}} \models (\text{legal } r\ m)$. Here, S^{true} is the collection of facts $\{(\text{true } f_1), \ldots, (\text{true } f_k)\}$ that compose the current state $S = \{f_1, \ldots, f_k\}$. A *joint move* assigns each role $r \in R$ a legal move. The *state transition* from state S by joint move M results in the state $\{f : G \cup S^{\text{true}} \cup M^{\text{does}} \models (\text{next } f)\}$. Here, S^{true} is as above and M^{does} denotes the collection of facts $\{(\text{does } r_1\ m_1), \ldots, (\text{does } r_{|R|}\ m_{|R|})\}$ such that joint move M assigns m_i to player r_i. Finally, a *terminal state* is any S such that $G \cup S^{\text{true}} \models \text{terminal}$; and a *goal value* for player $r \in R$ in state S is any v for which $G \cup S^{\text{true}} \models (\text{goal } r\ v)$ holds.

We adopt the convention that random is a special role constrained to select its action uniformly at random among its legal moves [13]. This is necessary to model games involving chance events such as throwing a die or tossing a coin.

The recursion restriction ensures that only a finite number of predicate instances are derivable from a fixed set of clauses. However, the set of clauses $G \cup S^{\text{true}}$ in the semantics of GDL is a dynamic. As a result, the recursion restriction is not enough to guarantee a bounded number of predicate instances over the course of a game. We therefore propose the following stronger restriction on GDL programs.

Definition 2. *Let Δ be a GDL program. Let Δ' be the program Δ extended with the set of rules* $\{(\leftarrow(\textbf{true}\ ?f)\ (\textbf{next}\ ?f)),\ (\leftarrow(\textbf{true}\ ?f)\ (\textbf{init}\ ?f)),\ (\leftarrow(\textbf{does}\ ?r\ ?m)\ (\textbf{legal}\ ?r\ ?m))\}$. *We say that Δ satisfies the* General Recursion Restriction (GRR) *exactly when Δ' satisfies the recursion restriction.*

The GRR makes the dependency between the `true`, `init`, and `next` as well as the `does` and `legal` predicates explicit. Intuitively, the recursion restriction bounds the size of terms for a fixed set of clauses, and the GRR bounds the size of terms across a sequence of sets of clauses related by the GDL dynamics.

Consider the game of *Tic-tac-toe*. We can distinguish two sets of features: the `control` fluent determines which player is going to mark a cell, and the `cell` fluent determines which player, if any, has marked a given location of the board. `control` instances alternate as the game is played, but `cell` instances are more static. If a predicate instance of the form (**true** (cell m n x)) appears in a state, then it must appear in all subsequent states. Conversely, if a predicate instance of the form (**true** (cell m n b)) does not appear in a state, then it cannot appear in any subsequent states. Thus, the instances of the fluent `cell` are monotonic while the instances of `control` are not.

Definition 3. *A fluent f is* persistent *if for every state s where f holds, f holds in every successor of s. f is* anti-persistent *if for every state s where f does not hold, f does not hold in any successor of f. A fluent is* monotonic *if it is either persistent or anti-persistent.* [1]

Variables, non-monotonic fluent instances, and sets of clauses not satisfying the GRR are source of computational complexity in GDL reasoning. To study their influence formally, we define the following fragments of the Game Description Language.

Definition 4. *A game description is in* bounded domain *if it satisfies the GRR. A game description is* propositional *if it satisfies the GRR and has a bounded number of variables. A description is* monotonic *if the number of non-monotonic fluents is bounded by a constant.* [2]

Table 3 summarizes the dependency between the game features and the GDL fragment considered.

Game features such as the maximum number of fluents holding in any one state, or the number of legal moves depend mainly on whether variables are

---

[1] We can actually have a more general definition where we just bound for each fact the number of alternations between being true and false.

[2] As usual in complexity theory, we implicitly consider sets of descriptions. For example, a set of descriptions corresponds to generalized chess, and each board size maps to one GDL description. When the number of variables is bounded, increasing the size of the chess instance can polynomially increase the size of the GDL code but not the number of variables.

Table 3. Game features

Class	Query	# fluents # different moves	# different states	Longest acyclic path
Prop. and Monot.	$\in$ P	poly	expo	poly
Propositional	$\in$ P	poly	expo	expo
Monotonic	EXPTIME-c	expo	2-exp	expo
Bounded	EXPTIME-c	expo	2-exp	2-exp
Full	EXPTIME-c	unbounded	unbounded	unbounded

allowed. Variables also impact static state queries: the complexity jumps from P-complete to EXPTIME-complete when variables are allowed in the representation [3]. Conversely, as long as the GRR is satisfied, the nesting depth of function symbols remains polynomial. The game description can therefore be rewritten so that nested symbols are only allowed to depth 2 (to accommodate the fixed arity of the predefined keywords).

The number of facts is at most linear if there are no variables, and singly-exponential if there are variables. As the number of facts n_f and the number of possible states n_s are linked by the relation $n_s = 2^{n_f}$, the number of different states is singly-exponential or doubly-exponential depending on whether there are variables. The number of legal moves, in a given state, is at most linear if there are no variables, and singly-exponential if there are variables.

The following proposition justifies our definition of *propositional*.

Proposition 1. *One can transform a GDL encoding with a constant number of variables into a polynomial size GDL encoding without variables (in polynomial time).*

Proof. For each rule featuring a variable, write down all the possible instantiated rules. This has constant blow-up d^c where d is the size of the domain and c is the constant number of variables.

3   Turing Machines and Complexity Classes

The reader can find the following standard definitions in [8].

Definition 5. *A Turing Machine (TM) is a tuple $\langle Q, q_1, \Delta, g \rangle$ where Q is a finite set of states; $q_1 \in Q$ is a distinguished initial state; $\Delta \subseteq Q \times \{0, 1\} \times Q \times \{0, 1\} \times \{\leftarrow, \rightarrow\}$ is a set of transition rules; and $g : Q \rightarrow \{\exists, \forall, ?, \top, \bot\}$ is a labeling of the states. The labels denote respectively existential, universal, stochastic, (final) accepting, and (final) rejecting states.*

Definition 6. *A configuration is a triple $\langle w_1, q, w_2 \rangle$ where q is the current state, $w_1 w_2$ is the content of the tape, and the head is upon the first letter of w_2.*

Definition 7. *The probability p that a configuration $\langle w_1, q, w_2 \rangle$ is accepting can be defined inductively as follows. If q is accepting then we set $p = 1$ and if q is rejecting then $p = 0$. Else let n be the number of possible transitions and for each transition i, let p_i be the probability that the resulting configuration is accepting. If q is existential then we set $p = \max_i p_i$, if q is universal then $p = \min p_i$, and if q is stochastic then $p = \frac{\sum_i p_i}{n}$.*
A word w is recognized if the probability that configuration $\langle \varepsilon, q_1, w \rangle$ is accepting is greater than $1/2$.

Equivalently, the acceptance condition can be seen as a game between Existential player who chooses the transition applied from existential states and Universal player who does so from universal ones.

Definition 8. *A TM is* deterministic *if in each non-final configuration there is exactly one applicable transition. A TM is* non-deterministic *if all non-final states are existential,* alternating *if they are existential or universal,* probabilistic *if they are stochastic, and* stochastic-alternating *if they are existential or stochastic.*

DTIME($f(n)$) is the class of deterministic machines working in time $O(f(n))$. DSPACE($f(n)$) is the class of deterministic machines working in space $O(f(n))$. NTIME($f(n)$) and NSPACE($f(n)$) are their non-deterministic counterpart and ATIME($f(n)$) and ASPACE($f(n)$) are their alternating counterpart.

Theorem 1 (Savitch [11]). NPSPACE = PSPACE *and* NEXPSPACE = EXPSPACE.

Theorem 2 (Chandra et al. [2]). APTIME = PSPACE, APSPACE = EXPTIME, AEXPTIME = EXPSPACE, *and* AEXPSPACE = 2EXPTIME.

SATIME($f(n)$) is the class of stochastic-alternating machines working in time $O(f(n))$. SAATIME($f(n)$) is the class of machines working in time $O(f(n))$ with existential, universal and stochastic states. SASPACE($f(n)$) and SAASPACE($f(n)$) are defined similarly for space.

Proposition 2. *For any function $f \in \Omega(n)$ growing no slower than linearly,* SAATIME($f(n)$) = SATIME($f(n)$) = ATIME($f(n)$), *and* SAASPACE($f(n)$) = SASPACE($f(n)$) = ASPACE($f(n)$).

Proof. We recall an idea first used to show that NP $\subseteq$ PP [5], and to show that APTIME $\subseteq$ SAPTIME [7]. This idea, more generally, allows to show that ATIME($f(n)$) $\subseteq$ SATIME($f(n)$) and that ASPACE($f(n)$) $\subseteq$ SASPACE($f(n)$).

To simulate an alternating machine with a stochastic-alternating machine, one can start on a stochastic state. In the first branch all the runs are rejecting but one, and in the second branch the alternating machine is mimicked by switching the universal states to stochastic states. To win the Existential player needs to win all his games "against nature" in the second branch, which is equivalent to defeating Universal player.

Now, we show that $\mathrm{SAATIME}(f(n)) \subseteq \mathrm{NSPACE}(f(n)) = \mathrm{ATIME}(f(n))$. Let $\mathcal{A}$ be a general machine (existential, universal and stochastic states) working in time $O(f(n))$.

Without loss of generality, we can assume that in every non-final configuration there are exactly two applicable transitions; that all the runs have the same length $3f(n)$; and, besides the transition towards final state, that there are only three possible kinds of transition: from existential state to universal state, from universal state to stochastic state, and from stochastic state to existential state [7].

We traverse the computing tree of $\mathcal{A}$ as follows. We maintain on the tape of our $\mathrm{NSPACE}(f(n))$ machine $\mathcal{A}'$ two counters c_W and c_L up to $2^{f(n)}$ and a pointer which represents our position in the computing tree. We maintain one additional counter c which indicates how many stochastic states have been encountered along the branch. This can be done using space $O(f(n))$. Basically, c_W will count the number of accepting runs, and c_L the number of rejecting runs. If the state is existential, we guess which transition to apply. If the state is universal, we check all the transitions one after the other. If the state is stochastic, we increment c, and we check the left transition, then the right one. When we reach a leaf, we add $2^{f(n)-c}$ to c_W if the final state is accepting, or we add $2^{f(n)-c}$ to c_L if the final state is rejecting. When the entire computation tree has been explored, we accept if c_W contains a bigger number than c_L.

$\mathrm{SAASPACE}(f(n)) \subseteq \mathrm{DTIME}(2^{f(n)}) = \mathrm{ASPACE}(f(n))$. Indeed, the configuration graph of the general machine has $O(2^{f(n)})$ vertices, and we can decide the value of the stochastic reachability game in polynomial time in the number of vertices, i.e., $O(2^{f(n)})$.

4   Upper Bounds

A GDL state is defined by a set of (true) facts. An *extensive* representation of a state is an exhaustive list of grounded facts. An *implicit* representation of a state is a list of terms, such that all the possible instantiations of the terms should exactly match the set of true facts. In the former case, we say that the state is *implicitly represented*, and in the latter, *extensively represented*. An extensive representation can be exponentially (in the arity of the function constant) larger than an implicit representation. For instance, if the set of constants is $D = \{0,1\}$, $\{g\ ?x_1\ ?x_2, h\ 1\ ?y\}$ is the implicit representation and $\{g\ 0\ 0, g\ 0\ 1, g\ 1\ 0, g\ 1\ 1, h\ 1\ 0, h\ 1\ 1\}$ is the extensive representation of the same state. In the multi-agent case, the problem is to decide whether the first agent can win even if the other agents cooperate against him. Thus, we can merge all the opponents into one unique opponent, and we can consider that there are only two agents. In the following propositions, we show the corresponding result for the single-agent case, and Theorem 2 on alternation transfers the result from the single-agent to the multi-agent case.

Proposition 3. *Single-agent propositional monotonic GDL is in* NP. *Multi-agent propositional monotonic GDL is in* PSPACE.

Proof. The length of a shortest win is polynomial. Indeed, from a winning sequence of joint moves, you can remove all those joint moves which have no effect on the list of facts. It is still a winning sequence. Now, the list of facts is different from one state to the next. As it is propositional, the total number n_f of facts is linear in the GDL encoding. As it is monotonic, one can fully characterize the winning sequence by a set of n_f intervals representing the period of validity of each fact. At each state, one interval starts or ends, so the winning sequence is of size at most $2n_f$.

A strategy for the single agent consists of finding the one move to apply, at each move. The number of (propositional) moves is linear in the description of the game. Thus, you can guess a polynomial word encoding all the moves to apply from the beginning to the end of the game. Check if that word corresponds to a winning strategy can be done in polynomial time. At each step, you maintain the list of facts by applying a linear number of "next" rules, and you check if the moves are legal by considering a linear number of "legal" rules. If you reach the desired *goal value* at the end then you accept.

Proposition 4. *Single-agent propositional GDL is in* PSPACE. *Multi-agent propositional GDL is in* EXPTIME.

Proof. A state can be extensively represented in polynomial space. The number of legal moves in a given state is linearly bounded. Non-deterministic polynomial space allows to guess which move to play and maintain the current list of facts. Thus, it belongs to NPSPACE, which is equal to PSPACE by Savitch's theorem (Theorem 1).

Proposition 5. *Single-agent monotonic GDL is in* NEXPTIME. *Multi-agent monotonic GDL is in* EXPSPACE.

Proof. The number of facts is singly-exponential, but the depth of a game is also only singly-exponential 2^{n^c} since it is monotonic. The number of legal moves in a given state is exponentially bounded by $2^{n^{c'}}$. Deriving in GDL the next state from the current state, and that a state is terminal, is of singly-exponential depth bounded by, say, $2^{n^{c''}}$. Thus, a certificate for a winning strategy of the single-agent is of size at most $n^{c'} 2^{n^c} 2^{n^{c''}}$. Hence, it belongs to NEXPTIME.

Proposition 6. *Single-agent bounded GDL is in* EXPSPACE. *Multi-agent bounded GDL is in* 2EXPTIME.

Proof. A state can be represented extensively in exponential space. The number of legal moves in a state is exponentially bounded. Non-deterministic exponential space allows to guess which move to play and maintain the current list of facts. Thus, it belongs to NEXPSPACE, which is equal to EXPSPACE by Savitch's theorem (Theorem 1).

Listing 1. GDL simulation of a TM: generic termination and acceptance.

```
1  (← (role ?r) (label ?r ?q))
2  (← terminal (true (state ?t ?q)) (accept ?q))
3  (← terminal (true (state ?t ?q)) (reject ?q))
4
5  (← (goal exists 100) (role exists) (true (state ?t ?q)) (accept ?q))
6  (← (goal exists   0) (role exists) (true (state ?t ?q)) (reject ?q))
7  (← (goal univer   0) (role univer) (true (state ?t ?q)) (accept ?q))
8  (← (goal univer 100) (role univer) (true (state ?t ?q)) (reject ?q))
```

5   Lower Bounds

In this section, we obtain the lower bounds for the complexity results described in Table 1. We describe how we can encode TMs with various restrictions in different fragments of GDL in a three-step reduction.

The first part is a set of generic axioms of constant size. The second part is a set of machine specific axioms encoding the transition rules and the labeling of the states. The third part encodes the restriction set on the running time or the tape space used by the machine. There, we provide a different encoding for each specific restriction.

The choice of the third part alone determines to which fragment of GDL the program belongs. Indeed, the number of variables appearing in the first and second part is constant and the fluents introduced in the first part can be made monotonic in the third part.

Generic Axioms. In our description, variables starting with `?p` are GDL variables ranging over tape *position* indices. The variables starting with `?t`, `?q`, `?a`, `?d`, and `?r` range respectively over the *time* domain, the states of the machine, the letters of the *alphabet*, the *direction* of transitions, and the players (or *roles*).

We use the following auxiliary predicates. `accept` and `reject` take a state index as argument and characterize final states. Similarly, `label` characterizes non-final state labels and indicates their type. `delta` takes 5 arguments a, i, b, j, d such that a and b denote alphabet symbols, i and j represent states, and d represents a direction. This rigid predicate records the transition rules of the machine: there are as many instances of `delta` as there are elements in Δ.

The `zerop` and `succp` predicates encode the relation between the possible positions of the machine cursor on the tape. (`zerop` p) holds for the unique leftmost position p of the cursor on the tape. (`succp` p_1 p_2) holds exactly when p_2 represents a cursor position immediately to the right of p_1. `zerot`, `succt` encode the relation between the different times represented. `input` takes a possible cursor position i and a tape symbol a and denotes that the ith letter of the input word is a. `now` characterizes the current time.

We also use three main sets of fluents. The `tape` fluent encodes the content of the machine tape. `state` encodes the current state of the machine. `head` encodes the position of the cursor on the tape.

We have one agent per non-final state label and the game ends when the machine reaches a final configuration (line 1–3, Listing 1).

Listing 2. GDL simulation of a TM: generic initial configuration.

```
 9   (← (init (head ?t ?p)) (zerot ?t) (zerop ?p))
10   (← (init (state ?t 1)) (zerot ?t))
11   (← (init (tape ?t ?p ?a)) (zerot ?t) (input ?p ?a))
12   (← (init (tape ?t ?p2 0)) (zerot ?t) (less ?p1 ?p2) (endinput ?p1))
13
14   (← (less ?p1 ?p2) (succp ?p1 ?p2))
15   (← (less ?p1 ?p3) (succp ?p1 ?p2) (less ?p2 ?p3))
```

Listing 3. GDL simulation of a TM: generic applicable transitions.

```
16   (← (legal ?r (apply ?a2 ?q2 ?d)) (delta ?a1 ?q1 ?a2 ?q2 ?d)
17      (true (head ?t ?p)) (true (tape ?t ?p ?a1))
18      (label ?q1 ?r) (now ?t) (true (state ?t ?q1)))
19   (← (legal ?r2 pass) (role ?r2) (distinct ?r1 ?r2)
20      (label ?q ?r1) (now ?t) (true (state ?t ?q)))
```

The goal of an existential player, if such a player exists for the game, is to bring the game into an accepting configuration (lines 5 to 6). Conversely, the goal of a universal player, if such a player exists for the game, is to bring the game into a rejection configuration (lines 7 to 8). When we simulate TMs without existential (resp. universal) states, the predicate **role** does not hold for **exist** (resp. **univer**) and the utility of the existential (resp. universal) player does not need to be defined. A player **random** may also be introduced if the machine has stochastic states but we do not need to specify goal values for that player. Note that the **random** role is a distinguished player in GDL which is assumed to select a move uniformly at random among its legal moves.

At the beginning, the head is on the first cell of the tape, the machine is in the initial state, and the tape contains the input word and then blank symbols (line 9 to 12 in Listing 2). We have introduced the **less** predicate such that (**less** p_1 p_2) holds when p_2 if situated further right than p_1. It can be based on the more elementary successor predicate **succp**.

The semantics of GDL assume simultaneous actions by all agents. However in our reduction from TMs, only the agent corresponding to the label of the current state makes a meaningful decision at a time. To comply with the semantics of the language, we use two kinds of actions: an **apply** action taking a letter, a state, and a direction as arguments and recording the transition effects, and a **pass** action. The mapping from possible transitions into legal agent moves is given in Listing 3. For instance, if the current state has label ∃ then the player **exists** chooses among the instances of **apply** to select a transition for the TM, and the other agents, if any, perform a **pass** action.

The evolution of the configuration of the machine as the transitions are selected is described in Listing 4. The cell under the head changes according to the transition effects, but the rest of the tape remains unaffected (line 21 to 25). The next state is determined by the transition effects recorded in the **apply** action. After a transition, the head moves one cell to the left or one cell to the right depending on the kind of transition performed (line 30 to 33).

Listing 4. GDL simulation of a TM: generic evolution of the configuration.

```
21  (← (next (tape ?t2 ?p  ?a)) (now ?t1) (succt ?t1 ?t2)
22      (does ?r (apply ?a ?q ?d)) (true (head ?t1 ?p)))
23  (← (next (tape ?t2 ?p2 ?a)) (now ?t1) (succt ?t1 ?t2)
24      (true (tape ?t1 ?p2 ?a)) (true (head ?t1 ?p1))
25      (distinct ?p1 ?p2))
26
27  (← (next (state ?t2 ?q)) (now ?t1) (succt ?t1 ?t2)
28      (does ?r (apply ?a ?q ?d)))
29
30  (← (next (head ?t2 ?p2)) (now ?t1) (succt ?t1 ?t2) (succp ?p2 ?p1)
31      (true (head ?t1 ?p1)) (does ?r (apply ?a ?q  left)))
32  (← (next (head ?t2 ?p2)) (now ?t1) (succt ?t1 ?t2) (succp ?p1 ?p2)
33      (true (head ?t1 ?p1)) (does ?r (apply ?a ?q right)))
```

Listing 5. GDL simulation of a TM: machine specific axioms.

```
34  For all states qi ∈ Q, add
35  (accept  i)   when g(qi) = ⊤
36  (reject  i)   when g(qi) = ⊥
37  (label exists  i)   when g(qi) = ∃
38  (label univer  i)   when g(qi) = ∀
39  (label random  i)   when g(qi) =?
40
41  For all transition rules (a, qi) → (b, qj, d) ∈ Δ, add
42  (delta a i b j   left)   when d =←
43  (delta a i b j  right)   when d =→
```

Machine-dependent Axioms. Assuming numbered states, $Q = \{q_1, \ldots, q_{|Q|}\}$, Listing 5 collects the machine-dependent GDL axioms: state labels and transitions.

The number of variables appearing in the fragments described so far is bounded by a constant that does not depend on the size of the input. Indeed, variables only appear in the generic part of the translation that does not depend on the specific machine to be simulated. The size of Listing 5 naturally depends on the specific machine but it only contains ground terms and it does not introduce any new fluent.

Time and Tape Axioms. Let us detail how we can ensure that a fragment satisfies the monotonicity assumption. Listing 6 provides axioms to be included when monotonicity is needed. We first add *inertia rules* that guarantee the persistence of the **state**, **head**, and **tape** fluents (Line 1 to 3 in Listing 6).

This importance of the time argument for these fluents now becomes clearer. We can have monotonicity without the head of the machine always pointing at the same cell at every stage of the game. The monotonic fact that is remembered throughout the rest of the game is that at some fixed time t, the head pointed at a given cell.

Since past configurations are remembered when monotonicity is enforced, we need to distinguish which is the current one. Recall that fluents need to be monotonic but not arbitrary predicates. We can therefore define a non-monotonic **now** predicate. To do so, we introduce a persistent **past** fluent such that (**true**

Listing 6. Ensuring monotonicity: inertia axioms and linear time axioms.

```
1   (← (next (state ?t ?q))      (true (state ?t ?q)))
2   (← (next (head ?t ?p))       (true (head ?t ?p)))
3   (← (next (tape ?t ?p ?a))    (true (tape ?t ?p ?a)))
4
5   (← (next (past ?t)) (true (state ?t ?q)))
6   (← (now ?t) (true (state ?t ?q)) (not (true (past ?t))))
7
8   (← (zerot ?x) (zerop ?x))
9   (← (succt ?x ?y) (succp ?x ?y))
```

Listing 7. Dummy time axioms.

```
1   (now dummy) (zerot dummy) (succt dummy dummy)
```

(past ?t)) only holds for past time points ?t (Line 5 to 6 in Listing 6). past is persistent since it only depends on state which is persistent.

Finally, we give time a linear structure mapped from the linear structure of the tape. Thus, the simulation length inherits any bound on the size of the tape (Line 8 to 9 in Listing 6). When monotonicity is not required, history is not kept in the state and time points need not be distinguished. In that case, simpler axioms are used (Listing 7).

We now provide the axioms defining the tape structure, zerop and succp, as well as the axioms defining the input word, input and endinput. If w is an input word of size n, then for each $i \in \{0, \ldots, n-1\}$, w_i denotes the $i+1$-th letter of w. Listing 8 gives a linear encoding such that a polynomial number of consecutive tape positions can be represented. This encoding uses a polynomial number of axioms and does not use any variable. Listing 9 gives a binary encoding such that an exponential number of consecutive tape positions can be represented. The additional bit predicate provides the domain of bit variables, namely 0 and 1. This encoding uses a polynomial number of axioms and a polynomial number of variables. Listing 10 gives a unary encoding such that an unbounded number of consecutive tape positions can be represented. The additional monotonic access fluent denotes the tape positions potentially reachable. This encoding uses a polynomial number of axioms and a constant number of variables.

Combining the Listings. We have now described all the elements needed for the reduction of a TM to a GDL program.

Listing 8. Tape of size n^c and input w of size n: linear encoding.

```
1   (zerop 0)
2   (succp h h')    for all h ∈ {0, ..., n^c − 1} and h' = h + 1
3   (input i w_i)   for all i ∈ {0, ..., n − 1}
4   (endinput n)
```

Listing 9. Tape of size 2^{n^c} and input w of size n: binary encoding.

```
1   ( bit  0)   ( bit  1)   ( zerop  ( bin  0 ... 0))
2   (←  ( succp  ( bin  ?b_{n^c} ... ?b_{h+1}  0  1 ... 1)  ( bin  ?b_{n^c} ... ?b_{h+1}  1  0 ... 0))
3      ( bit  ?b_{h+1})  ...  ( bit  ?b_{n^c})) for all h ∈ {1,...,n^c}
4
5   For i ∈ {0,...,n − 1} with the binary writing b_{log n} ... b_1, add
6   ( input  ( bin  0 ... 0  b_{log n} ... b_1 )  w_i )
7   If the binary writing of n − 1 is b_{log n} ... b_1, then add
8   ( endinput  ( bin  0 ... 0  b_{log n} ... b_1 ))
```

Listing 10. Tape of unbounded size and input w of size n: unary encoding.

```
1   ( init  ( access  zero ))
2   (←  ( next  ( access  ?x ))  ( true  ( access  ?x )))
3   (←  ( next  ( access  ( incr  ?x )))  ( true  ( access  ?x )))
4   ( zerop  zero )
5   (←  ( succp  ?x  ( incr  ?x ))  ( true  ( access  ?x )))
6
7   For i ∈ {0,...,n − 1}, add
8   ( input  ( incr  ...  ( incr  zero ))  w_i )    with i nested incr.
9   ( endinput  ( incr  ...  ( incr  zero )))    with n nested incr.
```

Theorem 3. *Let c be a fixed constant. Propositional monotonic GDL can simulate a TM working in $\mathrm{TIME}(n^c)$. Propositional GDL can simulate a TM working in $\mathrm{SPACE}(n^c)$. Monotonic GDL can simulate a TM working in $\mathrm{TIME}(2^{n^c})$. Bounded GDL can simulate a TM working in $\mathrm{SPACE}(2^{n^c})$. GDL can simulate an unrestricted TM, using a bounded number of variables and only monotonic fluents.*

Proof. By combining Listings 1–5 with one time listing (6 or 7) and one tape listing (8, 9, or 10), we obtain a GDL description simulating a given TM M. The chosen listings determine the constraints on M and the properties satisfied by the description as indicated in Table 4.

Listings 9 and 10 are the only ones not using a constant number of variables or not satisfying the GRR, so we obtain a propositional GDL program as long as none of these two fragment is used. Similarly, the GRR is satisfied as long as Listing 10 is not used.

Positions of the game correspond to configurations of the machine and joint moves correspond to transitions. If we assume the players **exists** and **univer** to be rational and the player **random** to be making each decision uniformly at random, then we can conclude that the likelihood of reaching a position such that **accept** holds is more than $1/2$ if and only if M accepts w.

The potential time/space constraint on the TM result in potential properties satisfied by the GDL program, and the type of the machine (non-deterministic, alternating, ...) induces the number and type of agents in the corresponding game. Using Theorem 1, 2, 3 and Proposition 2, we derive the lower bounds for the results in Table 1.

Table 4. Effect of the time and tape listings added to Listings 1–5 on the TM restrictions and the GDL properties satisfied by the encoding

Listing		Restriction on the TM	GDL properties		
Time	Tape		Monot.	GRR	Prop.
6	8	TIME(n^c)	✓	✓	✓
6	9	TIME(2^{n^c})	✓	✓	✗
6	10	—	✓	✗	✗
7	8	SPACE(n^c)	✗	✓	✓
7	9	SPACE(2^{n^c})	✗	✓	✗
7	10	—	✗	✗	✗

6   Conclusion

We have established the complexity of the adversarial reachability problem in the most natural fragments of GGP. That is, can a specified agent ensure a win assuming the other agents are adversaries or are playing a fixed mixed strategy. Using backward induction, our results directly generalize to finding Nash equilibria in GGP when the number of agents is polynomial in the size of the GDL description. However, it is possible to create contrived GDL descriptions involving exponentially many agents. Whether our results carry over to finding Nash equilibria in arbitrary GDL games remains open at this stage.

GDL has recently been extended to allow defining imperfect information (II) games [13]. The only extensions to the language are that of the official specification of the **random** role and the introduction of **sees**, a new keyword indicating the knowledge of each player on the state of the game. We have investigated how a **random** role affected the complexity. A natural avenue for future work is to extend the complexity landscape when the predicate **sees** is allowed.

A recent paper shows that the General Game Playing problem is universal in the sense that there is a tight relation between extensive-form games and models of GDL programs [14]. We have focused here on another dimension of universality: computability and complexity. Besides the Turing-completeness of GDL, we have shown that a wide range of standard complexity classes could be captured as finding a winning strategy in GGP via natural syntactic assumptions.

Acknowledgement. The second author was supported by the Australian Research Councils (ARC) Discovery Projects funding scheme (project DP 120102023).

References

1. Bylander, T.: The computational complexity of propositional STRIPS planning. Artificial Intelligence 69(1), 165–204 (1994)
2. Chandra, A.K., Kozen, D.C., Stockmeyer, L.J.: Alternation. Journal of the ACM 28(1), 114–133 (1981)

3. Dantsin, E., Eiter, T., Gottlob, G., Voronkov, A.: Complexity and expressive power of logic programming. ACM Computing Surveys 33(3), 374–425 (2001)
4. Genesereth, M., Love, N.: General Game Playing: Overview of the AAAI competition. AI Magazine 26, 62–72 (2005)
5. Gill, J.: Computational complexity of probabilistic turing machines. SIAM J. Comput. 6(4), 675–695 (1977)
6. Love, N.C., Hinrichs, T.L., Genesereth, M.R.: General Game Playing: Game Description Language specification. Tech. rep., LG-2006-01, Stanford Logic Group (2006)
7. Papadimitriou, C.H.: Games against nature. Journal of Computer and System Sciences 31(2), 288–301 (1985)
8. Papadimitriou, C.H.: Computational complexity. Addison-Wesley, Reading (1994)
9. Rintanen, J.: Complexity of planning with partial observability. In: 14th International Conference on Automated Planning and Scheduling (ICAPS), pp. 345–354. AAAI Press (2004)
10. Ruan, J., Van der Hoek, W., Wooldridge, M.: Verification of games in the Game Description Language. Journal of Logic and Computation 19(6), 1127–1156 (2009)
11. Savitch, W.J.: Relationships between nondeterministic and deterministic tape complexities. Journal of Computer and System Sciences 4(2), 177–192 (1970)
12. Schiffel, S., Thielscher, M.: A multiagent semantics for the Game Description Language. In: Filipe, J., Fred, A., Sharp, B. (eds.) Agents and Artificial Intelligence (ICAART). CCIS, vol. 67, pp. 44–55. Springer, Heidelberg (2010)
13. Thielscher, M.: A general Game Description Language for incomplete information games. In: 24th AAAI Conference on Artificial Intelligence (AAAI), pp. 994–999. AAAI Press, Atlanta (2010)
14. Thielscher, M.: The general Game playing Description Language is universal. In: 22nd International Joint Conference on Artificial Intelligence, pp. 1107–1112. IJCAI (2011)

Efficient Grounding of Game Descriptions with Tabling

Jean-Noël Vittaut and Jean Méhat

LIASD - University of Paris 8, France
{jnv,jm}@ai.univ-paris8.fr

Abstract. We present a method to instantiate game descriptions used in General Game Playing with the tabling engine of a Prolog interpreter. Instantiation is a crucial step for speeding up the interpretation of the game descriptions and increasing the playing strength of general game players.

Our method allows us to ground almost all of the game descriptions present on the GGP servers in a time that is compatible with the common time settings of the GGP competition. It instantiates descriptions more rapidly than previous published methods.

1 Introduction

General Game Playing (GGP) aims at conceiving programs capable of playing a large variety of games without knowing the rules in advance. The Game Description Language (GDL) [8] has been used to communicate the rules of the game to be played at the beginning of a match in the General Game Playing competition since 2005.

Fast interpretation of GDL is important because it can significantly improve the strength of a player. Björnsson and Schiffel [1] [13] have compared the speed of several GDL reasoners[1] and they show that the reasoners are at least two to three orders of magnitude slower than hard coded versions of games. The two fastest reasoners they tested use a Prolog interpreter.

An approach to speed up a reasoner is to ground the rules, binding all variables with atoms. This instantiation of the rules can lead to better performance because it saves the time used to bind variables during unification and it eases the building of Propositional Nets [4]. Kissmann and Edelkamp [6] have shown that instantiation can allow from about 4 to 250 times more node expansions in a Monte-Carlo search on the tested games. Instantiation is also useful in the domain of action planning [7].

We use the tabling engine built in a Prolog interpreter. Tabling consists in storing answers for subgoals and reusing them whenever the same subgoal is called again. It was first implemented in the XSB programming language [9]. At the cost of a modification of the unification process, it avoids redundant sub-computations and deals with infinite loops. We use here the tabling as implemented in the YAP Prolog interpreter because of its performance, its availability and our familiarity with this interpreter [10], [11], [12].

This paper is structured as follows. First, we describe the Game Description Language. Next, we describe our method of instantiation of GDL programs which makes use of the Prolog tabling engine and we compare the performance of our method against other approaches.

---

[1] Flux Player, Cadia Player, Java Eclipse, Java Prover, GGPBase Prover, C++ Reasoner.

T. Cazenave et al. (Eds.): CGW 2014, CCIS 504, pp. 105–118, 2014.
© Springer International Publishing Switzerland 2014

2   The Game Description Language

The Game Description Language (GDL) allows to describe combinatorial perfect information games. It has also been extended to handle incomplete and imperfect information games (GDL-II). It uses first order logic and is similar to Datalog with negation as failure. Its syntax consists of Lisp S-expressions. A game is described with a set of facts and rules; a few keywords are reserved for logic and game-specific features (see Table 1); variables begin with a question mark.

Table 1. GDL Keywords

Logical operators
`<=`	clause declaration
`or`	disjunction
and	implicit in the premises of a rule
`not`	negation
`distinct`	evaluates to true only if the two terms differ

Static predicates
`role`	defines the names of the players
`init`	defines initial state of the game
`input`	defines a superset of possible moves
`base`	defines a superset of the game state components

Dynamic predicates
`terminal`	true if the game state is terminal
`goal`	player's rewards
`legal`	legal moves in the current game state
`next`	transition to the next game state
`does`	player's moves
`true`	defines the game state components

Numerical atoms
integers from 0 to 100 defined for `goal`

We distinguish the *dynamic* predicates depending on the state of the game from the remaining *static* ones, the instantiated values of which are independent from the state of the game and can be computed once and for all upon receiving the game description. GDL missing arithmetic, game descriptions usually contain the description of arithmetic operations on the numbers they need: it usually leads to a large number of static rules.

The predicates `true` and `does` are always dynamic because they trivially depend on the state of the game. The dynamic property is recursively extended to all predicates using at least one dynamic predicate even if it appears within a negation or a disjunction.

The other predicates mentioned as dynamic in Table 1 are marked as such to keep them in the grounded rules even in the rare cases where they are static e.g. when the goal of a player is independent from the final position of the game.

By extension, a term is dynamic or static, depending on the predicate it is formed on. Note that terms of the form (or T_1 $T_2 \ldots T_n$) or (not T_1) are: dynamic if they contain at least one dynamic term T_i; static if all of the T_i are static terms. Likewise a rule is dynamic if its conclusion is dynamic.

3   Instantiation of GDL Rules

The instantiation of GDL rules is done in successive steps. We firstly present an overview of the whole process and then give some details on these steps and justify their usefulness.

3.1   Overview

The instantiation starts with a cleaning step where or is removed from any rule. Then we compute base and input facts if they are not provided in the description.

Next we rewrite each rule, removing negated terms, renaming true and does as base and input and adding a side effect. This side effect stores, in the instantiated game description, a grounded version of the initial rule with static terms removed.

In the Prolog engine we use, tabling is enabled at the predicate level. Then, to force the tabling engine to process each and every rule, we change the predicate name of every rule conclusion so we can use tabling at the rule level. To keep our program correct, we add a new rule the role of which is allowing to call the new predicate with its old name.

Then we add a series of rules the conclusion of which is always the ground atom and premises are queries asking for all the answers related to the new predicate introduced previously.

Finally, we call the Prolog interpreter with the ground goal. The grounded description is stored into a data structure shared between Prolog and the driver program by the Prolog interpreter solving the ground goal. This instantiated description is only made of grounded terms, called fluents, and logic connectors.

3.2   Eliminating (or T_1 $T_2 \ldots T_n$) Terms

The or operator has been deprecated in GDL since 2007 [3]. However, it is used in old game descriptions and players need to support it to play these games. As it is easy to rewrite a game description into a game description without or or use the built in Prolog *or* operator, most players support this feature. Even in the 2013 official GGP competition, the game description of Eight Puzzle used it.

Removing any instance of the or operator ensures that we obtain at the end a grounded program in a disjunctive form. It also simplifies the next steps in case there is a disjunction between static and dynamic terms.

If a rule contains a term T of the form (or T_1 $T_2 \ldots T_n$), we simply duplicate the rule replacing T with T_i. We proceed recursively on the new rules which could still contain some term using or. Table 2 shows an example of this transformation from the Connect Five game description.

Table 2. A rule containing an or with 4 sub-terms is rewritten as 4 different rules

Rule with or	Rules without or

`(<= (conn5 ?r)`
`    (or (col ?r) (row ?r)`
`        (diag1 ?r) (diag2 ?r)))`
	`(<= (conn5 ?r) (col ?r))`
	`(<= (conn5 ?r) (row ?r))`
	`(<= (conn5 ?r) (diag1 ?r))`
	`(<= (conn5 ?r) (diag2 ?r))`

3.3 Adding `Input` and `Base` Predicates

The `base` predicate is used to enumerate all the terms that can be used in any reachable game state. Similarly, `input` allows one to pre-compute all the moves that can become legal in the course of any match of the described game. These predicates are a recent addition to GDL and we suppose they were introduced to facilitate the instantiation of game descriptions.

However, older GDL game descriptions do not provide `input` and `base` but are still in use on the servers running permanent tournaments that we use as a test bed for GGP competitions. The set of game descriptions including these predicates is small and does not contain many games that are commonly used for testing and performance comparison purposes.

Moreover, different descriptions of these predicates can lead to dramatic differences between grounded game descriptions, for instance the `input` predicate of the Breakthrough game description is defined more lazily on the Tiltyard server than on the Stanford server. It leads to a grounded description that contains 20 times more rules.

For these reasons, we do compute them when the game description does not provide them. Separating their computation from the strictly speaking grounding phase allows us to distinguish their respective computation times. It also allows us to discard undesirable rational tree terms which are infinite terms that this method can generate.

This step is detailed in section 4 in which we propose a method sharing many steps with the instantiation method we are currently describing.

Once computed, the `input` and `base` fluents are added to the description so there will be no difference with the case where the predicates are provided with the GDL description.

3.4 Eliminating `Not`, Renaming `True` and `Does`

From each rule R, we construct a new rule $g(R)$ by removing every (not T) term where T is a dynamic term; renaming every (true T) and (does T_1 T_2) term respectively with (base T) and (input T_1 T_2).

Removing the not operator in dynamic predicates allows us to compute any possible instantiation without risking an elimination by the negated term. It is a safe operation since GDL guarantees that any negated term always has to be fully instantiated. Consequently, the elimination cannot lead to a situation where one of the variables remains not instantiated. It is also necessary since the tabling engine we use cannot handle recursion through a negation. A drawback is that the process will produce useless grounded rules, since the `not` operator is never checked: these useless rules would never prove anything when used by a reasoner working with the instantiated description.

Replacing (`true` T) and (`does` T_1 T_2) by (`base` T) and (`input` T_1 T_2) allows us to ground all the rules in one pass, without computing `base` and `input` if they are already provided by the description.

Table 3 contains an example of this step on some rules of the Connect Five game description.

Table 3. Computation of $g(R)$: the negations are eliminated and `does` are replaced by `input`

R	$g(R)$
(<= (goal x 50) (not line_of_5))	(<= (goal x 50))

(<= (legal ?r noop)
    (role ?r)
    (not (true (ctrl ?r))))
	(<= (legal ?r noop)
	    (role ?r))

(<= (next (cell ?x ?y ?r))
    (does ?r (mark ?x ?y)))
	(<= (next (cell ?x ?y ?r))
	    (input ?r mark ?x ?y)))

3.5 Removing Static Terms

Terms formed on static predicates do not need to appear in the instantiated rules since their truth is known regardless of the state of the game: if true they can be removed; if false the entire rule can be discarded; conversely if they appear within a `not`, they can be removed if false and the rule can be discarded if true.

Consequently, we compute a rule $s(R)$ from the initial rule R by removing any static term or its negation from R.

This step could be skipped with no effect on the correctness of the method but without it, we would have to either post-process the instantiated rules to eliminate any true static term or include all of the static terms from the game description.

3.6 Adding the Side Effect and Introducing a New Symbol

The rules $g(R)$ and $s(R)$ are combined to produce the two new rules that will be part of our final grounded description. Given a rule $g(R)$ of the form:

$$(<= (p\ U_1 \ldots U_p)\ T_1 \ldots T_n)$$

we derive the two new rules:

$$(<= (p\#\ U_1 \ldots U_p)\ T_1 \ldots T_n\ (\text{store}\ s(R)))$$
$$(<= (p\ U_1 \ldots U_p)\ (p\#\ U_1 \ldots U_p))$$

where p is the original predicate symbol of the conclusion of $g(R)$. The `store` predicate has the side effect of storing the $s(R)$ instantiated rule in a data structure shared between the Prolog interpreter and the driver program; it always evaluates as true. $p\#$ is a new unique symbol, different for each processed rule. It is necessary to prevent the tabling engine from tabling rules with side effects because it would lead to missed instantiations: the rule including the side effect is not tabled while the second is.

These two rules are logically equivalent to the rule $g(R)$ since the side effect always evaluates as true.

An example of this step on rules from the Connect Five game description is shown in Table 4

Table 4. Each original rule is transformed into two new rules: one with a new conclusion symbol and a side effect; the other with the original conclusion

Initial rule	Derived rules

`(<= (goal x 50)`
`    (not line_of_5))`
	`(<= (goal# x 50)`
	`    (store (<= (goal x 50)`
	`               (not line_of_5)))))`
	`(<= (goal x 50)`
	`    (goal# x 50))`

`(<= (legal ?r noop)`
`    (role ?r)`
`    (not (true (ctrl ?r))))`
	`(<= (legal# ?r noop)`
	`    (role ?r)`
	`    (store (<= (legal ?r noop)`
	`               (not (true (ctrl ?r))))))`
	`(<= (legal ?r noop)`
	`    (legal# ?r noop))`

`(<= (next (cell ?x ?y ?r))`
`    (does ?r (mark ?x ?y)))`
	`(<= (next# (cell ?x ?y ?r))`
	`    (input ?r (mark ?x ?y))`
	`    (store (<= (next (cell ?x ?y ?r))`
	`               (does ?r (mark ?x ?y)))))`
	`(<= (next (cell ?x ?y ?r))`
	`    (next# (cell ?x ?y ?r)))`

3.7   Tabling Predicates and Creating the Instantiation Query

Finally, to generate all instantiations in one Prolog query, we add a new predicate `ground`, the goal of which is to query all the rules with side effects. Therefore, a rule like

$$(<=\ \mathtt{ground}\ (p\#\ U_1\ U_2\ \ldots U_n))$$

is added for each new symbol $p\#$ introduced in the previous step.

We set up the Prolog interpreter to table all predicates with the only exception of the new predicate symbols introduced in the previous subsection and the `ground` predicate which does not need to be tabled. By querying all the solutions to the `ground` goal, the `store` predicate inserts instantiated rules into the data structure shared between the Prolog interpreter and the driver program. In Table 5 we show the result of the instantiation of one rule of Connect Five.

Table 5. One of the rules of Connect Five is instantiated in two rules

Initial rule	Grounded rules

```(<= (legal ?r noop)```
 ```(role ?r)```
 ```(not (true (ctrl ?r)))))```
	```(<= (legal x noop)```
	 ```(not (true (ctrl x))))```
	 ```(<= (legal o noop)```
	 ```(not (true (ctrl o))))```

4   Computing `Input` and `Base`

Our instantiating method requires we generate the `input` and `base` predicates when not provided in the GDL description. We describe two ways of computing them: an *iterative* method which is equivalent to the one used by Kissmann and Edelkamp [6]; and our method using tabling which can be performed in *one step*.

4.1   Iterative Method

We compute two sets B and I that contain all the fluents that can occur in a game state or as a legal move. We initialize B with the facts defined via `init` in the game description; I is initially empty:

$$I = \emptyset$$
$$B = \{(\texttt{true}\ T)\ \text{s.t.}\ (\texttt{init}\ T)\ \text{is true}\}$$

We temporarily redefine the `not` operator as always true. We then iterate, generating legal move fluents, adding the new ones to I and the new game state fluents to B until reaching a fixed point:

$$I = I \cup \{(\texttt{does}\ T_1\ T_2)\ \text{s.t.}\ (\texttt{legal}\ T_1\ T_2)\ \text{is true}\}$$
$$B = B \cup \{(\texttt{true}\ T)\ \text{s.t.}\ (\texttt{next}\ T)\ \text{is true}\}$$

We use tabling for all the predicates at each iteration and flush the tables at every update of I and B.

The performance of this method strongly depends on the number of iterations required to reach the fixed point. It often happens that only a few elements are added to B at each iteration. It is, for instance, the case in many games where the state of the game contains a `step` term which simply counts how many moves have been played to prevent infinite matches (see Figure 1).

When this kind of counter is present in the game description, the method must be iterated the number of times that the counter needs to be incremented before reaching its final value.

To alleviate this specific problem, we first use the original GDL description to simulate a fake match from the initial position; we repeatedly compute the next state of the game that can be reached without playing a move. We halt this process when the reached state is empty or when a game state has already been seen. All the fluents that appeared in any game state are used to seed the B set along with the `init` predicates.

```
(<= (next (step 1))   (true (step 0)))
(<= (next (step 2))   (true (step 1)))
...
(<= (next (step 100)) (true (step 99)))
```

Fig. 1. A step counter is commonly used in many descriptions to prevent infinite matches. This fragment of a game description allows it to increment until a maximum figure of 100.

More generally, the aforementioned procedure processes any next rule not depending on the does predicate to compute fluents in order to initialize the B set. It provides an amelioration for many game descriptions however, it would not be difficult to conceive game rules capable of defeating this procedure.

4.2 One Step Method

We process the original GDL description with the same transformations we detailed in section 3, the only difference being that we do not add the side effect to the rules.

We also enable tabling for the same predicates that we mentioned in section 3.7 and add the three following rules to seed the B set with the initial state and add new fluents to B and new legal moves to I:

```
(<= (base ?x)    (init ?x))
(<= (base ?x)    (next ?x))
(<= (input ?r ?m) (legal ?r ?m))
```

Then by querying the Prolog interpreter with goals (base ?x) and (input ?r ?m), we obtain all the fluents of these predicates enabling the instantiation of the whole game description more efficiently.

5 Experimental Results

We collected the 246 different game descriptions that were active in February 2014 on the Dresden server[2].

We firstly measured the time necessary to generate input and base on the vast majority of game descriptions that do not include them using the *iterative* and *one step* methods.

Then we measured the time necessary to instantiate the game description enriched with the input and base fluents computed in the previous step except for the six game descriptions that already include them: for these, we used the predicates of the original game description. The time measured takes into account the translation of GDL terms from the Prolog interpreter into the driver program representation.

The experiments were run on one core of an Intel Xeon E5-4610 2.40GHz with 520Gb RAM. This amount of memory was more than enough to compute the instantiations. We measured that our method needs about 500Mb to compute one million

---

[2] The Dresden server is available at http://ggpserver.general-game-playing.de

instantiated rules. We used YAP 6.2.2 Prolog interpreter [2] as a library for our driver program written in C++.

5.1 Computing `Input` and `Base`

The `input` and `base` were successfully computed for the vast majority of the 240 game descriptions that did not already contain them, with the exception of two games for the *one step* method (`othello_comp2007` and `othellosuicide`) and 13 games for the *iterative* one. The two failures of the *one step* method were caused by a crash in the Prolog interpreter, whereas the *iterative* one was halted after 30 minutes as it had not yet converged. However, at least one method succeeded for each game description.

Figure 2 compares the two methods for the 225 games of the Dresden collection successfully processed by both. The x-axis represents the time used by the *one step* method and the y-axis the time used by the *iterative* one. The diagonal represents the location where the two methods take the same amount of time. A game plotted above the diagonal means that the *one step* method takes less time than the *iterative* one. Except for the 10 games plotted below the diagonal, the *one step* method is always faster than the *iterative* one. We also observed that the iterative method is only competitive when the number of iterations remains low.

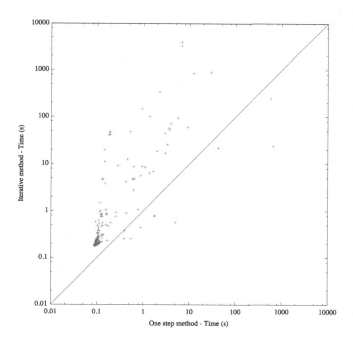

Fig. 2. Comparison of the computation of the `input` and `base` predicates between the *one step* and the *iterative* method

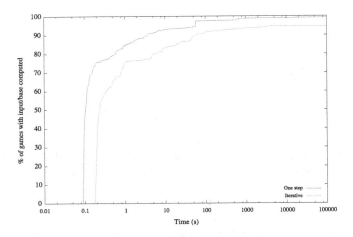

Fig. 3. Percentage of game descriptions of which input and base can be computed within the time budget on x-axis

In Figure 3 we plotted the percentage of games of which input and base fluents have been computed in less than the time budget represented in the x-axis with a logarithmic scale. It shows that a large majority of computations take less than one second.

With the *one step* method, 45% of the games had the fluents computed in less than 100ms, 84% in less than one second and 98% in less than one minute. With the *iterative* method, none of the games had the fluents computed in less than 100ms, 75% in less than one second and 90% in less than one minute.

5.2 Instantiation of the Rules

We tested the instantiation of the rules on all of the 246 games of the Dresden collection. Six of them already contained the input and base predicates. For the remaining 240, we added the fluents computed either by the *one step* or the *iterative* method. The processing of three games (racer, ruledepthquadratic and laikLee_hex) was halted after 30 minutes of computation.

In Figure 4 we plotted the time performance of our grounding method where the time of the step computing input and base is not taken into account. We represented the percentage of games that can be instantiated within the time budget represented in the x-axis. 24% of the games were instantiated in less than 100ms, 72% in less than one second and 94% in less than one minute.

The remaining 6% that were grounded in more than one minute are battlebrushes, merrills, amazons, racer4, farmers, the two instances of battlesnakes, and 8 of the 13 instances of vacuumcleaner. All of these game instantiated descriptions contained more than 10^7 rules and facts.

Figure 5 demonstrates that the time to ground increases almost linearly with the size of the grounded game description when it is greater than 10^4. We also observed that

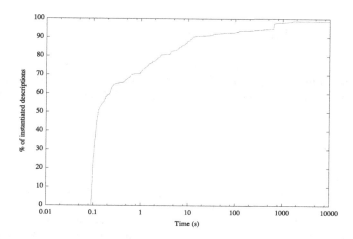

Fig. 4. Percentage of instantiated game descriptions that were grounded within the time budget in the x-axis

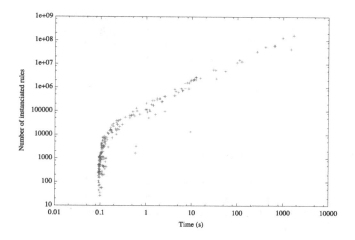

Fig. 5. The number of generated rules as a function of instantiation time for the 243 successfully instantiated games

a significant part of the time is used to translate the fluents from the Prolog internal representation into the GDL representation in the shared data structure.

6   Comparison with Other Works

It is somewhat difficult to compare our method with existing grounders, given that their measure of performance is usually mixed with the time used for building the Propositional Net. We examine here the results available from [6] and the time we measured with the *GGPBase flattener*.

6.1   The *GGPBase Flattener*

The *GGPBase flattener* is a freely distributed GDL grounder[3]. We compared the time to instantiate a few game descriptions that were of increasing difficulty for our grounder. We used a different machine that was more convenient to run the GGPBase flattener. The results are presented in Table 6. The time needed by the flattener seems to increase at least quadratically with the size of the grounded program whereas the time needed by our method has been established to increasing linearly.

The GGPBase flattener has primarily an educational purpose and its performance is not its main goal.

Table 6. Comparison of our method with GGPBase-flattener on an Intel Core 2 Duo 1.86GHz with 2Gb RAM

Game	Time to instantiate (seconds)	
	GGPBase	Our method
connectfour	0.844	0.560
CephalopodMicro	19.8	1.14
breakthrough	115	5.46
chinesecheckers4	Out of memory	14.9

6.2   The Kissmann and Edelkamp Approach

Kissmann and Edelkamp presented two approaches of grounding in [6]. They were able to instantiate 96 of 171 game descriptions in less than one minute with their Prolog-based approach, and 90 of 171 with their method using dependency graphs which are proportions that we attain in less than one second.

Their article lacks precise figures but similar results are presented in Kissmann PhD thesis for the 124 game descriptions their method was able to successfully process [5]. Their experiments were carried out on an Intel i7-920 2.67GHz with 24Gb RAM with

---

[3] The set of GGPBase Java libraries is distributed at
http://www.ggp.org/developers/players.html

a different Prolog interpreter (SWI-Prolog). Their method also includes a computation of mutually exclusive fluents.

The comparison of the percentage of game descriptions instantiated within a computational budget is given in Figure 6 for the best result of their two approaches and our method applied to the same 124 game descriptions. We observe that our implementation needs a setup time of approximately 0.2s. Our method appears to be of two orders of magnitude faster when the instantiation time becomes significant.

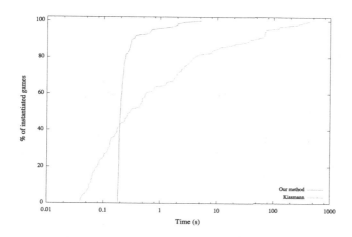

Fig. 6. Comparison of the percentages of instantiated game descriptions that were grounded within the time budget in the x-axis for the 124 game descriptions successfully processed in [5, pp. 129–130]

7 Conclusion

We have demonstrated that it is possible to ground almost all the game descriptions found on the GGP servers in a time span compatible with the current GGP competition time settings. This relies on the use of tabling in a Prolog interpreter.

This result should be considered in relation to the study of [1] and [13] in which Prolog-based GDL reasoners greatly outperform other approaches: the Prolog interpreters benefit from decades of optimization from their maintainers.

We have also established that the new predicates input and base introduced in the 2013 competition, probably with the aim of helping programs to ground game descriptions and generate Propositional Nets, can be considered as superfluous. The few game descriptions in which they can be useful have a grounded size that is so large that building alternative representations such as Propositional Nets is problematic. Tweaking the Game Description Language for specific tasks is somewhat dubious since the description language should be as agnostic as possible in relation to methods that could be used by players.

As a future work, we are interested in finding mutually exclusive terms and rules in the game description that could lead to more concise instantiations and facilitate the generation of Propositional Nets.

References

1. Björnsson, Y., Schiffel, S.: Comparison of GDL reasoners. In: Björnsson, Y., Thielscher, M. (eds.) Proceedings of the IJCAI-13 Workshop on General Game Playing (GIGA 2013), pp. 55–62 (2013)
2. Costa, V.S., Rocha, R., Damas, L.: The YAP prolog system. Theory and Practice of Logic Programming 12(1-2), 5–34 (2012)
3. Finnsson, H.: CADIA-Player: A General Game Playing Agent. Master's thesis, School of Computer Science, Reykjavík University (2007)
4. Genesereth, M., Thielscher, M.: General Game Playing. Synthesis Lectures on Artificial Intelligence and Machine Learning. Morgan & Claypool Publishers (2014)
5. Kissmann, P.: Symbolic search in planning and general game playing. Ph.D. thesis, Universität Bremen (2012)
6. Kissmann, P., Edelkamp, S.: Instantiating general games using prolog or dependency graphs. In: Dillmann, R., Beyerer, J., Hanebeck, U.D., Schultz, T. (eds.) KI 2010. LNCS, vol. 6359, pp. 255–262. Springer, Heidelberg (2010)
7. Koehler, J., Hoffmann, J.: Handling of inertia in a planning system. Tech. Rep. 122, Institute for Computer Science. Albert Ludwigs University, Freiburg, Germany (1999)
8. Love, N., Hinrichs, T., Haley, D., Schkufza, E., Genesereth, M.: General game playing: Game description language specification. Tech. Rep. LG-2006-01, Stanford Logic Group, Computer Science Department, Stanford University, Stanford, CA (2008)
9. Ramakrishnan, I., Rao, P., Sagonas, K., Swift, T., Warren, D.S.: Efficient access mechanisms for tabled logic programs. The Journal of Logic Programming 38(1), 31–54 (1999)
10. Rocha, R., Silva, F., Costa, V.S.: A tabling engine for the YAP prolog system. In: Proceedings of the 2000 APPIA-GULP-PRODE Joint Conference on Declarative Programming (AGP 2000), La Habana, Cuba (2000)
11. Rocha, R., Silva, F., Santos Costa, V.: Dynamic mixed-strategy evaluation of tabled logic programs. In: Gabbrielli, M., Gupta, G. (eds.) ICLP 2005. LNCS, vol. 3668, pp. 250–264. Springer, Heidelberg (2005)
12. Rocha, R., Silva, F., Santos Costa, V.: Yaptab: A tabling engine designed to support parallelism. In: Conference on Tabulation in Parsing and Deduction, pp. 77–87 (2000)
13. Schiffel, S., Björnsson, Y.: Efficiency of GDL reasoners. IEEE Transactions on Computational Intelligence and AI in Games 6(4) (2014)

SHPE: HTN Planning for Video Games

Alexandre Menif[1], Éric Jacopin[2], and Tristan Cazenave[3]

[1] Sagem Défense et Sécurité, 100 Avenue de Paris, 91300 Massy Cedex, France
[2] MACCLIA, CREC Saint Cyr, Écoles de Coëtquidan, F-56381 GUER Cedex, France
[3] LAMSADE, Université Paris-Dauphine, 75016, Paris, France

Abstract. This article describes SHPE (Simple Hierarchical Planning Engine), a hierarchical task network planning system designed to generate dynamic behaviours for real-time video games. SHPE is based on a combination of domain compilation and procedural task application/decomposition techniques in order to compute plans in a very short time-frame. The planner has been able to return relevant plans in less than three milliseconds for several problem instances of the *SimpleFPS* planning domain.

1 Introduction

Automated planning is now being used in popular games to satisfy the need of more realistic behaviours for Artificial Intelligence (AI) agents. The advantage of automated planning is twofold for the game industry. First, planners dynamically generate sequences of actions by reasoning according to goals, and thus go beyond simple reactive behaviours. Secondly, the use of a planner improves software maintenance, as an AI designer would only have to define sets of goals and actions, without worrying too much about the interactions between them. Planning has also drawbacks: it is known to require significant CPU time, while modern game engines are already consuming most resources of common gaming hardware. Early games implemented the STRIPS-like GOAP (Goal-Oriented Action Planning) system developed for the AI of F.E.A.R. [9], but nowadays several games have switched to Hierarchical Task Network (HTN) [2] planners. The latter requires to model and maintain an additional amount of planning knowledge, but also achieves better performance. However, the use of planning in games is still limited.

A recent study conducted in some popular video games [4], brings an interesting insight into two games implementing HTN based planning: *Killzone 3* (2011) and *Transformers 3: Fall of Cybertron* (2012). The study reveals the current performance of both games: (i) plan lengths hardly exceed 4 actions (longest plans, up to 12 actions, may appear, but they are rare), (ii) the number of Non-Playable Characters (NPCs) simultaneously handled by the planning system is below the size of a squad (less than 12 AI entities), and (iii) approximately one plan per second and per NPC is generated in average. As a comparison, our goal is to simulate the tactical behaviour of an entire platoon of soldiers (nearly 30

T. Cazenave et al. (Eds.): CGW 2014, CCIS 504, pp. 119–132, 2014.

to 40 NPCs), with plans potentially more complex than sequences of 4 actions. To preserve playability and immersion, the planner must be able to return plans for any agent in less than one second of real time. AI usually benefits from 10% of the overall computation time in a game (about 100 ms), thus only 2 to 3 ms per NPC are available in order to plan for a platoon.

This paper introduces the Simple Hierarchical Planning Engine (SHPE). This planning system is based on the same HTN planning techniques currently implemented in games, but achieves better performance thanks to an alternative encoding of planning data. Section 2 describes the main features of the system, some algorithmic details and how to operate the planner. Section 3 focuses on some additional features currently under study. Finally, Section 4 evaluates the performance of the planner using the *SimpleFPS* domain [11], a planning domain designed to emulate a game-world environment and test planners according to game mechanics.

2   SHPE: Simple Hierarchical Planning Engine

2.1   Planning Data Representation

Planning data are classically represented by a first-order logical language. A state of the world is described by a set of predicates, which represent properties holding for some objects of the world. Possible changes are described with operators. An operator is defined with a precondition, some effects, and may also have a numerical cost. Preconditions and effects are logical formulas on predicates, and they respectively represent the condition to apply the operator and the changes occurring on a state after the application of this operator. The set of definitions for predicates and operators is called a planning domain. Plans can be sequences or partially ordered sets of operators, and an optimisation criterion can be defined on the costs of these operators. A classical planner expects as input a goal condition on the predicates as well as an initial state, and returns a plan transforming the initial state into one satisfying the goal. A standard planning domain language conforming to these principles is PDDL [8]. Figure 1 shows some samples of planning data expressed in this language.

HTN planning introduces tasks into the planning domain. There are two types of tasks. Primitive tasks are associated with operators, while compound ones are designed to be decomposed into a partial plan made of subtasks, called a task network. For each compound task, alternative decompositions are defined through several HTN methods. This paper adopts the formalism for methods of the Simple Hierarchical Ordered Planner (SHOP [5]) and its successor SHOP2 [6]. Thus, our methods are defined as successive pairs of preconditions and task networks (each pair is called a branch, and the planner only decomposes the method for the first satisfied branch). Figure 2 presents some examples of such methods. The purpose of an HTN planner is different from a classical one: instead of building a plan fulfilling a goal from the initial state, an HTN planner decomposes an initial task network down to a plan only made of primitive tasks, and applicable to the initial state.

```
; a definition of an action in PDDL, here this action
; applies to a NPC that uses a gun to shoot at the player
(:action shoot-player
 :parameters    (?npc ?gun ?wpt1 ?wpt2)
 ; to perform the action, the NPC needs a loaded gun and
 ; a clear line of sight to the player
 :precondition (and (at ?npc ?wpt1) (player-at ?wpt2)
                    (holding ?npc ?gun) (loaded ?gun)
                    (visible ?wpt1 ?wpt2))
 ; the player is wounded and the gun is no longer loaded
 :effect        (and (not (loaded ?gun)) (player-wounded)))

[...]


; a description of the initial situation
(:init (at npc0 wpt0) (player-at wpt1) (visible wpt0 wpt1)
       (visible wpt1 wpt0) (gun gun0) (loaded gun0)
       (holding npc0 gun0) [...])
; the goal we want to achieve
(:goal (player-wounded))
```

Fig. 1. An operator (action) described in the PDDL planning representation language, along with an initial state and a goal formula. Here, *(shoot-player npc0 gun0)* is a valid plan according to the initial situation and the goal.

```
; method for attacking the player at range
(:method (attack-player ?npc)
 ; a first branch, when the NPC already has
 ; visibility with the player
 (and (at ?npc ?wpt1) (player-at ?wpt2) (visible ?wpt1 ?wpt2)
      (gun ?gun) (holding ?npc ?gun))
 ((!shoot-player ?npc ?gun))
 ; a second branch that moves the NPC to a waypoint where it
 ; will have visibility to the player location
 (and (waypoint ?wpt1) (player-at ?wpt2) (visible ?wpt1 ?wpt2)
      (gun ?gun) (holding ?npc ?gun))
 ((move ?npc ?wpt1) (!shoot-player ?npc ?gun)))

; method for attacking the player in melee combat
(:method (attack-player ?npc)
 (and (at ?npc ?wpt) (player-at ?wpt) (knife ?knife)
      (holding ?npc ?knife))
 ((!stab-player ?npc ?knife)))
```

Fig. 2. Two methods that define alternative decompositions for the compound task *(attack-player ?npc)*. The first method provides the behaviour to attack the player with a ranged weapon, while the second one makes the NPC use a close combat weapon. The LISP-like syntax is the one used by SHOP for its input data, where the exclamation mark "!" denotes a primitive task.

From a programming viewpoint, logical formulas (preconditions, effects) in operators and methods are generally encoded as lists of atomic propositions evaluated by an inference engine. Pyhop [7], a SHOP-like HTN planner coded in Python, follows another approach supposed to be more suited to games. First, world states are represented as Python data structures containing state-variables, an alternative representation for facts in planning, instead of sets of predicates. Secondly, operators and methods are Python functions taking a state as input, and respectively returning a new state and a sequence of subtasks. Figure 3 provides an insight on what such functions look like. The entire domain is therefore written in Python, and not with a logical language as usual. For SHPE, we decided to follow the same rules for reason of both system simplicity and expectation of a runtime improvement. Indeed, there is no need to code an inference engine and state-variables can be instantly accessed in a structure to read or modify their values, while we have to find a predicate to add or delete it from a state. But unlike Pyhop, we did not choose Python but C++ in order to implement our planning system. First, this is a commonly used language for video games and we expect our choice to ease the integration of the planner in most game engines. Secondly, being a low-level compiled language, C++ seemed to be an appropriate option to achieve the best runtime.

```
def shoot_player(state, npc, gun):
    if state.visible[state.at[npc]][state.player_at] and \
       state.holding[npc][gun] and state.loaded[gun]:
        state.loaded[gun] = False
        state.player_wounded = True
        return state
    else: return False
```

Fig. 3. The same operator as defined in Figure 1, but encoded in Python this time

2.2   Algorithm

SHOP, Pyhop and SHPE use the same algorithmic principle. They conduct a depth-first, backtracking search in the space of partially decomposed task networks, combined with a forward state-space search. When the planner selects the next task to process, it always picks one that has no predecessor in the task network. Doing so results in constructing the plan in the same order as it will be executed. The planner always has a full description of the current state of the world at its disposal, thus logical expressions in operators and methods can be written with very expressive logical formulas. For instance, the domain modeling language of SHOP2 allows for existential and universal quantifiers, disjunction, implication and even more specific expressions [6]. Not only does this type of search provide the domain modeler with a powerful way to encode good strategies for decomposing task networks, but it also justifies why operators and methods can be encoded as functions in Pyhop.

However, the implementation of SHPE differs from Pyhop in several ways. We do not actually define operators and methods, and associate them with tasks. As primitive tasks are in one-to-one correspondence with operators, we simply blend both of them together into a single primitive task definition. We do not define each method separately either. Instead, they are all gathered in the body of a single function named *decompose*. This function is defined for all compound task types, and it returns a list of all the decompositions for each method. Besides, an operator/primitive task is not considered as being a single function, but is split into three parts:

1. The function *applicable* returns the evaluation of the precondition (a boolean value).
2. The function *apply* returns the new value of the state after the application of all effects.
3. The function *cost* returns the cost of the operator/task.

Another difference is the iterative structure of the algorithm implementation. It provides the ability to interrupt and resume the planner, which is a nice feature to have with some game engines in order to time-slice planning through multiple frames. The last addition is the "branch-and-bound" optimization technique implemented for SHOP2 [6] in order to search for a least-cost plan, along with the standard procedure returning the first plan found. The optimal version, combined with the ability to interrupt the planner, can work more or less as an "anytime-like" algorithm [1]: when a first solution is found, possibly not optimal, it keeps running in order to find a better plan as long as it has not been interrupted. The procedure executed at each iteration of the planner is described in Algorithm 1. Algorithms 2 and 3 are respectively the standard and optimal procedures to run the planner (without interrupting it).

2.3   Operating the Planner

SHPE is implemented as a C++ template library. The planner is provided in a template *Planner<MyState>* class, and the template parameter must be specialized with the C++ structure type defined for the state. The implementation of the planner provides the necessary member functions to be run in different ways: *run*, and *run_best* are used to operate the planner directly in the standard and optimize mode, while the function *next* is publicly visible to enable the integration of the planner according to one's requirements. For example, it can be used to run the planner for a limited amount of iterations or time.

All primitive and compound tasks must be implemented by inheriting the provided *Task<MyState>* virtual class and overloading its virtual member functions: either *applicable*, *apply* and *cost* if this is a primitive task, or *decompose* if it is a compound one. Also, a task is supposed to be implemented with all its parameters as class member attributes. Due to the use of polymorphism, an instance of the *Planner<MyState>* class only deals with references to tasks, therefore the actual task objects need to be stored in a global memory space.

Algorithm 1. next(*stack*, *best_plan*, *best_cost*)

(*plan*, *cost*, *state*, *task_network*) ← top(*stack*)
pop *stack*
if *cost* ≥ *best_cost* **then**
  return
end if
if *task_network* is empty **then**
  best_plan ← *plan*
  best_cost ← *cost*
  return
end if
tasks ← all tasks in *task_network* without predecessor
for all *t* ∈ *tasks* **do**
  if *t* is a primitive task **then**
    if *t*.applicable(*state*) **then**
      plan ← append *t* to *plan*
      cost ← *cost* + *t*.cost(*state*)
      remove *t* from *task_network*
      push (*plan*, *cost*, *t*.apply(*state*), *task_network*) on *stack*
    end if
  end if
  if *t* is a compound task **then**
    for all *tn* ∈ *t*.decompose(*state*) **do**
      replace *t* in *task_network* with *tn*
      push (*plan*, *cost*, *state*, *task_network*) on *stack*
    end for
  end if
end for

Algorithm 2. find_first_plan(*state*, *task_network*)

---

stack ← []
best_plan ← []
best_cost ← ∞
push ([], 0, *state*, *task_network*) on *stack*
while *best_cost* = ∞ and *stack* is not empty **do**
  next(*stack*, *best_plan*, *best_cost*)
end while

Algorithm 3. find_best_plan(*state*, *task_network*)

---

stack ← []
best_plan ← []
best_cost ← ∞
push ([], 0, *state*, *task_network*) on *stack*
while *stack* is not empty **do**
  next(*stack*, *best_plan*, *best_cost*)
end while

For this purpose, and also to limit dynamic heap allocation, a caching system registers all allocated instances of a type of task. But if a task class only has few different instances, they can also be stored in static attributes of this class. Figure 4 provides a practical example of how a task can be implemented for SHPE.

So, in order to get plans from SHPE, one needs to execute the following steps:

1. Define a C++ structure for the state (*MyState*). Some variables of the domain are never modified and can be easily identified as they do not appear in any effects; thus a good practice is to define a constant state structure, and make all constant variables from a state pointing to the constant structure. This technique significantly reduces memory usage and runtime as states are copied many times in the planner's stack.
2. Define all primitive and compound tasks of the domain as C++ classes inheriting from *Task<MyState>*.
3. Include the C++ files for your domain and the ones from SHPE within a project, and write some code to instantiate and use the specialized instance of the *Planner<MyState>* class.
4. Compile and run this domain-specific planning program.

3   Planning Domain Design and Pre-compilation

3.1   High Level Modeling Language

When it comes to modeling a planning domain, C++ is anything but an appropriate language. Being a low-level programming language, it is already quite verbose. Besides, our way to implement tasks does not help either. On several occasions, a domain written with a few hundred lines of LISP code was expanded into a few thousand of C++ lines. Thus, a much more convenient high-level planning domain modeling language is needed. Neither PDDL nor the LISP syntax of SHOP were appropriate as this language should support state-variable representation and HTN decompositions. By contrast, the ANML language [10], currently under development at NASA, provides these elements. Therefore, we have started to design a language based on ANML as a tool for domain modeling.

However, ANML is quite a comprehensive language for planning and already supports many features. As some of these features are out of scope for SHPE, they were simply discarded. The removal of temporal qualifications on preconditions is probably the most noticeable change (indeed SHPE does not support temporal networks, but this may be a further improvement). Some minor changes on the syntax were also included in order to conform the language to the task-based HTN formalism of SHOP. Figure 5 provides an insight on some elements of a planning domain expressed with this language.

The language was also expanded with *sort-by* and *first* preconditions, two features available in SHOP and SHOP2. *sort-by* preconditions allow to sort the variable bindings satisfying the precondition according to the value of a numerical expression and *first* preconditions allow to consider only the first binding

```cpp
class ShootPlayer : public Task<MyState> {
public:
    // the class constructor
    ShootPlayer(const Npc& npc, const Gun& gun) : primitive(true),
                                                  npc(npc),
                                                  gun(gun)
    {
    }

    // evaluate the precondition according to the current state
    bool applicable(const MyState& state) const
    {
        return state.visible[state.at[npc]][state.player_at] and
               state.holding[npc][gun] and state.loaded[gun];
    }

    // apply the effects of this task on the current state
    void apply(MyState& state) const
    {
        state.loaded[gun] = false;
        state.player_wounded = true;
    }
protected:
    // print this task for debugging purpose
    std::ostream& print(std::ostream& out) const
    {
        return out << "ShootPlayer(" << npc << ", " << gun << ")";
    }
private:
    Npc npc;
    Gun gun;
};
```

Fig. 4. An example of a C++ definition for the primitive task *ShootPlayer(npc, gun)*. The *cost* function is not overloaded here. In this case, the default implementation of this function, inherited from *Task<MyState>*, returns 1. It is a primitive task, so the virtual function *decompose* is not overloaded either and a call to this function will return an empty set of decompositions.

```
task ShootPlayer(Npc npc, Gun gun) {
    cost := 1;
    {
        visible(at(npc), player_at);
        holding(npc, gun);
        loaded(gun) == true :-> false;
        player_wounded := true;
    }
}

task AttackPlayer(Npc npc) {
    // method for attacking the player at range
    method {
        // a first branch, when the NPC already has
        // visibility with the player
        branch {
            exists (Gun gun) {
                visible(at(npc), player_at);
                holding(npc, gun);
                ordered(ShootPlayer(npc, gun));
            }
        }
        // a second branch that moves the NPC to a waypoint
        // where it will have visibility to the player location
        branch {
            exists (Waypoint wpt, Gun gun) {
                visible(wpt, player_at);
                holding(npc, gun);
                ordered(Move(npc, wpt), ShootPlayer(npc, gun));
            }
        }
    }
    // method for attacking the player in melee combat
    method {
        exists (Knife knife) {
            at(npc) == player_at;
            holding(npc, knife);
            ordered(StabPlayer(npc, knife));
        }
    }
}
```

Fig. 5. Primitive and compound tasks defined with a high-level modeling language, in a state-variable based representation

```
task RestoreHealth(Npc npc) {
    method {
        // a first branch, when the NPC already has a medikit
        branch {
            first (Medikit medikit) {
                holding(npc, medikit);
                ordered(UseMedikit(npc, medikit));
            }
        }
        // a second branch when the NPC needs to
        // find a medikit
        branch {
            sort-by (Medikit medikit; distance(at(npc),
                                                at(medikit)); <) {
                ordered(Move(npc, at(medikit)),
                        UseMedikit(npc, medikit));
            }
        }
    }
}
```

Fig. 6. A method using both *sort-by* and *first* expressions. In the first branch, it would be pointless to generate a decomposition for each medikit the NPC holds as the choice of the medikit would not alter the quality of the plan, so it makes sense to consider the first satisfier only. In the second one, a medikit in the neighborhood is more likely to be the best option in order to find one in fewer steps, so exploring this option first is a good heuristic.

(Figure 6). The ability to insert calls to external user-defined functions is also under study.

3.2   Domain Pre-compilation

Having a convenient language for domain modeling is one thing, but currently the domain still requires to be translated by hand into C++ code. Depending on the size of the domain, this task quickly becomes tedious and error-prone, and completely goes against the requirement for a system simple enough to be used by a non-programmer (for example by a game designer). Therefore, an additional piece of software is required to parse the domain from the high-level modeling language and generate a C++ domain definition automatically. At the end of the process, the generated C++ classes containing the domain elements as well as the specialized planner would be integrated in a game project or even compiled as an independent dynamic link library to achieve modularity. Nevertheless, this tool has not been implemented yet.

4   Performance Evaluations

4.1   The *SimpleFPS* Planning Domain

The *SimpleFPS* domain [11] has been designed specially to produce planning problems that could serve as benchmarks to evaluate planners according to FPS (First-Person Shooter) game mechanics. *SimpleFPS* problems stage a NPC and a player in a game level made of several areas connected to each other, and each area includes various types of points of interest (items such as weapons, medikits or keys, doors between areas, cover-points...). A comprehensive description of the domain can be found in the original paper.

As this domain is provided in a PDDL format, it was necessary to convert the predicate based representation into a state-variable one. It was also necessary to add tasks and methods in order to operate the domain with an HTN planner, as *SimpleFPS* has only been designed to evaluate goal-oriented classical planning techniques. The hierarchical structure of the domain makes use of the tools provided by SHOP2 to encode heuristics in methods (*sort-by* expressions...) in order to make the planner more likely to find near-optimal solutions. To achieve this, we added a *distance* predicate/state-variable to encode the distances between all areas (this distance is used as the criterion to sort the areas and the point of interest in the methods). In an actual game environment, this information could be computed with the Euclidean distance between points of interest.

4.2   Experiments

For the first set of experiments, we wanted to compare the performance of SHPE with a similar planner. We selected JSHOP2 [3], a java implementation of SHOP2 [6]. JSHOP2 is a problem specific planner: a specialized instance of the planner is compiled for each domain and problem. This feature provides JSHOP2 with an advantage over SHPE, which can only be optimized for the planning domain. Besides, JSHOP2 already compared favorably to other more academic implementations (it has been shown to run by a polynomial order of magnitude faster than SHOP2). So it revealed itself to be an appropriate candidate to compete with SHPE in our benchmark. Several problems with various numbers of points of interest were randomly generated (the number of areas is set to 10).

The computer used for all experiments is equipped with an Intel core i5 CPU (2.66 GHz), 4 GB of RAM, and it runs a 64 bits version of Debian 7.0. This configuration is equivalent to an average *Steam Box*, a new PC-based gaming concept currently developed by *Valve*. The running-time results for SHPE and JSHOP2 are presented in Figure 7: each measure is the average running time for a collection of one hundred samples of the same size. The results indicate a clear advantage on the side of SHPE, which solves each set of problems 10 to 15 times faster than JSHOP2. Moreover, the running times are short enough (less than 3 ms for each instance) to assume that SHPE should be able to plan for several squads of NPCs in a game or a simulator.

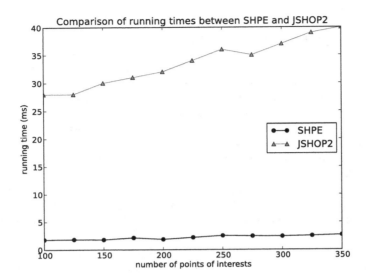

Fig. 7. SHPE and JSHOP2 performance comparison on different instances of problems from the *SimpleFPS* domain. The instances were generated with ten areas and a varying amount of points of interest. For these scenarios, SHPE outperforms JSHOP2 by at least a factor of 10.

The results show that SHPE runs quite fast, but what about the quality of the plans? There is actually no reason to evaluate SHPE on this aspect against JSHOP2. Indeed plan quality is related to the designed decomposition hierarchy, and both planners share the same. Our hierarchy generally performs well: it provides a satisfactory near-optimal plan in most cases, and sometimes it even returns an optimal one. However there are situations when it does not: for instance, a sequence of 70 actions is returned when the optimal plan only contains 30 of them. In this case, will the "branch-and-bound" optimization technique be of any help? In order to get an idea about it, we ran the planner until it had returned an optimal solution for two scenarios. In the first one, the planner first returned a plan far from being optimal; thus it was interesting to measure how long the game would have to wait for a satisfactory solution. In the second scenario, the returned plan was already satisfactory, but could still be improved. The answer is shown in Figure 8. In both cases, the optimal solution is out of reach: it requires several seconds in the already near optimal case, and several minutes in the other case. When the initial solution is far from being optimal, it also requires several minutes to get an acceptable one. So this optimization option does not seem very useful and the ability to obtain a good solution from the planner mainly relies on the designed decomposition methods.

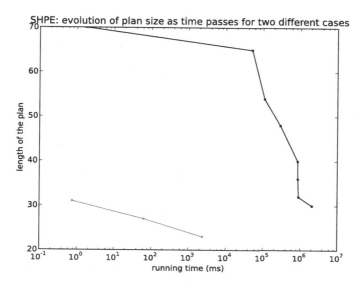

Fig. 8. SHPE using the "branch-and-bound" optimization techniques to search for the best solution in two scenarios. One when the first plan found is far from being optimal (the uppermost graph, starting with 70 actions), and another case with a first plan almost optimal, but still improvable (the lower graph, starting with 31 actions).

5   Conclusion

The ideas introduced with Pyhop [7] were put into application in SHPE in order to provide fast planning capabilities to video games. The system has reached the targeted performance: it has been evaluated against various problems with properties similar to FPS games, and was able to solve them in a few milliseconds. In addition, a high-level modeling language can be used to design the planning knowledge required to operate the planner efficiently. To bridge the gap between this high-level language and the C++ encoding expected by the planner, a pre-compiler should be implemented. This component would enable AI designers to modify the behaviour of game characters, without any skills in low-level C++ programming.

But even if this system achieves its initial goal in terms of performance and maintenance, it does not address issues like real-time re-planning in dynamic environments such as games. Besides, even if plans containing more than twenty actions can be computed in a few milliseconds, this time is still partially a waste, as it is likely that most of the plan will no longer be relevant to the evolution of the situation. Thus, our future plan for this system is to study and incorporate partial and delayed decomposition. A hierarchical planner including these features could decompose a plan into primitive tasks for imminent acting only, keep the more distant tasks at a more abstract level and eventually expand them at the appropriate time.

References

1. Dean, T.L., Boddy, M.S.: An Analysis of Time-Dependent Planning. In: AAAI 1988, pp. 49–54 (1988)
2. Ghallab, M., Nau, D., Traverso, P.: Automated Planning: Theory and Practice. Morgan Kaufmann (2004)
3. Ilghami, O., Nau, D.S.: A General Approach to Synthesize Problem-Specific Planners. Tech. rep., CS-TR-4597 and UMIACS-TR-2004-40, University of Maryland (2003)
4. Jacopin, É.: Game AI Planning Analytics: Evaluation and Comparison of the AI Planning in three First-Person Shooters. In: AIIDE (2014)
5. Nau, D., Cao, Y., Lotem, A., Muñoz-Avila, H.: SHOP: Simple Hierarchical Ordered Planner. In: IJCAI 1999, pp. 968–975 (1999)
6. Nau, D., Au, T.-C., Ilghami, O., Kuter, U., Murdock, J.W., Wu, D., Yaman, F.: SHOP2: An HTN Planning System. Journal of Artificial Intelligence Research (JAIR) 20, 379–404 (2003)
7. Nau, D.: Game Applications of HTN Planning with State Variables. In: ICAPS Workshop on Planning in Games (2013) Invited talk
8. McDermott, D., Ghallab, M., Howe, A., Knoblock, C., Ram, A., Veloso, M., Weld, D., Wilkins, D.: PDDL – The Planning Domain Definition Language. Tech. Rep. CVC TR-98-003/DCS TR-1165, Yale Center for Computational Vision and Control (1998)
9. Orkin, J.: Three States and a Plan: The AI of F.E.A.R. In: Game Developer's Conference (GDC) (2006)
10. Smith, D.E., Frank, J., Cushing, W.: The ANML Language. In: ICAPS 2008 (2008)
11. Vassos, S., Papakonstantinou, M.: The SimpleFPS Planning Domain: A PDDL Benchmark for Proactive NPCs. In: AIIDE Workshop: Intelligent Narrative Technologies, pp. 92–97 (2011)

Predicting Player Disengagement
in Online Games

Hanting Xie *, Daniel Kudenko **, Sam Devlin * * *, and Peter Cowling †

Department of Computer Science
University of York
YO10 5GH, York, UK

Abstract. Game engagement, as one of the most fundamental objectives for game designers to achieve, has become an attractive industrial and academic topic. An important direction in this area is to construct a model to predict how long a player could be engaged with a game. This paper introduces a pure data driven method to foresee whether a player will quit the game given their previous activity within the game, by constructing decision trees from historical gameplay data of previous players. The method will be assessed on two popular commercial online games: *I Am Playr* and *Lyroke*. The former is a football game while the latter is a music game. The results indicate that the decision tree built by our method is valuable to predict the players' disengagement and that its human-readable form allow us to search out further reasons about what in-game events made them quit.

Keywords: Game Data Mining, Player Modelling, Decision Trees.

1   Introduction

In the global game industry, over 1500 commercial games are published annually [8]. Nevertheless, only a few of them gain popularity and become memorised by the history of games. For the continual growth of the games industry, more companies could succeed if they could fully understand their players. Therefore, how to shape an in-depth understanding of players has become a big issue in the area of games. Recently, game data mining has become popular in this area to help developers to understand more about their customers. Some research focuses on how players behave in the game [14] especially whether they play in a legal way [6]. Others concentrate on classifying players by their play styles [10], which would be advantageous for the developer to better satisfy their customers.

For many players, except for external factors, a predominant reason which may lead to their disengagement is design flaws in the game. Therefore, it would

---

* hx597@york.ac.uk
** daniel.kudenko@york.ac.uk
* * * sam.devlin@york.ac.uk
† peter.cowling@york.ac.uk

T. Cazenave et al. (Eds.): CGW 2014, CCIS 504, pp. 133–149, 2014.
© Springer International Publishing Switzerland 2014

be helpful if we could discover some rule-sets based on the game that could predict whether a player will quit (or disengage). To be more precise, if one's actions match all the rules in a set, he/she would be highly likely to leave the game without hesitation.

In this work, we promote a pure data driven method to investigate the causes of disengagement in games. The data are collected from two commercial online games in different genres; 'I Am Playr' [1], a first-person football game, and 'Lyroke' [2], a music game, both developed by 'We R Interactive' [3].

2   Background

In this section we cover the relevant background material and terms necessary for the comprehension of this work.

2.1   Game Telemetry

To understand players, collecting data from users is always the first step. A widely utilized technology in the game industry is called *game telemetry*. Telemetry refers to obtaining data through remote access, in the sense of games, that is to transmit data collected from a game sever to a collection server and formatted there to support further analysis [11]. The data collected usually includes different types which are related to the genre of the game. For example, in sport games, valuable game metrics could be *match type*, *team selection* and *country chosen* etc. In the game industry, game telemetry data could be used both externally and internally. As an example of external use, the *World of WarCraft Armory* [5] provides its players with statistics about its characters and guilds. As an internal tool, developers could take advantage of game telemetry data to detect bugs and adjust the settings of the game [15].

2.2   Game Data Mining and Player Modelling

Game data mining or game analytics is the application of data mining in the area of games [11]. Its intention is to train models from game telemetry data using machine learning algorithms. Player Modelling is one example of this where the models trained are intended to represent a behaviour of the player. For example, how they play or experience the game.

The method introduced in this paper is based on *supervised learning*. The problem of supervised learning can be considered as classification (or regression). In this case, a set of attributes or *features* to be analysed is selected. A single instance in a dataset refers to a specific vector of corresponding values of those selected features. Each instance of the dataset used to train the model is given a *label* corresponding to its classification or the group it belongs to. The model generated by supervised learning intends to uncover the correlation between a group of selected features and the labels. So that after training, the model should be able to assign labels to new incoming instances automatically.

2.3   Decision Tree

The model learnt in this paper is a *decision tree*; a tree data structure which is generated by a divide-and-conquer strategy [7]. Decision trees are one of the most easily interpretable data structures in data mining and have been chosen, therefore, as this will be helpful to demystify what events are likely to result in players' disengage. Given the human readable output of this model the resultant decision tree can be used by game designers to inform future development of the game without the designer requiring in-depth knowledge of data mining.

A decision tree includes a root with several nodes connected by paths. The root and each non-terminal (or leaf) node are features of the dataset whilst the leaf nodes are the labels that would be assigned to a new data instance provided they had all the features given by the nodes from the root to that leaf. An example of decision tree is shown later in Figure 1. While building, every node could also be taken as root to be linked to more nodes until it has reached a leaf node. The decision tree is in fact another form of rule sets. Because the process of heading to leaves is just the same with matching rules.

There are various algorithms for building up decision trees, the specific algorithm used in this paper is called *C4.5* [9] but any decision tree learner could be used with our methodology. This paper will follow the original algorithm without any specific modification. Our contribution is the methodology of applying decision trees to predict player disengagement not a refinement of the learning algorithm. We have chosen C4.5 because the algorithm is widely used in data mining and so that the method we introduce in this paper can be easily implemented by interested game developers.

2.4   Feature Selection

In data mining, features are those factors related to outcomes. In terms of decision trees, they are the things that utilised to branch the tree. However, having too many redundant features can affect both the accuracy of the model built, the time to train the model and the memory needed. It is not rare that there are thousands of possible features to be analysed in a game. For example, one of the games to be analysed in this paper, I Am Playr, has 6408 key assorted events that could be useful features. Considering this, it is important to apply feature selection to prune those irrelevant ones.

There are many algorithms to perform feature selection. In this paper, we conduct feature selection (and model learning) using of WEKA [4]. The algorithm used by WEKA is called Correlation based Feature Selection (CFS). It is an algorithm based on an evaluation formula including both correlation measure and heuristic search strategy [12]. As with our motivation to use decision tree, the reason to apply CFS is that it is widely used, well developed and would be convenient for further investigations.

3 Games

To test our method, we applied it to two existing commercial games of distinct genres, both developed by *We R Interactive*. An introduction to both is included in this section and is intended to emphasise the significant differences in the games.

3.1 I Am Playr

I Am Playr is a *free to play*, first person, football game on the social network *Facebook*. Like other free to play games, I Am Playr offers different items such as boots, cars and other luxury items that players can purchase in the game.

Our method focussed on data regarding the occurrence of events in the game. In I Am Playr there are currently a total of 6048 events possibly experienced by players. Worldwide, most of those events happened nearly hundreds of times in only one minute. Those events in game originate from gameplay events and system events. The former is about the actions performed by players, for instance, 'Wining Matches', 'Playing Videos' and 'Training'. Whilst the latter, system events, the game decides when the player will experiences, for example promotions such as a 'Daily Bonus' or 'Free Coins'.

3.2 Lyroke

Lyroke is a commercial music game available on multiple platforms including Facebook, iOS and Android. The main mechanism of this game is that a song is played with most of the lyrics displayed, the players need to respond with the missing lyrics before the singer reaches them. The most common purchases in game are to unlock new songs.

Similar to I Am Playr, the events are from gameplay and system. However, the event types are very different due to the different genres or the games. In Lyroke, gameplay events include 'Using Power Up Items' and 'Answering Lyric' whereas system events include 'System Gifts' and 'Achievements'.

4 Methodology

The objective of our method is trying to predict the disengagement of users as a result of the events they experienced. Specifically, we predict whether there will be a decrease in a players' activity from one month to the next on the basis of their behaviour in the first month. In this section, we will show how our method is assessed in both games.

4.1 Data Collection

The data from these two games is all gathered by game telemetry and stored in a web data server. All the raw data we used for analysis are downloaded from this sever. As mentioned before, the event data will be the only dataset covered in this paper, Table 1 shows a general description of its compiled format on the server.

As can be seen in Table 1, a complete event type includes 'st1', 'st2', 'st3' and the corresponding action of the event type, attribute 'n'. So, the format of events we use as features for training is 'st1-st2-st3-n'. Thus, as an example, the event (feature) appeared in Table 1 would be 'Item-Equip-Boots-IAmHelios'.

Another attribute should be noticed is the 'game week' ('i' in Table 1) which represents the in game week that the player has currently reached. Game week (or any similar measure of a player's progression through the game) could also be a relevant feature because the same event in game could generate contrasting meanings in different game weeks. Since it is not an event, and is partially game specific, we built models both with and without this attribute with the latter being for the purpose of generalisation. However, most games will have a similar metric that could be used in place of game week with similar results expected to the models generated using this feature.

With permission and help from We R Interactive, we are able to access up-to-date data. For I Am Playr, we analysed datasets from January to March 2014. Whereas in Lyroke, we had datasets from March to April 2014.

Table 1. Event data format with Example Instance from I Am Playr

Attribute Name	Descriptions	Examples Instance
Timestamp	The Unix Time	'1388534450669'
Type	The type of this dataset	'event'
s	Anonymous User ID	'00008'
n	The specific action related to event	'IAmHelios'
v	Values related to action	'1'
i	The week in game that player is currently in	'3'
st1	Level 1 description of event	'Item'
st2	Level 2 description of event	'Equip'
st3	Level 3 description of event	'Boots'

4.2 Data Labelling

Before training, we must label players' change in engagement between months. This is necessary for training and evaluating the decision tree only. Afterwards, when deploying the model, players can be classified as one of the following types simply by observing the events they experienced in the previous month. For the purpose of future research on players' full retention trends, we decide to not only assign *Decreasing* labels but also consider labels of *Increasing* and *Stable*. Those three labels are distributed by the following steps described in Algorithm 1.

Firstly, in step 1, we take only users that exist both in January and February into consideration. Next, in steps 2 to 6, each user's (usr) event counts in both January ($EventC_{Jan}(usr)$) and February ($EventC_{Feb}(usr)$) will be calculated and recorded in the event count lists ($EventCList_{Jan}$ and $EventCList_{Feb}$). And then, in step 7 and 8, the two lists are sorted. After that, in step 9 to 12, for each user, if his/her event counts belongs to the first quarter of sorted January event count list, then we say the rank of this user is 1 in January. Likewise, his/her rank would be 2, 3 or 4 if they were in second, third or fourth quarter in January. Repeating the same thing for February. Finally, for each user, if his/her rank in January ($C_{Jan}(usr)$) minus his/her rank in February ($C_{Feb}(usr)$) surpasses 2, then he/she would be allocated to the Decreasing Group. Similarly, if a user's rank in February minus his/her rank in January is bigger than 2, it means he belongs to the Increasing Group. In comparison, players with ranks lower than 2 will be categorised into the Stable Group.

Algorithm 1. Label Distribution Algorithm

1: $U \leftarrow U_{Jan} \cap U_{Feb}$
2: **for** user in U **do**
3:     $EventC_{Jan}(usr)$, $EventC_{Feb}(usr)$
4:     $EventCList_{Jan} \leftarrow EventCList_{Jan} \cup EventC_{Jan}(usr)$
5:     $EventCList_{Feb} \leftarrow EventCList_{Feb} \cup EventC_{Feb}(usr)$
6: **end for**
7: Sort $EventCList_{Jan}$
8: Sort $EventCList_{Feb}$
9: **for** user in U **do**
10:     $C_{Jan}(usr) \leftarrow$ 1, 2, 3 or 4 if user in 1st, 2nd, 3rd or 4th quarter of $EventCList_{Jan}$
11:     $C_{Feb}(usr) \leftarrow$ 1, 2, 3 or 4 if user in 1st, 2nd, 3rd or 4th quarter of $EventCList_{Jan}$
12: **end for**
13: **for** user in U **do**
14:     **if** $C_{Jan}(usr)$ - $C_{Feb}(usr) \geq 2$ **then**
15:         $Label(usr) \leftarrow$ Decreasing
16:     **else if** $|C_{Jan}(usr)$ - $C_{Feb}(usr)| < 2$ **then**
17:         $Label(usr) \leftarrow$ Stable
18:     **else if** $C_{Jan}(usr)$ - $C_{Feb}(usr) \leq$ -2 **then**
19:         $Label(usr) \leftarrow$ Increasing
20:     **end if**
21: **end for**

4.3   Model

As discussed in the preceding section, to train a supervised model, we need a set of instances with labels. In our case, an instance is a complete event history of a player with his/her label; decreasing, increasing or stable.

I Am Playr. In I Am Playr, since we use players' actions in January to predict the trend of their retention between January and February, the feature set contains all events the player experienced in January. Subsequently, for each instance, we use the number of occurrences of an event (feature) as the value of this feature. At the same time, the labels are decided by use of the Algorithm 1.

After the data is prepared, we make use of the C4.5 (called J48 in WEKA) decision tree learning algorithm in WEKA to build the models. Modelling with and without feature selection are both tried and their performances are compared. At the same time, as discussed in Section 4.1, we will also consider models both with and without the attribute 'game week'. Finally, for completeness, we will consider models with both feature selection and 'game week'.

In this paper, we conduct two experiments to assess the performance of our method. In the first we split players from the January-February dataset into 10 training and testing sets, and then perform 10-fold cross validations on them to observe the average performance. In this experiment, we randomly pick 3000 instances from each group (decreasing, increasing and stable), thus there are 9000 instances in total in this test. Those 9000 instances would be separated into training set and testing set automatically. The reason to use 3000 instances is that the smallest group merely contain around 3000 instances, so the use of this number to limit instances from other groups could ensure that the training data has a same size for each group.

The other one is to validate the decision tree trained by the trend between January and February to predict the trend between February and March. In this experiment, we use exactly the same model trained from the preceding experiment to test on 3000 (1000 instances for each group) randomly picked instances from February-March data.

Lyroke. The method of training decision tree of Lyroke remains the same with I Am Playr. However, the dissimilarity is that since we only hold the data about March and April, only the 10-fold cross validation test could be examined. In this experiment, we pick 900 instances randomly from each group(decreasing, increasing and stable), thus there are totally 2700 instances in this test. In 10-fold cross, those 2700 instance would be divided into training set and testing set automatically. We choose 900 instances since this is the size of our smallest set.

4.4   Evaluation Metrics

In order to evaluate our method, 'Recall', 'Precision', 'F-Measure' and 'Accuracy' will be used as metrics of performance. Among them, 'Recall' refers to the true positive rate or sensitivity in the context of classification while 'Precision' represents the positive predictive value. 'F-Measure' is a harmonic mean of those two. As a commonly used metric, 'Accuracy' cares both true positives and true negatives. In formulas below, 'true positives', 'true negatives', 'false positive' and 'false negative' are represented by 'tp', 'tn', 'fp' and 'fn' respectively.

$$Recall = \frac{tp}{tp + fn} \tag{1}$$

$$Precision = \frac{tp}{tp + fp} \tag{2}$$

$$FMeasure = 2 \cdot \frac{precision \cdot recall}{precision + recall} \tag{3}$$

$$Accuracy = \frac{tp + tn}{tp + tn + fp + fn} \tag{4}$$

5   Result and Discussion

In this section we will discuss the relative performance of the models in predicting player engagement in both games. For comparison, we compare our method to a naive method of randomly guessing player engagement based on the known distribution of example instances.

5.1   I Am Playr

There are in total four different models constructed for I Am Playr. The size of the original model is 1705 nodes with 853 leaves and was learnt from 6408 features. After applying feature selection, the number of features is reduced to 79, which results in 1451 nodes with 725 leaves in the tree. Another tree built with the 'game week' feature contains 117 nodes with 59 leaves and was learnt from 6409 feature. Compared with the original model, it is clear including the 'game week' prunes the tree. Finally, the last model with both feature selection and the 'game week' feature included is 69 nodes 35 leaves and was learnt from only 35 features. The first four layers of this model are illustrated in Figure 1.

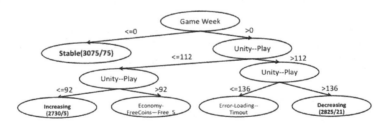

Fig. 1. Top of Decision Tree Learnt for I Am Playr with Feature Selection and the 'Game Week' Feature Included

As demonstrated by Figure 1, the decision tree is clear and easy to be interpreted. To classify the expected engagement of a new player, start from the root feature, 'game week', if its value is 0, the instance will be labelled as stable. Otherwise, we then consider the feature 'Unity-Play' (right child), this process continues until one of the 3 labels (decreasing, increasing or stable) is reached. One thing should be noticed is that many instances are classified as stable by only considering 'game week'. This could be a sign of overfitting and may mislead the prediction, perhaps explaining the performance in Figure 7.

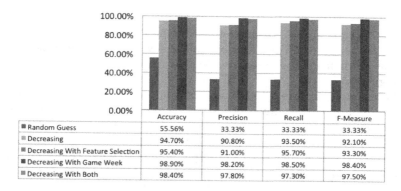

Fig. 2. 10 Fold CV Performance on Decreasing label in I Am Playr

10-Fold Cross Validation. Figure 2 indicates the performance of predicting decreasing engagement. As shown in the chart, the accuracy, precision, recall and F-Measure are high for all models. This shows our method can reliably predict player disengagement. At the same time, we could see that the feature selection process and 'game week' attribute further improve the accuracy. Nevertheless, if we use both of them, the accuracy is not as high as when we use 'game week' without feature selection. This might be because when we use 'game week', some other important features are filtered by the feature selection.

Since the four methods (except for random guess) are showing close performance, it is needed to check the RMSE (Root mean squared error) on them to identify which one is the best. The accuracies with RMSE are $94.70\% \pm 0.4362$, $95.40\% \pm 0.4197$, $98.90\% \pm 0.1063$ and $98.40\% \pm 0.1207$ respectively. This further supports that 'Decreasing With Game Week' is the best model, but it also shows that all models perform statistically significantly better than random guessing.

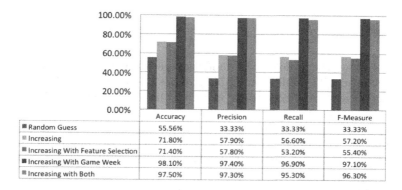

Fig. 3. 10 Fold CV Performance on Increasing label in I Am Playr

Figure 3 illustrates the 10-fold cross validation performance of predicting the increasing labelled group. Apart from predicting disengagement, we also try to find out whether we could predict which players would get more addicted to this game. The graph here shows that we achieve a significantly higher accuracy than random guess.

In this example, feature selection does not improve these metrics, but it does speed up the process of training. Adding feature selection reduces the time cost from 539.9s to 3.3s which is because it shrinks the number of features from 6048 to only 79. Therefore, it also helps to save memory for storage. An important thing to be noticed is that when we apply 'game week' attribute on this, the performance is improved dramatically, as 'game week' is an important feature to show whether a player is experienced or not. Thus it helped to improve the accuracy of model by dividing and conquering. However, since the two methods with 'game week' are showing close accuracies, an RMSE check of them is necessary. The accuracies with RMSE are 98.10% ± 0.1063 and 97.50% ± 0.1207 respectively. Therefore, the method with only 'game week' is the best again, but the significant reduction in training time that occurs when adding feature selection may be favoured over the small improvement in these metrics.

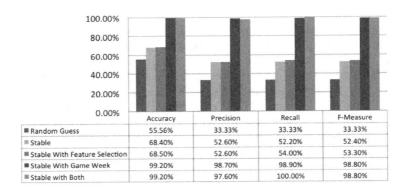

	Accuracy	Precision	Recall	F-Measure
■ Random Guess	55.56%	33.33%	33.33%	33.33%
▤ Stable	68.40%	52.60%	52.20%	52.40%
■ Stable With Feature Selection	68.50%	52.60%	54.00%	53.30%
■ Stable With Game Week	99.20%	98.70%	98.90%	98.80%
▤ Stable with Both	99.20%	97.60%	100.00%	98.80%

Fig. 4. 10 Fold CV Performance on Stable label in I Am Playr

Figure 4 shows the 10-fold cross validation performance of predicting the stable labelled group. To predict the stable group is the most demanding task in the research as players could keep stable in entirely different situations. For example, those players who only play once a week belong to stable group whereas some frequent players are also in the Stable Group as a result of certain play patterns shaped by their timetable. This result shows that the original model performs significantly better on all metrics than random guessing. The application of feature selection is shown to be of no substantial use once again on performance, however as discussed above, feature selection is essential to reduce the time cost. Similar to what happened to increasing group, including the 'game week' feature significantly improves all metrics. Likewise, the RMSE check is needed to distinguish the two accuracy bars related to 'game week'. The accuracies with RMSE are 99.20% ± 0.1063 and 99.20% ± 0.1207. So there is no longer a significant difference between using 'game week' with and without feature selection and, therefore, if predicting stable players was a priority we would recommend using feature selection for its benefits in reducing the memory and time requirements when training the model.

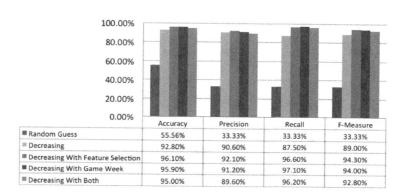

	Accuracy	Precision	Recall	F-Measure
■ Random Guess	55.56%	33.33%	33.33%	33.33%
▨ Decreasing	92.80%	90.60%	87.50%	89.00%
■ Decreasing With Feature Selection	96.10%	92.10%	96.60%	94.30%
■ Decreasing With Game Week	95.90%	91.20%	97.10%	94.00%
▨ Decreasing With Both	95.00%	89.60%	96.20%	92.80%

Fig. 5. Verified on February - March Performance on Decreasing label in I Am Playr

Verified on February - March Data. Figure 5 reveals the result of testing on the February-March data. It shows that the performance on the decreasing group (disengagement) still remains great. So it proves that our model has a desirable function to predict disengagement in the case of generalisation. In addition, the performance could be further improved by applying feature selection or 'game week' attribute. Similar to what we did in 10-fold cross validation, RMSE would be performed for all accuracy bars (except random guess) to figure out which method is the best. The accuracies with RMSE are 92.80% ± 0.4535, 96.10% ± 0.4175, 95.90% ± 0.4827 and 95.00% ± 0.4855 respectively, and it indicates that the model with only feature selection performs the best.

Figure 6 shows less improvement in predictions using our model. However, the performance of all decision trees is still higher quality than that of random guess. So it means the patterns of increasing playtime players tend to change considerably during different months. However, one thing should be noticed is that with the help of 'game week' attribute, the recall of the increasing group could be boosted noticeably. According to the formula of recall, it is to say that the number of true positives has been increased. As the accuracies of original model and the model optimised by feature selection performs similar with each other, RMSE should be applied to show the details. The accuracies with RMSE for those two methods are 70.50% ± 0.4535 and 70.90% ± 0.4175. According to this, the best remains the model with just feature selection applied.

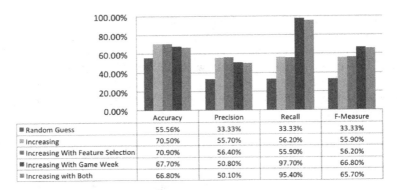

Fig. 6. Verified on February - March Performance on Increasing label in I Am Playr

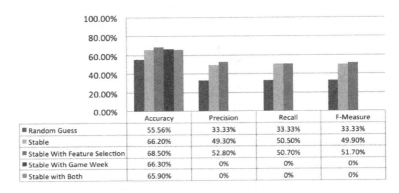

Fig. 7. Verified on February - March Performance on Stable label in I Am Playr

Figure 7 displays a similar result as the increasing group. Furthermore, for this group, if the 'game week' is included, the precision, recall, and F-Measure drop to 0. According to the formulas, this occurs because these models give no true positives. Which is also to say that no instances are correctly assigned to the stable group. This is possible as in the original model of January-February, the 'game week' attribute is trained to be the only important feature to predict whether a player is in the stable group or not. This fact could be clearly seen in Figure 1. However according to the February-March data, the patterns of stable users generate another type of tendency. Since the accuracies of all methods are close to each other, the RMSE is used. The accuracies with RMSE for all methods are $66.20\% \pm 0.4535$, $68.50\% \pm 0.4175$, $66.30\% \pm 0.4827$ and $65.90\% \pm 0.4855$ individually. So as can be seen, the conclusion remains again that the model with only feature selection performs the best.

5.2   Lyroke

As with I Am Playr, there are also four models for Lyroke. The size of the original model is 589 nodes with 295 leaves and was learnt from 7382 features.

After applying feature selection, only 33 feature are left. This resulted in a tree with 413 nodes and 207 leaves. The tree with the 'game week' feature included contains 149 nodes with 75 leaves learnt from 7383 features. Including the 'game week' has again reduced the tree size. Finally, the last model with both feature selection and the 'game week' feature is 39 nodes with 20 leaves and was learnt from only 23 features.

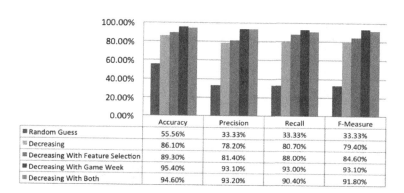

	Accuracy	Precision	Recall	F-Measure
■ Random Guess	55.56%	33.33%	33.33%	33.33%
▨ Decreasing	86.10%	78.20%	80.70%	79.40%
■ Decreasing With Feature Selection	89.30%	81.40%	88.00%	84.60%
■ Decreasing With Game Week	95.40%	93.10%	93.00%	93.10%
▨ Decreasing With Both	94.60%	93.20%	90.40%	91.80%

Fig. 8. 10 Fold CV Performance on Decreasing label in Lyroke

10-Fold Cross Validation. Figure 8 suggests that we attain a great performance in the decreasing group once more, which could be further enhanced by feature selection and the 'game week' attribute. The accuracies with RMSE are $95.40\% \pm 0.2120$ and $94.60\% \pm 0.2166$ for the last two bars with 'game week' respectively. Therefore, the model with only 'game week' performs best.

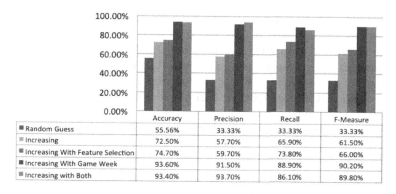

	Accuracy	Precision	Recall	F-Measure
■ Random Guess	55.56%	33.33%	33.33%	33.33%
▨ Increasing	72.50%	57.70%	65.90%	61.50%
■ Increasing With Feature Selection	74.70%	59.70%	73.80%	66.00%
■ Increasing With Game Week	93.60%	91.50%	88.90%	90.20%
▨ Increasing with Both	93.40%	93.70%	86.10%	89.80%

Fig. 9. 10 Fold CV Performance on Increasing label in Lyroke

Figure 9 shows again that all our models acquire a significantly higher accuracy than random guess. The accuracy without the 'game week' feature exceeds 70% and could be used for problems at a reasonable error standard. At the same time, feature selection also boosted both the performance and speed. Especially the speed, as adding feature selection reduced the time cost of training the model from 61.88s to 0.28s. Also the number of features to be analysed decrease from 7382 to only 23. Like I Am Playr, the accuracy could be improved to higher than 90% by applying 'game week' attribute too. Similar to decreasing group, the accuracy bars related to 'game week' should be checked with RMSE. The results are 93.60% ± 0.2120 and 93.40% ± 0.2166 correspondingly. In this case, there is no significant difference in performance. Therefore, the speed and memory advantages of using feature selection may be favourable if predicting this class of players is a priority.

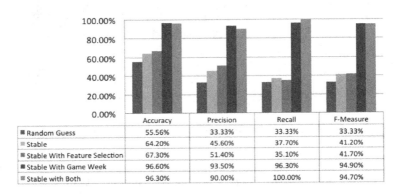

	Accuracy	Precision	Recall	F-Measure
Random Guess	55.56%	33.33%	33.33%	33.33%
Stable	64.20%	45.60%	37.70%	41.20%
Stable With Feature Selection	67.30%	51.40%	35.10%	41.70%
Stable With Game Week	96.60%	93.50%	96.30%	94.90%
Stable with Both	96.30%	90.00%	100.00%	94.70%

Fig. 10. 10 Fold CV Performance on Stable label in Lyroke

Figure 10 shows a similar result as the increasing group. As discussed above, the task of distinguishing stable players is a much more complicated process. Despite this, we still observe a significant improvement compared with random guess. With 'feature selection' applied, the performance could be improved once again. Also, as we discussed before, the time cost of it has been reduced a lot. Similar to increasing group, the performance could be improved to higher than 90% by including the 'game week' attribute. Likewise, the accuracies of those bars related to 'game week' should be investigated by RMSE. The corresponding accuracies with RMSE are 96.60% ± 0.2120 and 96.30% ± 0.2166. This indicates again that there is no significant difference and, therefore, the model with both feature selection and the 'game week' feature may be favourable.

5.3 Summary

From the results above, we conclude our method is accurate and stable to predict disengagement cases in varying conditions. The findings can be applied to other genres of games, which means it is possible to track players' certain behavioural patterns for detecting their disengagements.

For the increasing and stable groups, the original model could offer an accuracy around 60%-70% which is significantly higher than that of random guess. Furthermore, including the 'game week' feature could significantly improve the performance. Although it is not a general attribute in all games, most should have similar attributes used to record the progress of players. However, when the model is used to perform classifications in a later month slot (February-March), the performance turned out to be of inferior quality. This means that the action patterns of players who belong to increasing/stable group are changeable between month slots.

Finally, using feature selection typically does not have a significant effect on the accuracy of the model but does significantly reduce the time taken and memory required when training the model.

6 Related Work

Relevant existing research in this domain tend to be based on two concepts: *player modelling* and *game design by data mining*. The main directions of player modelling are: *player analysis, behaviour detection* and *character simulation*

In the direction of *player analysis*, the purpose of work by Mahlmann et al. [13] resembles that of this paper. In that paper, the authors introduced how to utilize the system records (e.g. Playing time, Total number of deaths, Causes of deaths etc.) of players to predict when players are going to leave the game *Tomb Raider: Underworld*. This work differs from ours because we focus on the events experienced by players within a period of time in different game genres. By focusing on events the resultant model includes only features developers can manipulate the occurrence of directly.

Another paper focusing on players' interests also shows similar intention. Except instead of investigating when players will leave, Bauckhage et al. [8] focus was more about the abstract interest of player. The authors built a model which could smoothly match the change of interests and predict the likelihood of players' exit with distinct modelling methods. They focused more on fitting existed random process models while we try to build new models based on actual activities from players.

In terms of the utilization of players' behaviour, another related paper is written by Ahmad et al. [6] aiming at detecting gold-farmer player in a massively-multiplayer online role-playing game (*MMORPG*) game called *EverQuest II*. In this paper, the authors used the pre-processed behavioural data of players to perform a binary classification on whether players are gold farmers (who acquire in-game currency and sell for real-world money) or not. So its purpose is dissimilar with ours but the methods could be used interchangeably, with decision trees on events used to predict gold farmers. The advantage of an interpretable model could also be useful for understanding critical behaviours of gold farmers.

For tuning design, the work by Weber et al. [15] is an example. In this paper, the authors put forward a method to build up a model consists of game features and player's retention so that the most valuable game features could be found according to the sorted features list. The purpose of this paper is also different as it used games features rather than events to predict, which means it also covered factors such as control settings. Weber gave priority to adjusting game features (game settings) rather than the disengagement of players.

7   Conclusion

We introduced a method which could be used to predict the disengagement of players as a result of their recent activities. To validate our method, we tested it on two online games of different genres and achieved desirable outcomes.

Moreover, we endeavoured to use the same method in testing participants in the increasing and stable groups. The performance was better than that of random guess and could possibly be used under the condition of an accepted error standard.

The method has potential practical significance for two reasons. First, data analysts could better understand players and indicate what type of designs are not welcomed or accepted by users. Second, it would potentially become a very high-level tool for developers to adjust their design in games. The developers, however, do not have to understand the complicated mechanism and relationships in their event space to find out what will lead customers to quit as the resultant model is human readable and easily interpreted. One thing to be mentioned is that, our method assumes that events in game are frequently generated which could reflect the activities of players. Nevertheless, games which contain only sparse events might still be analysed as login information of players is frequent events that happened in every online game.

Future work will aim to improve the prediction of the increasing and stable groups. The next attempt could be using more users' information to classify players' behaviour. Also, as discussed earlier, the stable group contains too many players facing different conditions. Therefore perhaps if the players in this group could be clustered into more groups/labels, the performance of the model could possibly be improved. Finally, experimenting with targeting the players predicted to disengage with adverts and/or special offers could be useful to help maintain their engagement and prevent or delay them quitting.

References

1. I am playr, http://www.iamplayr.com/ (accessed May 23, 2014)
2. Lyroke, https://game.lyroke.com/ (accessed May 23, 2014)
3. We r interactive, http://www.werinteractive.com/ (accessed May 23, 2014)
4. Weka, http://www.cs.waikato.ac.nz/ml/weka/ (accessed May 23, 2014)
5. World of warcraft armory, http://www.wowarmory.us/ (accessed May 23, 2014)
6. Ahmad, M.A., Keegan, B., Srivastava, J., Williams, D., Contractor, N.: Mining for gold farmers: Automatic detection of deviant players in mmogs. In: International Conference on Computational Science and Engineering, CSE 2009, vol. 4, pp. 340–345. IEEE (2009)

7. Alpaydin, E.: Introduction to machine learning. Adaptive computation and machine learning. MIT Press (2010)

8. Bauckhage, C., Kersting, K., Sifa, R., Thurau, C., Drachen, A., Canossa, A.: How players lose interest in playing a game: An empirical study based on distributions of total playing times. In: 2012 IEEE Conference on Computational Intelligence and Games (CIG), pp. 139–146. IEEE (2012)

9. Bouckaert, R.R., Frank, E., Hall, M., Kirkby, R., Reutemann, P., Seewald, A., Scuse, D.: WEKA Manual for Version 3-7-10. University of Waikato, Hamilton, New Zealand (2013)

10. Drachen, A., Sifa, R., Bauckhage, C., Thurau, C.: Guns, swords and data: Clustering of player behavior in computer games in the wild. In: 2012 IEEE Conference on Computational Intelligence and Games (CIG), pp. 163–170. IEEE (2012)

11. El-Nasr, M., Drachen, A., Canossa, A.: Game Analytics: Maximizing the Value of Player Data. Springer (2013)

12. Hall, M.A.: Correlation-based feature selection for machine learning. Ph.D. thesis, University of Waikato, Hamilton, New Zealand (1999)

13. Mahlmann, T., Drachen, A., Togelius, J., Canossa, A., Yannakakis, G.N.: Predicting player behavior in tomb raider: Underworld. In: 2010 IEEE Conference on Computational Intelligence and Games (CIG), pp. 178–185 (2010)

14. Thurau, C., Bauckhage, C.: Analyzing the evolution of social groups in world of warcraft®. In: 2010 IEEE Conference on Computational Intelligence and Games (CIG), pp. 170–177. IEEE (2010)

15. Weber, B.G., John, M., Mateas, M., Jhala, A.: Modeling Player Retention in Madden NFL 11. In: IAAI (2011)

Coordinating Dialogue Systems and Stories through Behavior Composition

Stefano Cianciulli, Daniele Riccardelli, and Stavros Vassos

Department of Computer, Control, and Management Engineering
Sapienza University of Rome, Italy
{stefano.cianciulli,dan.riccardelli}@gmail.com,
vassos@dis.uniroma1.it

Abstract. We exploit behavior composition in AI as a formal tool to facilitate interactive storytelling in video games. This is motivated by (i) the familiarity of transition systems, on which behavior composition is based, in video game development, and (ii) the fact that behavior composition extends the spectrum of approaches for non-linear storylines by introducing a new paradigm based on planning for a target desired process instead of a goal state. Moreover, this approach provides support for the debugging of deadlocks in stories at design level. We describe the behavior composition framework, and show the details for an interactive dialogue system scenario in order to illustrate how interactive storytelling can be phrased in terms of it. We also report on a simple architecture for implementing a demo game over the scenario using existing behavior composition tools.

1 Introduction

In this work we employ the AI method of behavior composition to facilitate interactive storytelling through a dialogue system. Behavior composition is concerned with *orchestrating* a set of *available behaviors*, expressed as transition systems, in order to accommodate an intended *virtual target behavior*, also described as a transition system [5]. The aim is to synthesize a controller that is able to realize the desired target behavior by exploiting execution fragments of the available behaviors.

The motivation for exploring behavior composition as a method for interactive storytelling is twofold. First, transition systems are ubiquitous in game development: finite-state machines (FSMs), which are variants of transition systems, are a popular model for specifying the reactive behavior of non-player characters (NPCs) in game-worlds. This familiarity makes behavior composition well-suited for orchestrating the behavior of NPCs also at a higher-level that relates to an underlying storyline.

Second, as the community explores ways for a non-linear, adaptive, and interactive storyline in video games by means of automated (reactive or proactive) planning, e.g., [2,8,1,9,14], behavior composition can be used either as an alternative or a complementary tool to existing approaches. In particular, the main

T. Cazenave et al. (Eds.): CGW 2014, CCIS 504, pp. 150–163, 2014.

difference is that unlike planning for a *desired target state*, behavior composition is about *offline* synthesizing a *strategy* for allocating plot units to characters in such a way that a *desired target process* can always be realized at runtime in an *online* fashion.

In the setting we explore, the NPCs of the game may feature any preferred method for specifying and realizing their actions and behavior in the game-world, but we also assume that there is one additional interaction layer that specifies the *role* of the NPCs with respect to the *plot units* or events of the storyline. For each NPC, then, a FSM is assumed that specifies which events in the storyline may be initiated and handled by the NPC and how they further affect their role expressed using states. For example, a particular NPC may be used to initiate a conversation with the player that reveals a clue or initiates a quest, but only if in the course of the game the player has not previously engaged in combat with the NPC. Different states of the FSM may be used to represent the internal state of the NPC, and transitions may be used to encode available storyline interactions at each state. The set of these FSMs constitute the so-called *available behaviors* for behavior composition.

As far as the intended storyline is concerned, a desired *target behavior* describes how the events in the storyline may unfold. The target is not a fixed sequence of events, but rather another FSM that provides a high-level view of the process that the storyline should follow. Each state in the target FSM corresponds to a *decision point* allowing a number of available plot events to be invoked as transitions that lead to other states accordingly. These decision points essentially provide flexibility for a *drama manager* to decide how the story should continue, while keeping it structured under the specification of the FSM of the target behavior.

The rest of the paper is organized as follows. First, we illustrate the use of behavior composition for interactive storytelling using a scenario in which the story unfolds through a dialogue system. Then we discuss on available tools for implementing such a scenario and report on a demo game that we developed based on the presented scenario and a simple architecture. Finally, we discuss ways that other interactions can be encoded so as to facilitate wider cases in interactive storytelling, and close with related work and conclusions.

2   The Uncommon Crime Scene (UCS) Scenario

In order to show how behavior composition can be employed to coordinate a dialogue system in video games, we report on a simple scenario, called "Uncommon Crime Scene" (UCS), in which the player is a detective whose task is to solve a crime. The scene is populated by 5 characters-suspects that the player-detective is asked to interrogate in order to unmask the thief.

2.1   The Target Behavior as FSM

Figure 1 shows the target FSM representing the target process that the storyline should comply with. Such an FSM simply states, at each point of the game,

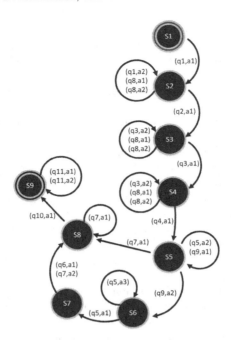

Fig. 1. The UCS storyline as a target FSM

which events the player could experience and how past interactions influence the unfolding of the narration. Inspired by the scenarios of dialogue-based adventure video games, the only events that influence the narration are player-triggered dialogues between the player and the witnesses of the crime.

For example consider state S1 which is the initial story state when the player starts the game: the only interaction allowed is "q1,a1", which serves as a "tutorial interaction" that introduces the player to the game context. "q1,a1" stands for "Question1, Answer1", the identifier of an interaction listed in the game script that we describe shortly, which means that the player can ask "Question1" and in return the character he is asking this question will answer with the corresponding line labeled as "Answer1". Once the introductory interaction is completed, the story moves to state "S2", where the player can start interrogating the witnesses.

The target FSM features elements such as:

- *Primary interactions* that take the story further. E.g. "q2,a1", which reveals an important detail about the story, labels an outgoing transition from S2, the state where the player just learned what the game is about, to S3 where the player just discovered that one of the characters knows something about the crime.
- *Texture interactions* that keep the story in the same state. Such interactions are not relevant for progressing into the story, but make the scenario more credible and appealing by giving the chance to the author to show interesting

Q1: Hey there, what's going on?

A1: There is a terrible thing that just happened here! Go inside and investigate! Quick!
A2: Still here?!? Run inside! The one responsible might still be around!

Q2: You, little kid, do you know anything about this crime?

A1: I could tell you... if only you could give me something in return.

Q3: That kid is looking for something hes lost. You know what it is?

A1: Oh, I guess I do! I found this in the yard, this morning.
A2: Hmm, I have no idea. I barely see that kid around.

Q4: Here you are. Can you tell me now?

A1: If I were you, I would ask Mrs. White over there...

Q5: Confess! It's you the one who committed the crime!

A1: I don't know what you're talking about! I dont even like cookies!
A2: Prove it, you disrespectful investigator!
A3: Ahah, nice try, my friend!

...

Fig. 2. Part from the UCS script

details, e.g., about the setting and the characters. This is what happens, for instance, in state S2 with interactions "q8,a1", "q8,a2", that reveal different thoughts from different characters about the setting, but do not add clues toward solving the crime, which is the player's main task.

- *Story branching* according to which different player interactions could drive the story to different states, augmenting player control over the unfolding the story. In state S5, for example, being suspicious about a particular character instead of another character, progresses the story to state S6 rather than S8, forming a different experience. While not necessary in the general case, in this scenario the branches will eventually converge to state S8 leading essentially to a single ending for this simple scenario. A different scenario may feature multiple endings, maybe with different criminals to unmask, having a Target FSM include multiple final states.

2.2   Game Script

The game script is a table where all the dialogue-based interactions of the game are stored, as a list of questions with related answers. Figure 2 shows a part of the script written for this scenario. This is an exhaustive list of all questions and all possible answers to each question by any character participating in the story. In particular, the same question may have different answers according to when (i.e., in which story state) and who the player asks this question to. For example, referring to Figure 1, if the player asks Q1 again when the story is in state S2, the answer this time will be "q1,a2" which is different from what they

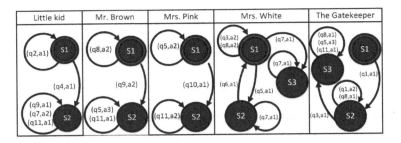

Fig. 3. The FSMs of the characters in the UCS scenario

received in S1, since the player has already been introduced to the scenario with "q1,a1" and they are now ready to start investigating.

2.3   Character Behaviors as FSMs

The role of each of the five characters in the story is also expressed as an FSM as shown in Figure 3. Each of these characters essentially function as *resources* that can facilitate transitions in the target FSM. Each resource, called available behavior, specifies what interactions they can facilitate and also how possible interactions affect their internal state. They are responsible for accommodating the target process described by the Target FSM as follows: an interaction labeling a transition from a certain state in the Target FSM, in fact, indicates that there must be at least one Character FSM designed in such a way that can facilitate that same interaction at that point of the story, so to accommodate the desired story unfolding. Referring to the Target FSM in Figure 1, let us assume that the story has reached state S8. According to the Target FSM, then, in the game world there must be characters (at least one) capable of facilitating interactions labeled as "q7,a1" and "q10,a1".

While behavior FSMs can model various things such as the mood or disposition of a character with respect to the player, in this scenario they model a type of memory of past events: a character can use the FSM to remember the fact that a dialogue interaction has already occurred between the player-detective and the character, and thus avoid repeating it. For example, referring to the Mrs. Pink character in Figure 3: once she confesses her crime ("q10,a1"), her state changes so that she is not allowed to evade accusations ("q5,a2") anymore, but, instead, manifest concern for her future ("q11,a2").

Note that the target behavior FSM and the available character behavior FSMs are designed separately and provide a form of decomposition of the story and the resources that can realize it. One can first focus on the target behavior and the desired narration unfolding, designing the high-level overall experience, and then look into appropriate single character behaviors. In fact, the target behavior FSM does not specify which characters should facilitate certain interactions but only the interactions themselves.

LK	MrB	MrsW	MrsP	GK	Target	QA	Assign
S2	S1	S1	S1	S3	S5	(q5,a2)	MrsP
S2	S1	S1	S1	S3	S5	(q7,a1)	MrsW
S2	S1	S1	S1	S3	S5	(q9,a1)	LK
S2	S1	S1	S1	S3	S5	(q9,a2)	MrB

Fig. 4. Controller Generator

2.4 Controller Generator

So, how can one run this scenario while keeping consistency with the target behavior and character behavior specifications? Also, how can one make sure that, for any given run, there will always be characters able to accommodate the target process so as to avoid deadlocks? We are interested in building a mechanism that can tell us if the target process could, for each run, be accommodated and, in case it can, which characters should facilitate what dialogue part for every possible configuration of the target and character behaviors states.

The solution is to compute a Controller Generator (CG) [5], a strategy expressed as a look-up table that, in each state of the story, specifies which character should facilitate a certain interaction. Figure 4 shows what the CG table looks like: for each possible combination of target and character behaviors states the player could take the game to, the CG lists the corresponding set of dialogues available, including, for each of them, the character that could facilitate it.

The CG is computed offline, receiving as input the target along with the character behavior FSMs, and can be used at run-time to instruct the system managing this scenario in order to offer to the player, at each point of the story and for each possible run, a set of dialogues to choose from that always guarantee the realization of the story until the end.

2.5 Design and Debugging of the Storyline

The fact that the target behavior is not directly linked to the available behavior, i.e., the target takes into account which dialogue parts to facilitate but not who actually facilitates them, makes it easy for the designer of the story to edit, add, and remove characters modeled as available behaviors, as the story is being designed.

For example, at some point the author may decide that a new character should also able to facilitate "q1,a1". Then he simply needs to add this behavior to the scenario leaving the rest of the modeling of behaviors (the target included) untouched. Similarly, if he decides that some behavior should be removed from the scenario.

Relying on behavior composition for managing the scenario yields another great benefit: when a CG is computed successfully, it is granted that no deadlock might arise for any possible unfolding of the storyline expressed by the target

Fig. 5. The NPCs' lower-level FSM

FSM. Even in the presence of loops in the target process specification, which is the case of the UCS scenario, the output strategy, if existing, is guaranteed to be valid for any possible way the target may be run. In a sense the CG is like a "global conditional plan" that takes into account any possible combination of target and available behavior states achievable at run-time and precomputes what the appropriate course of action should be.

Let us consider now the case where the behavior composition problem has no solution. While this is obviously a crucial fact to know, which tells us that the experience may yield to narration deadlocks, it is not very helpful on its own unless enriched with some diagnostic information. Interestingly, a CG computation can prove useful also in case the composition problem we design is not solvable. The adopted approach is based on the fact that when no composition exists, this is due to presence of some problematic history for the target behavior. Thus, it would be of great help to obtain an indication about the problematic histories that prevented the composition problem from being solvable.

We can, in fact, add temporarily a stateless "debug behavior" to the scenario, which is able to facilitate any dialogue that appears in the Target FSM, and request a CG computation again. This time the problem will obviously be solvable, and the CG returned will help us spot the problematic histories or traces of our scenario: since the debug behavior is necessary to obtain a composition, this CG must, in fact, contain some (CG) states where the only behavior able to execute some action is the debug behavior itself. This turns out to be a powerful tool for storyline design debugging, as one can spot quickly where the design flaw in their scenario lies and can either adjust the other behaviors so to be able to accommodate the target process, or remove the interactions that are causing problems from the target FSM. The latter approach, though, while being formally valid, may be less desirable in practice, as it narrows the set of possible alternatives for the player.

The reader may have noticed, at this point, how an approach based on behavior composition is substantially different in relation to other search-based mechanisms, e.g., planning. Compared to planning-based approaches for interactive storytelling, e.g., based on reactive planning such as ABL [8] or proactive planning such as the PDDL-based approach of [10], our work is different in the specified objective that the deliberation system achieves.

While the planning-based approaches are able to form joint goals for ensuring appropriate interaction of characters, our work aims for stronger guarantees over the intended storyline, prescribing all possible unfoldings in a concise way and precomputing how to achieve them by means of coordinating the available characters. The proposed method (*i*) decouples all storyline requirements from the behavior of characters into a target behavior for the entire system; (*ii*) guarantees at design time whether it can be always enforced (and how) by means of the computed strategy; (*iii*) is able to deliberate and plan ahead also taking into account loops in the story; and (*iv*) provides built-in debugging capabilities for identifying deadlocks and storyline design flaws.

We now proceed to report on a demo game that we developed based on existing behavior composition tools and a simple architecture inside a popular video game engine.

3 Unity Mini-game

Over the UCS scenario introduced earlier in this paper, a short video game has been developed using the Unity Game Engine[1] and the JACO web service [3] as the composition engine for computing the CG. The video game is a first-person investigation game where the five crime witnesses are non-player characters (NPCs) wandering around the crime scene, and the player can interact with them by approaching and interrogating them one by one until eventually the guilty one is unmasked.

3.1 Non-player Characters

The NPCs are simple-behaving characters who, unlike the player-detective, have no interest in starting a dialogue with the player on their own. Along with a high-level behavior FSM, which captures the NPC role into the game and serves as input for JACO for computing the CG, each NPC features a lower-level behavior FSM, which describes their physical interactions in the game world. As shown in Figure 5, NPC physical interactions consist simply of walking around (WALK state) when they are alone and focusing their attention on the detective (TALK state) when he is around.

3.2 Jaco

The NPC and Target behaviors are encoded into separate XML files that serve as input for JACO in order to compute and, if the corresponding composition problem is solvable, return a CG: a look-up table also encoded in XML. This computation has to be done at design time, once each time the behavior set is edited, i.e., when we modify, delete behaviors, or add new ones to the scenario. Each time we request a computation, assuming such problem is solvable, the new CG will replace the older one so that the game will always use the CG from the most recent scenario. The stand-alone mini-game ships with a ready-to-use CG, so no communication with the JACO server or computation for updating

---

[1] http://unity3d.com/

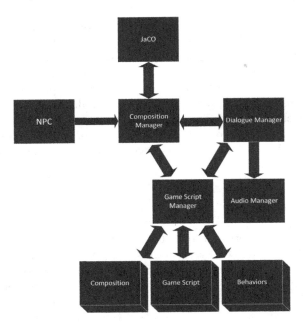

Fig. 6. Dialogue System components

the output strategy is necessary, as all the information we need to orchestrate the behaviors is included in the pre-computed CG. If the user wants to change the specification of the available behaviors and target behavior, JACO server can then be used to obtain a new GC.

The entity who takes care of running the CG, serving as a *drama manager*, is the dialogue system whose components are shown in Figure 6, along with how they interface with other components such as JACO, the C# scripts that contain the NPCs' logic in the Unity game engine, the behavior files and the game script repository, which is an XML file storing all the dialogue lines written for the game.

3.3   Dialogue Interactions

In order to show how the dialogue system works, we present the steps that build up a dialogue interaction:

1. As soon as the player approaches the NPC they are willing to interrogate, the NPC fires an event.
2. The system gets notified, so it collects the NPC and Target state and checks, looking up the CG, if the NPC can facilitate any interaction at that point of the storyline.
3. If it can, the dialogue system loads the corresponding lines from the game script repository.
4. The dialogue window is shown, presenting to the player all the questions they can possibly ask to such an NPC at that point of the storyline.

Fig. 7. Screenshot from the UCS scenario mini-game

5. Once the player selects one of these questions, the related NPC answer is shown.
6. The system updates the NPC and Target states according to the player selection.
7. The player closes the dialogue window and goes on interrogating witnesses.

Figure 7 shows how the dialogue window looks like once the player has selected one dialogue option. In the top-right corner of the game viewport, the mini-game features a debug head-up display which indicates the state of the story and the state of each NPCs populating the scene.

All the details of the character and target behaviors can be found at the JACO website jaco.dis.uniroma1.it/#example3. A web player version of the game can be found at jaco.dis.uniroma1.it/docs/ucs/web-camp-v2/web-camp-v2.html.

4   Further Applications

While the UCS scenario introduced in this paper is simple, there are different ways it could be expanded, modeling additional aspects of the gameplay and the storyline into transition systems. An example direction is to model the target process so as to take into account also the player inventory, which is a common element of many commercial adventure games. Inventory items can, in fact, play a fundamental role over the unfolding of the story (e.g., particular items that are crucial such as keys, maps, etc.), and it would be very useful to expand the same formalism, exploited here for managing dialogues, in order to keep track of inventory state as well. This could support, for instance, different story states for different inventory configurations.

Another example is to model the functionality of interactive game-world objects as available behaviors. It comes indeed natural to design a behavior transition system for almost every entity the player is allowed to interact with. For instance, our scenario could feature a "door behavior" that facilitates the "unlock door" interaction, hence moving from the "LOCKED" to the "UNLOCKED"

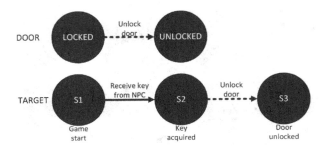

Fig. 8. Behaviors modeling inventory and interactive objects functionalities

state, only if the story is in state S2, which indicates that the player has received the door key, as shown in Figure 8.

Finally, there is a fundamental aspect of behavior composition that is not exploited in the presented scenario, namely the fact that available behaviors can be non-deterministic. This is a powerful feature that allows to express uncertainty about the internal transition of a character when an event is triggered, e.g., due to the low-level details of the actual execution of the event. Note that a computed CG (if exists) is able to provide a strategy that always realizes the target story also taking into account this uncertainty.

5   Related Work and Discussion

Interactive storytelling as behavior composition lies in the middle ground between manually authored and automatically generated stories with respect to authorial intent, following the landscape of interactive narrative research as presented in [11]. Intuitively, the target behavior circumscribes a variety of possible unfoldings for the story under a concise representation of a transition system. This allows for a predefined set of plot points and multiple options for realizing each one of them at run-time, while some basic structure is ensured by means of following the execution of the transition system that models the target behavior.

Note that in the transition system of the target behavior, nodes are decision points for the drama manager, and that recurring or repetitive tasks can be modeled via regular loops. Moreover, a special type of joint behavior called *the environment* can be used to also capture more detailed underlying causal rules that involve all of the available behaviors and further refine the executable narrative trajectories. We did not include this in our presentation for simplicity, but an account for this component has already been studied in [5].

As far as character autonomy is concerned [7], our approach lies also in the middle ground between strong story and strong autonomy, but closer to the strong story end of the spectrum. This is because characters are allowed to have flexibility to act as autonomous entities but only as long as they do not change their internal state captured in the corresponding behavior. One of the assumptions for this approach to work is that a change of state may only happen after the drama manager invokes some action execution. Since the transition systems for characters can be non-deterministic it is not sure what will be the next state for the available behaviors, but no change is assumed to take place unless it is invoked by the drama manager.

Note though that this can be a relatively mild restriction under conditions, as the term action in our framework refers to a higher-level of abstraction essentially wrapping the macro-actions, strategies or plot-related goals for the characters. In this sense, the restriction to the autonomy of the characters depends on the specification of the plot points and their relation to the high-level actions for agents. Each of these actions could be further specified using the reactive planning language ABL [8] or, in the terminology of IN-TALE [12], each of them can assign a goal that needs to be realized by means of invoking a corresponding Narrative Directed Behavior (NDB). Similarly, each action could be decomposed in a Hierarchical Task Network (HTN) manner following approaches such as [2].

Our approach is similar in spirit to many other approaches in the literature that are based on automated planning, including STRIPS and HTN planning, for example the aforementioned system I-Storytelling, GADIN [1], and MIST [9] as well as the work on the framework Mimesis [13] and Zócalo [14]. Nonetheless, the methodology of behavior composition is different from planning both in conceptual and technical terms as we explain next.

Firstly, the target behavior is not a specification of a goal situation to reach but, rather, a description of a set of *routines* one would like to be able to carry on *at runtime*. Moreover, such routines cannot be seen as (classical or non-deterministic) plans, either, in that they do not prescribe the actions to execute, but leave the choice to the executor. Further, they may contain loops, which are typically ruled out in planning. From this perspective, target behaviors are more similar to IndiGolog programs [4], i.e., high-level procedures definable on top of planning domains, for which one is typically interested to find an executable realization at runtime.

Secondly, in behavior composition, actions are not the subject of a planning task. Indeed, the controller does not select the actions to execute; instead it returns the index of the behavior that should execute the action selected by the drama manager. In this sense, actions constitute the input, not the output, of the reasoning task, but in a way that takes into account *all possible narrative trajectories*. From a more formal perspective, we observe that both behavior composition and *conditional planning* are EXPTIME-complete problems [5,6], thus some way of reducing composition to (non-deterministic) planning must exist. Nonetheless, how this can actually be done is not as straightforward as one might expect, as shown by the above considerations.

Finally, our implementation that relies on using behavior composition as a web-service is similar to the client-server based approach that is adopted in Mimesis and Zócalo. In fact as the web service JACO is built as a pure behavior composition engine that can be accessed via a REST API, one interesting direction for future work is to explore how it can be used as a service in such frameworks in order to provide high-level orchestration of characters, either as an alternative or in pair with the embedded narrative planner.

6 Conclusions

In this paper we propose the technique of behavior composition as an alternative tool for facilitating interactive storytelling in video games. We illustrate some of the most basic functionality of this approach using a scenario of an interactive dialogue system and a demo game that is built over a simple architecture.

In the wider context of interactive storytelling, behavior composition represents a different view that is based on planning for a desired process, rather than a goal state. In particular, the process is a specification of the possible stories that the drama manager can decide to realize at runtime. In contrast to other approaches, the generated stories are not bounded in length, as the target process may contain loops that can be unfolded an unbounded number of times.

Behavior composition includes a framework based on the specification of behaviors as transition systems, and a solution technique that returns a finite-state machine, called the *composition generator (CG)* , from which all solutions can be generated. We believe that the framework itself is valuable, as it represents a useful abstraction of both NPCs and storylines, that is general enough to accommodate many relevant approaches in the literature, e.g., in the special case of the target behavior being a sequence, the framework captures a basic scenario where the storyline requires the execution of a classical plan, and the controller generator contains all possible ways of executing such plan, by resorting to the actions that the NPC behaviors make available.

Acknowledgements. The authors acknowledge support of Sapienza Award 2013 "Spiritlets" project.

References

1. Barber, H., Kudenko, D.: Generation of adaptive Dilemma-Based interactive narratives. IEEE Transactions on Computational Intelligence and AI in Games 1(4), 309–326 (2009)
2. Cavazza, M., Charles, F., Mead, S.J.: Character-Based interactive storytelling. IEEE Intelligent Systems 17(4), 17–24 (2002)
3. Cianciulli, S., Vassos, S.: Planning for interactive storytelling processes. In: Proceedings of the 3rd International Planning in Games Workshop (2013)
4. De Giacomo, G., Lespérance, Y., Levesque, H.J., Sardina, S.: IndiGolog: A High-Level programming language for embedded reasoning agents. In: Multi-Agent Programming: Languages, Tools and Applications, pp. 31–72. Springer (2009)
5. De Giacomo, G., Patrizi, F., Sardiña, S.: Automatic Behavior Composition Synthesis. Artif. Intell. 196, 106–142 (2013)
6. Littman, M.L.: Probabilistic Propositional Planning: Representations and Complexity. In: Proc. of AAAI 1997 and IAAI 1997, pp. 748–754 (1997)
7. Mateas, M., Stern, A.: Towards integrating plot and character for interactive drama. Working Notes of the Social Intelligent Agents: The Human in the Loop Symposium. AAAI Fall Symposium Series, Menlo Park, pp. 113–118 (2000)
8. Mateas, M., Stern, A.: A behavior language: Joint action and behavioral idioms. In: Life-like Characters: Tools, Affective Functions and Applications (2004)

9. Paul, R., Charles, D., McNeill, M., McSherry, D.: MIST: An interactive storytelling system with variable character behavior. In: Aylett, R., Lim, M.Y., Louchart, S., Petta, P., Riedl, M. (eds.) ICIDS 2010. LNCS, vol. 6432, pp. 4–15. Springer, Heidelberg (2010)

10. Porteous, J., Cavazza, M.: Controlling narrative generation with planning trajectories: The role of constraints. In: Iurgel, I.A., Zagalo, N., Petta, P. (eds.) ICIDS 2009. LNCS, vol. 5915, pp. 234–245. Springer, Heidelberg (2009)

11. Riedl, M.O., Bulitko, V.: Interactive narrative: An intelligent systems approach. AI Magazine 34(1), 67–77 (2013)

12. Riedl, M.O., Stern, A.: Believable agents and intelligent story adaptation for interactive storytelling. In: Göbel, S., Malkewitz, R., Iurgel, I. (eds.) TIDSE 2006. LNCS, vol. 4326, pp. 1–12. Springer, Heidelberg (2006)

13. Young, R.M.: An overview of the mimesis architecture: Integrating intelligent narrative control into an existing gaming environment. Working Notes of the AAAI Spring Symposium on Artificial Intelligence and Interactive Entertainment (2001)

14. Young, R.M., Thomas, J., Bevan, C., Cassel, B.A.: Zócalo: A service-oriented architecture facilitating sharing of computational resources in interactive narrative research. Working Notes of the Workshop on Sharing Interactive Digital Storytelling Technologies at the Fourth International Conference on Interactive Digital Storytelling (2011)

Author Index